# Jessie's Journal

## The road less travelled

The names have been changed to protect the innocent.

The facts remain to protect the truth.

Rebecca J Green

## DEDICATION

This book is primarily dedicated to the real and actual
Jessie.
You are now, as you always thought, famous!

Also, to all our friends and family, who have been on
this journey with us. We are forever grateful for your
continuous love and support. It would have been a
much harder journey without you.

# ACKNOWLEDGMENTS

To the original fan club of Jessie's Journal, when it was first released in its intended form, as a monthly update on the progress of one incredible, remarkable, smiley, courageous, yet totally crazy little girl.

# Preface

When I was a child I was told, "if you want to be just one of the crowd then follow the flow, like a sheep in a flock. If you want to be different, to see the world differently from the rest, then take the road less travelled." I had absolutely no idea what my mother was talking about.

Now I am older, and hopefully somewhat wiser, I kind of understand what I was being told back then. I see it this way. We always seem to be trying to get from A to B. The question is, how do we get there? Most of us like to take the direct route, like the motorway for instance. It is rarely scenic or fun, but it gets you there, and if you are lucky it is relatively fast. There are some who would rather drive across a field and through a river, rather than conform and take the more 'acceptable' route. I'm not exactly one of these adventurous types and I would have predicted I would be one of the millions on the motorway, trying to get wherever it is I am going, as fast as humanly possible. However, without any warning I found myself disappearing along a windy old back road, most definitely taking the road less travelled. I wasn't being brave or adventurous or anything - more just plain lost! And why? Well, my daughter Jessica was destined to do things that bit differently and by God, if she wanted to take the scenic route, then the rest of our family and friends were going to come along too!

# The beginning

Hi, I'm Jess. Well my real name is Jessica but I will also answer to Pickle or Jumbleweed. It is amazing I stayed sane amongst my crazy relations but I do believe I have almost achieved it. Well, where should I start? I was born in January and there were snowmen in the garden at home. And I was the first baby in the family. It was that kind of world I was being brought into! Anyway, to be honest, if I say so myself, the first 6 weeks of my life were entirely uneventful. Well for me they were. Mummy and Daddy on the other hand looked as if they were running marathons on a daily basis on almost no sleep. I have no idea what they were up to, but I'm sure it had nothing to do with me. So, 6 weeks old and all was fine. Then I went for the routine 6-week check-up at the doctors and there they found a heart murmur. "Nothing to worry about, just come back in a fortnight," they said.

You'd like to think nothing much could happen in 14 days, but during that time I was cruelly evicted from my cosy Moses basket in Mummy and Daddy's room and put in a proper cot in my very own bedroom. Allegedly I had grown out of the Moses basket already and it had to be moved to the loft. Had I mentioned I like my food? At only 5 weeks old, I was already on the extra thick formula milk 9 times a day! I can't help being peckish. I was used to food 24/7 before I was born, and now I am here I just expect the same level of service. Anyway, you get the gist. I was never ever one of these tiny frail babies. I like to think of myself as more of a cherub! Look, I'm digressing - where was I?

Oh yes, heart murmur. So, at 8 weeks old there I am back at the doctors only to find that the heart murmur is still there, large as life. So, the doctor recommends I see a consultant and have a few tests done, "nothing to worry about, just routine." Easy for him to say. However, all this talk of tests had made me a bit nervous and I just had to have a tinkle, right there and then. It's a shame he'd just taken my nappy off to examine me further. I'm sure his tie recovered once it had been washed a couple of times. So, over the next 2 months I had electrodes stuck to me for an ECG (an electrocardiograph... I think?!) and the most awful chest x-ray, which involved lying still and half naked, on a cold bit of metal. You try it. It was an understatement to say I wasn't happy and I admit most of the hospital were aware of this by the time I left. Thankfully after all this worry, when I did get to see the consultant with all the test results at 4 months old I was given the 'all clear'.

Oh well, I veered briefly off course there but I think we can now safely head back to join the other 'normal' babies. I think we had one, or was it even two weeks of normality when I went to the clinic for a weigh-in. It is a bit like weight-watchers but with completely opposite objectives. Anyway, I'm lying there, butt naked, minding my own business when the health visitor pipes up "did you know your daughter has a squint? I'll get her referred to the ophthalmologist." (posh term for optician). My mother, bless her, had no idea that being completely boss-eyed was not the way a baby was supposed to look and obviously hadn't given the thing a second thought. So here I am, a whole 4 and a half months old and already on my 2nd referral. Let's hope this isn't a sign of things to come.

Meanwhile I'm just carrying on as normal. Photo shoots, baby massage, swimming - that kind of thing. So as instructed by the health visitor (hereafter to be referred to as the hell visitor), Mummy and I went along to see the ophthalmologist. You know, I went there to get my eyes checked and they wave the tiniest toy in the world attached to the top of a pencil in front of my face and expect me to be able to see it. I mean, you'd need pretty good eyesight to see this thing and frankly I was not in the mood to humour the optician (now be known as the "bug-eyed monster") and play along. Thankfully Mummy had brought along my orange giraffe and that was eventually used instead. After numerous "where's the giraffe" which was wearing thin even for me, it was decided that I needed to see a consultant. It was then determined that I had something called an alternating convergent squint.

This means I only look out of one eye at a time and when I do, the other eye wanders in to have a look at my nose. It is quite understandable really as I do have a rather cute nose. So, it was decided that I may need to have glasses and that an appointment with the "big man" consultant was to be arranged. What a palaver!

Well, things are not quite going to plan so far, but it is still early days. Mummy is slowly coming to terms with the fact that she will have to go back to work in a few months and in preparation for that I am to start nursery just a couple of hours a week. I have to say I wasn't completely convinced at first. There were no tears or anything, like some of the other cry-babies, but I wasn't really sure it was the thing for me. But when I discovered that after breakfasting at home I could arrive at nursery and have a mid-morning snack, lunch, mid afternoon snack and then tea, plus all the toys I could play with, I soon warmed to the idea. The only thing was, the other babies in the room were crawling or rolling or at least doing something. I was not quite sure why they were all gadding about, when you could sit most comfortably in an inflatable ring and have people bring stuff to you all day long. I was soon likened to the Queen of Sheba - not looks or anything, but if I say so myself, I am pretty laid back. Well, horizontal in fact most of the time.

Before I knew it, my meeting with the "big man" optician consultant had arrived. Daddy wanted to be there (I know, because he told me) but he couldn't get the day off, so I had to settle for going with Mummy and Granny instead. The "big man" put horrible stuff in my eyes that made them sting and water, and then he shone lights at me, all while wearing something that looked like a miner's helmet. After a bit of muttering he came to the diagnosis that I was long-sighted. He sat there 2 feet in front of me, as blurry as anything, and told me I couldn't see too well. I could have told him that. The problem is, when you are so small no one actually asks you! So, I've got a squint and I am long sighted and will have to wear glasses all the time. Just to put the icing on the cake (there I go thinking of food again), if the glasses don't correct

6

the squint over time, then I will need an eye operation too. Not quite 6 months old, my contemporise are at home playing with not a care in the world, and here I am, in hospital, again, choosing glasses for heaven's sake! The good news is that the "glasses man" who fits and orders the glasses is the nicest man in the world. He thought the glasses we chose really suited me and said I looked lovely in them. What a charmer. Even Mummy was pleased when she was told to put her Barclaycard away as they were on the NHS. So, those were the ones we ordered.

I'm sure, just to take my mind off things; Mummy and Daddy took me to Norfolk for a holiday the very next day. Norfolk was lovely. Not exactly the Costa de Sol or anything, but we all had a nice time. A week exploring the countryside, climbing windmills, sailing on the broads and swimming in an outdoor pool. A pretty typical family holiday away from it all.

When we got back, the dreaded glasses were ready for collection. I have to say, I was really good the day I had my first pair of glasses fitted. I wore them in the fitting room, all through the hospital, back to the car and nearly all of the 1 mile home. After that I decided I had worn them plenty and the best place for them was the floor. Mummy and Daddy kept trying to put them back on me but I was insistent, I had worn them - honest - for over 5 minutes already. I'm sure the lovely glasses man didn't mean for me to wear them more than that. Eventually Mummy and Daddy gave up and put the glasses away. I thought they had gone for good, until the next day when it started all over again!

My first ever summer was an absolute scorcher. No exaggeration or anything but it topped 100 degrees. So, like the floozy I am, I spent weeks in just a nappy and a pair of frilly knickers. Very sexy. Come to think of it, it was about then I started seeing my boyfriend Harry on a regular basis. We'd lie there on a blanket in the sun hand in hand. It was quite romantic really. He's a toy boy you know! Nearly 3 weeks younger than me. But I won't let the age gap bother me.

So, the summer passed pretty uneventfully. Harry and the

other babies kept crawling around, but I was quite happy doing my own thing. Before I knew it, September was upon us and the security and routine of me and Mummy being at home and us sending Daddy to work was about to see quite a change.

# September 2003
## (age 7½ months)

Hi there, it is just little ole me writing to tell you all what I have been getting up to this month. Daddy now goes to work 3 days a week and has 3 Saturdays and a Sunday off. Alright for some, Mummy says. This, he tells me, is so he can look after me nicely. Well, I guess it beats being looked after badly.

I now have 4 teeny tiny toothy pegs, but you will have to look really hard to be able to see them all. If you get too close though, I may bite. By accident, obviously. I'm a baby, not an animal!

I now go swimming once a week with Mummy, but I don't like it when we jump in and sing Humpty Dumpty. My swimming teacher thinks it is because I don't like jumping in the water, but it's not that that makes me cry, it's Mummy's singing!

I've got a new winter coat. It is pink, but it's better than nothing. I've got matching hat and mittens too. I'm going to look a right wally.

Lots of slobbery kisses,

Jess xxx

# October 2003

Mummy has now had to go back to work. I could tell she didn't particularly want to go back. But someone has got to get out there and earn some money to keep me in the luxury I have become accustomed to. The two of us had been doing just fine for as long as I can remember. But now this means I will have to look after Daddy a couple of days a week. I have been keeping him busy and taking him to the supermarket, showing him what to get and where to find it. Although I am having trouble reaching everything I need from the seat of the trolley.

I've been a bit snuffly this last month so I've missed a few of my swimming lessons. To make sure I don't get too behind I've been practising in the bath with my 2 new bath buddies. Freddie (the fish) and Franc (the frog). I've been doing quite well with my kicking and splashing in the bath, although Mummy is starting to regret redecorating the bathroom a few weeks ago.

I've been to see the scary eye man and he says I need stronger glasses, so Daddy has chosen me a pair. Both me and Mummy are a bit worried what they are going to look like as Daddy isn't exactly what you would call a style guru. Oh well, I'm sure I'll be able to take them off just as quickly as the old pair. Mummy bought glasses for teddy too, with the idea we'd be matching. Although I take my glasses off as soon as no-one is looking! Unfortunately, teddy is pretty stupid sometimes, so I have to take his glasses off for him.

Everyone has been asking for a Christmas list from me and I am getting a bit concerned that the list has been written without anyone actually consulting me. So just in case, I thought I could let you all know that I would like; some paper to eat (as I haven't worked out the point of paper yet, and I'll eat anything), food to throw (or wear, I'm not fussy) and some more teeth, as with my appetite I've found 4 is not enough to do anything much with.

I have been playing bouncing in a thing that hangs from

the door frame, and I am getting quite good at it. However, my preference is to wind it around in circles and then lift my feet off the floor and then whizz back in the opposite direction. My record is just over an hour in the bouncer but I need quite a lay down afterwards to recover, as apart from anything else, you get pretty darn dizzy!

Lots of wet and sloppy kisses,

Jess xxx

# '7-9 month assessment'

In October, I had my '7-9 month assessment' at the doctors. It's a regular thing all babies go through apparently (or they at least they did when I was a baby!). Except Mummy held out until I was 3 days short of being 9 months old before she would take me. This was motivated by the concern that I would fail the tests. She's actually a good deal more perceptive than she looks! It was quite funny looking back on it, but at the time I really wasn't in a laughing mood. We got to the surgery and both the doctor and hell visitor were there. I showed them I could sit quite nicely for a minute or two, but then the floor got all wobbly and Mummy had to do an impressive rugby tackle to save me. They were apparently expecting a crawling demonstration or something, but I wasn't exactly up to that. They then wanted to see me stand. To be honest I thought we were doing the wrong test because I couldn't do any of this fancy stuff. They held me upright and I hung there with my feet up touching my bottom. They weren't at all impressed with that. So apparently, I failed on the first test, 'gross motor skills'. Next, they held out a tiny bell, rung it and then held it still in front of me. Well, I had taken my glasses off by now and couldn't even see this stupid bell let alone do anything with it. According to the rules of the game you are supposed to take the bell and ring it. How you are supposed to know this, I have no idea. I feel I should have attended a revision course or something and now feel seriously under prepared. Eventually I was handed said bell and I treated it like an unexploded bomb. Well you can't trust these hell visitors you know, I could have been given anything! I held it as still as possible, determined that it was not going to make a single noise. 'Fine motor skills' - FAILED. Next, the doctor put on a lovely show with a toy dragonfly while the hell visitor kept whispering in one ear. I have to say I thought it was quite rude to talk through this demonstration when I proved I could sit there quietly and watch the show. Unfortunately, this wasn't the point. 'Hearing' - FAILED. After that I really didn't feel in a chatty mood at all and as you could have predicted, 'Communication' - FAILED. I should mention I did actually get a 'satisfactory' in something. Eating!!! Well done me. Well, you have to be good at something I suppose. Well as a result of that I was referred for just about everything under the sun. The doctor explained that she was going to write a nice letter to the local Children's Development Centre where they've got some paediatric specialists that I could meet. Well, how nice I thought, that'll make a lovely day out!

# November 2003

I had my very first haircut this month. And as I was being particularly good that day, my stylist, even gave me my own L'Oréal baby mousse for my lovely blonde curls; 'because I'm worth it' don't you know!

I have a lovely fluffy pair of new slippers. They came all the way from the Antarctic!! Daddy says it is EVEN colder there than it is in Norfolk. He must be crazy.

I have been growing more teeth too this month. I now have 6 incy wincy toothy pegs and have decided it is much better to grow them in my order, rather than do it the way the book says. I haven't conformed with anything else yet so far, so I'm not about to start doing this the way people expect. So, I now have a couple of nice big back teeth. I'm sure they'll come in handy at some point.

I have been Christmas shopping with Mummy and chosen myself a nice present. It is a big red ladybird that you can push along the floor. I cuddled it in the shop and only let Mummy have it back long enough to pay for it. I then insisted that it really didn't need to go into a bag and instead I would help Mummy out by carrying it all the way through town and back to the car in my pushchair. Aren't I ever so helpful?

You'll be pleased to know that the glasses Daddy chose for me weren't too bad after all. I was a bit concerned when I found out he had picked them, but I have to say they do rather suit me.

Anyway, it is getting late and I had better go to bed as Santa knows who's naughty and nice.

Night, night and kiss, kiss.

Jess (and Bonnie, my dolly) xxx

# December 2003

Cool, or pretty chilly really, but I have had my very first Christmas. Mummy said I had just about been good enough to qualify for a stocking from Santa. This was very nice of him as I had only met him once at nursery. Mind you, he seemed a nice enough fellow, even if he did wear a funny outfit and have a big belly. Come to think of it, I may just have described my Pop Pop!

I was very clever at Christmas and almost mastered the art of opening parcels. Mind you, I did have quite a few presents to practice on. In the excitement of everything I forgot to ask - 'when is the next Christmas, so I can do it all over again?'. Daddy reckons I am going to need a container lorry to use as a toy box. I'm not completely sure he's joking either. On Christmas evening at the dinner table, everyone decided to pull their crackers at once. I wasn't expecting a noise like that. Frightened the life out of me.

Well, other than Christmas not much else happened. I have had a bit of a nasty cold, but anti- 'bionics' soon sorted that out. I was kind enough to remember to share my cold with Mummy and Daddy too. Thankfully as luck would have it, we were all better in time for the festivities.

I have been growing more teeth. I'm not very sure how many I am supposed to collect, but already I have more than I can count, which I'm starting to think must be plenty.

Lots of bite-y kisses,

Jess xxx

# January 2004

This month I had my very first birthday. I had loads of lovely presents. And a few dodgy ones too.

It snowed this month, just like it did this time last January. However, this year Mummy didn't build any snowmen. Spoil sport. I wanted to build a snow something or at least sit in the snow with the cat, but I was told I would get a wet bottom if I did. What they forget is, I wear a nappy and I frankly don't think I would have noticed any difference.

I saw the bug-eyed monster optician again. She is now dishing out career advice of all things. Apparently, I will never be able to be a pilot. I am not too upset as I have no idea what a pie-lot is. I assume it must have something to do with pies... and lots of them?!

I have also managed to break the arm off my glasses, so I am on my 3rd pair already. Good going, I think. However, now I know how to break them, I expect to be getting through pairs of glasses a lot quicker now.

I have seen the people at 'The Grange' (local Children's Development Centre) a couple of times this month. When we went to see them, Daddy thought it was hysterical when the Speech Therapist, Polly, offered him a cup of tea. It wasn't until he had pointed out that Polly had put the kettle on that we all laughed along too. He's hilarious sometimes. Gets it off me, you know.

In the last few weeks I have learnt to dance - sitting down of course (my legs only hold up my socks!!) Daddy has been trying to teach me rhythm; well that is what he calls it. Mummy and me are not sure what it is.

I grew another 4 teeth this month. It is now getting a bit ridiculous; I'm not quite sure where to put them all - I have 12. Apparently, I should come with a warning 'have teeth - will bite'. I think that's a bit unfair, they are a bit new to me and I'm just trying them out.

Anyway, it is way past my bedtime so I had better go.

Lots of wet kisses, Jess xxx

# February 2004

I had quite a few firsts this month - some good and some, well frankly, not good at all.

I went out to the Queen's Head pub for Uncle Billy-Bob's birthday with Nanny, Grandad, Mummy and Daddy. I was a really big girl and had my first ever 'kids' meals'. To make it extra special I also tried everyone else's lunch... whether they liked it or not.

This month has been an exciting time trying loads of new food. I like to be really helpful and feed myself. Although it can sometimes get a bit messy. I also learnt to wave this month too, but if you do it when you are practising your eating you can end up with tuna pasta in your hair or porridge on your glasses. It really can happen. I know. You have been warned.

The main event of the month though has been my trip up to Great Ormond Street Hospital. Us inmates, or is it inpatients? call it GOSH for short. The trip started well because I went on a train for the first time and loved it. When I got to my ward my name was already written on a white board. Just like they do on 'Casualty'. The doctors wanted to do lots of tests to see what was wrong with me, but I kept telling them, 'I'm okay, I'm marvellous'. I accidentally called the consultant 'da da' but I don't think anyone noticed. Easy mistake!

I'm sure they were trying to interrogate me at one point though, as they stuck electrodes to my head with glue and flashed a light in my face. You'll be pleased to know I just told them name and rank and no more. I was a bit miffed however as the glue played absolute havoc with my beautiful curls.

Anyway, we are off the Centre Parcs at the end of the month with Nanny and Grandad and I want to make sure my new swimsuit gets packed.

Lots of slobbery kisses,

Jess xxx

# GOSH. Oh, my, gosh.

I sort of glossed over the whole GOSH (Great Ormond Street Hospital) ordeal, but now I have nearly got over it I feel I can finally go into more detail about what actually went on.

As I said, it was good because it started with my first ever trip on a train. Unfortunately, because of the time I needed to check in at the hospital we had to travel at the tail end of rush hour. I tried reading the paper of some businesswoman next to me but she was having none of it. So, to get my own back I did a super smelly nappy and then sat there happily waving at people out of the window. It is funny watching people trying to casually breathe through their ears. So as soon as we got to the station, people fled off the train a whiter shade of green and I was rushed straight to the baby change unit. Then in my pushchair, I was wheeled into a London taxi. That was quite fun in itself. The day was becoming quite an adventure. Eventually we got to the hospital and were shown to my room. The first day was pretty easy. A few basic questions, some relatively painless tests. Although I did have a blood test and they wanted absolutely gallons of the stuff. I mean, I thought I was going to run out at one point. They also took the opportunity to swab everything... and I mean, almost anything that could house a cotton wool bud, got one! Thankfully before I knew it, it was time for bed. Only one person was allowed to stay the night with me so Mummy and Daddy flipped a coin. I don't know who won, but it was Mummy that stayed the night. They filled my nappy with cotton wool (for another test), which wasn't an entirely unpleasant experience and put me in this big cot with what I think were cardboard sheets. All things considered I had a good night. While I slept, decisions were made about what tests I would have done, along with discussions about the availability of people and machines and the possibility that I would be staying in hospital for several days at the very least. Thankfully I was not told I would have to go without food for about 8 hours the following day. If I'd known about that I would have had nightmares for sure. So, the next morning Mummy was being more insistent than usual that I eat up my toast, all the while keeping one eye on the clock. You could tell she was up to something; I just couldn't put my finger on it at the time. Shortly after breakfast Daddy arrived back at the hospital and I filled him in on the bits he had missed and warned him that Mummy had gone even weirder than usual.

That morning was absolutely frantic with tests.

There was an early appointment to have an EEG (I think?!). First of all, they drew spots across my forehead and in my hair with a special pen. Then on the spots they had drawn, they stuck on loads of electrodes with wires coming out, which was then attached to a machine. Then they got this huge lamp and flashed lights into my face at various speeds to see what it did to me!! Well, amazingly I didn't react adversely to any of it, although I have no immediate desire to go to a disco! I thought that was pretty grim, especially as the glue they use to stick the electrodes on doesn't come off very easily, so I'm now having a seriously bad hair day as well as everything else.

With hair stuck at right angles and everything that bit more blurry than usual, I was taken straight into another room. This time for an EMG. If you ever have the offer of having this test, turn and run and don't stop running. I would have done, but I can't walk, let alone run. I'm a bit like a sitting duck. Quack. To say I wouldn't exactly recommend an EMG to my worst enemy is a bit of an understatement. Picture the scene. I've been manhandled over the last hour or so, had the whole flashing light experiment and the whole time being exceptionally well behaved, if I say so myself. However, I'm due a bit of a nap now and I'm starting to get a bit peckish. A little snack-ette, some milk and a nap would have done just the job. Instead, more manhandling and I'm stripped half naked. And I really don't like being chilly. Then, with the most enormous needle I have ever seen, the other end of which is attached to a computer, they stick it straight in my leg. OUCHHHHHHHHHHHHHHHHH. And to make matters worse it stays there, half in, half out, while my feet are prodded and poked. That comes out and seconds later it goes in another part of my leg. OWWWWWWWWWW. Again, more wiggling of the needle while it is attached to me and the computer. I'm not feeling so well now. In fact, I'm feeling decidedly peaky. I don't recall how many times that happened, I just know it went on too long. So, when the consultant mentioned he still had the other leg to do, I cried and I do believe Mummy joined in! I had had enough now and was ready to go home. Even though the people were nice, you soon learnt to trust no-one.

At the point when I thought I could take no more, it was over and I was being carried back to my cot. I was there less than an hour before it was time for me to go and have an MRI brain scan! It had been discussed early that morning and the consultant had casually mentioned that they wanted to rule out the possibility of me having a brain tumour. I did wonder if they could have come up with something a little less drastic! So, off I went, just like someone in an episode of Casualty, being wheeled around in a cot. I was wheeled down the corridor and into a lift to the MRI suite. While down there, and after a reasonable amount of protesting, I succumbed to some exceptionally disgusting medicine. Before I knew it, I felt really, really s l e e p y. Apparently, I was then lifted onto the MRI machine and they put earphones on me that were as big as my head! Mummy, Daddy and a nurse stayed in the room with me and after lots of exceptionally loud clonking and banging, which wasn't me (I was oblivious to it all); it was finally over and back to my cot and onto the ward. I have to say that was more than enough for anyone for one day and I was able to sleep off the effects of the sedation for most of the afternoon.

When I woke up it was teatime, which was good because I was starving and I was sure I had missed lunch somewhere along the line. The problem is when you can't even count to 3 it is difficult to know whether you have been diddled out of a meal! Anyway, I was well fed and watered and thankfully just before bedtime I was given the all-clear regarding any obvious or hideous brain abnormalities, although they did say they would have to look at the results more closely over the next few weeks. At least they found a brain. Daddy was teasing me that there might not even be one!

After tea went down, I had a bath and hair wash, which considering the glue and pen in my hair and across my head, it was more of a necessity than a 'nice to have'. But at least I felt better for it. Even if the glue didn't all come out. Some medicine and milk later, and I was beginning to feel absolutely shattered. So, as it was Daddy's turn to stay the night, we waved bye bye to Mummy at bedtime and sent her on her way.

Yet again, while I slept, decisions about what further tests I would have done, and what people I needed to see were made. Next morning breakfast was nothing like as manic as the previous day. To keep me occupied doctors, nurses and consultants came and went. We got the comments like, "she's a really bendy baby", "isn't she a floppy one" and "isn't she gorgeous." Although, I may have imagined that last one! I had a lovely visit from the physiotherapist and we played nicely on the floor for ages, until I lost my balance and disappeared under my cot. People came and went, prodded and poked. The one thing they did all agree on was that I was clearly hypotonic. Clearly hypo WHAT?! Apparently, this is a medical term to mean I have low muscle tone, which means I'm naturally more floppy than I should be. It's quite a hard concept to grasp until you realise that if I had high muscle tone, I would have spastic tendencies. You just don't get the same leniency when you are all floppy, because it is not so visually apparent. In fact, you usually just get called 'laid back' or 'lazy'. Anyway, it was decided, after lots of talks with lots of people, that apart from a play in the sensory room, there was nothing else they could do at this time. It was more of a "wait for the results and we'll take it from there" kind of situation. So, we started packing bags and getting all my stuff together, including a beautifully soft yellow duck that I had been given by the nurses while I was in hospital and which we later named 'GOSH'. It was late afternoon by now and we were almost out of the door when they decided that one last blood test to look for chromosomal and genetic problems should be done. Frankly for me this was the last straw. I had become so wary of what they might do to me, bearing in mind I now have plasters on both hands and both feet from all the blood tests over the last few days, that every time they held my hand to put a needle in I would snatch it back. 13 months old and I will not trust anyone to even hold my hand. With a bit of persuasion and a little brute force they got the needle in. I have to say I didn't give this last blood sample willingly; in fact, I got so upset it made me sick. The more I cried the more I was sick, but they were determined to get enough blood in this one last attempt otherwise they'd have to get another needle in, so it just kept going. By the time they had finished, I was exhausted. Mummy looked nearly as bad as I felt and Daddy was nowhere to be seen! And they didn't even go near them with a needle. So, before they could think of anything else to test, swab or measure we got out of there as fast as we could. Once we were safely off the ward and a few floors away, Mummy and Daddy decided I should have a quick session in the sensory room. What a good idea. We all laid on this waterbed with dimmed lights and soothing music in the background for about 20 minutes. I have to say we all looked a little better for it. But we had to make a move as it would take hours to get home and none of us would be completely happy until we were all safe and sound at home again. So off we headed, homeward bound.

# March 2004

I have been to Centre Parcs. The one that burnt down. It wasn't me, honest. I had a lovely time on holiday. I went swimming with Nanny, Grandad, Daddy and Mummy and although they are better swimmers than me, I had the nicest swimsuit by far. I even went in an outdoor pool when it was snowing - it was really cool... I mean completely freezing!!! I went to a 'baby dolphin' class, but it was just lots of strange people singing nursery rhymes badly. While we were away, I ate out at a couple of restaurants and even let the others come along too. They were quite well behaved on the whole. I might even take them again sometime. Nanny definitely had too many glasses of wine as she managed to rename my buggy the 'shush-pair'.

The physio has been pleased with my progress so far - which is handy, as I am going as fast as I can. I now have one of The Grange's stools to practise sitting on nicely. Thank goodness I'm not potty trained yet, as wearing a nappy when you sit on it is practically essential. This chair needs all the padding it can get. I am seeing the physio again early next month and if she is really lucky I may even show her a few tricks that I'm working on.

I went to primary school this month. Not full-time or anything, as that would be just plain silly. I'm only just 1. I went to visit Granny for lunch. I always thought it was funny that Granny is still at primary school; you'd have thought she would have at least progressed to secondary school by now. Anyway, while I was there I tried my very first strawberry. I wasn't hugely keen on it to say the least. And as a result, Mummy ended up mopping up the staff room floor, her jumper and Granny's shoes. I did avoid getting too much down myself though as that would have been just disgusting.

I am pleased to say I did remember Mother's Day although silly old Daddy completely blew the budget. So, I made him pay for the present by himself.

Must go. Lots of sloppy kisses, Jess xxx

# April 2004

I have had quite a busy month. I took both Mummy and Daddy to a nearby farm to see some animals. I had a right laugh at the pair of them trying to feed the goats. I had to even send Mummy back for animal feed because she forgot to pick any up at the entrance. Sometimes I wonder how they ever managed without me.

I have also been on an Easter egg hunt with Granny. At first I thought the eggs were really dry and tasteless until Granny pointed out that I had to swap my half eaten cardboard egg for a chocolate one. As it was Easter I did have lots of chocolate, so I have been able to maintain my cherub-like figure without any real problem.

I have also been to an actual zoo this month too. Bit of animal overload really. It was my first ever trip to a zoo. It was a lovely hot day when we went, and in a moment of insanity I accidentally threw my sock at a rhino... but it missed. It was a shame, because I was really looking forward to seeing Daddy go in after it.

I have acquired some new talents this month. I can throw now, which livens things up when I'm in a ball pit. And I can sing, well sort of, which is kind of nice for everyone. I guess.

I have been having a few really bad hair days recently, so Daddy has invested in some detangle spray and a load of girlie hair clips. They are for me you understand - he hasn't got enough hair to accommodate a single clip. Mummy thinks I look dead pretty with clips in my hair, but to be honest they feel all tight and spikey and I am worried that I look like a right wally. And to top it all, they are a real pain in the head. Especially when you fall asleep on one. I think I may have to revisit my stylist and see what she can do with my hair instead.

Must go and make myself look gorgeous.

Lots of chocolatey kisses,

Jess xxx

# May 2004

Well, what a month. I was supposed to have another eye test with the grouchy old consultant, see the bug-eyed monster and I had a photo shoot booked. My hectic social calendar went totally to pot, or should I say to spot, when I caught the chicken pox. Also known as the 'poxy chicken'... well, it's called that in my household anyway. Figures. After spending ages covered in weird pink ointment I am finally feeling better now but I haven't been to nursery for weeks. I bet they have really missed me!

One thing I did get to go and do was see the nice GOSH Consultant about my trip up to London back in February. The good news is that all the tests were normal, which with my parents is more miraculous than lucky. Anyway, to cut a long story short, I don't have an official diagnosis as such, but I do have a muscle condition called 'hypotonia'. It means I am more floppy than I should be. The worst of it is, I am now referred to as 'Mummy's flopsy bunny'. If word gets out at nursery the others are going to have a field day and my street cred will go right out the window.

I have discovered that I can just about reach the tiles around the bath when I am having a splash, or is it a wash, I never remember. Anyway, I thought I'd help out a bit, so every time I am in the bath I wash 3 tiles with my flannel. Always the same 3 mind you, I can't reach any of the others. I can see a big improvement already. When I'm bigger I may even wash 4 tiles.

One BRILLIANT thing I did discover this month is that I can now stand, if someone holds me up round the middle though of course. I can't do it for long though as my legs go to jelly. It is very exciting and I am rather pleased with myself. I think I should warn you though that I only stand when I want to. I'm not in the circus you know, so don't expect a demonstration.

I went to a 3rd birthday party in May. I think it was the first party I'd ever been invited to. Other than my own, of course. So, I had a new outfit especially and looked dead cute. Well Daddy said I did. I had a lovely time and was even allowed to bring home a balloon. I think I rather like parties.

I'm off for a week's holiday in Norfolk (not Norfolk… again!) at the end of the month, so I had better make sure I pack my bikini, and my bucket and spade, just in case. I'll tell you all about it next month.

Lots of wet kisses,

Jess xxx

# June 2004

Mummy was a tad premature, but decided I should have my first pair of Clarke's shoes. They are the indoor ones, but it is still very exciting. They even took a photo of me in the shop. They are smart navy T-bars with pink bits on them. Even Daddy likes them. I was however rather concerned that they clash rather hideously with my red and white gingham shorts, but no one seemed to care that I was not properly colour co-ordinated. Just wait till I can talk, I'm sure 'Childline' would be interested!

After having the poxy-chicken last month I have finally caught up on my social calendar. I saw both the bug-eyed monster optician and the grouchy old consultant and ordered some new stronger glasses (stronger lenses not frames), although I could do with reinforced armour plated frames as they do kind of fall apart in my hands. They also don't last too long when I leave them on the floor and Mummy steps on them. This new pair of glasses were more trendy than the last pair. The only problem was, when they did arrive they didn't fit me at all well. So after just one week, they had to go back and I've ordered yet another pair. That'll be 5 pairs of glasses in less than a year - not bad going, eh!

I also had my photo shoot at a real studio. They were, as always, very impressed with me. But I am a natural model/poser you know.

I've been on my 'summer' holidays this month although you'd have never known it. It was wet, cold, wet, windy, wet and then on the day we came home, we had lovely sunshine. Typical. I had packed shorts, bikini and everything and spent the week in an anorak. Next time I'm going to choose where we go on holiday and it'll be somewhere a good deal warmer than Norfolk! Despite the weather, we still did loads. I saw penguins (they were in a sanctuary - it was cold, but not THAT cold), I went to a countryside park and I got to go on a boat trip to see seals. And on our last day I was able to go to the beach and play sandcastles. It was there I discovered that sand isn't actually edible. I wished someone had mentioned it before I took a mouthful. Yuck... way too crunchy for my liking.

Anyway, I'm too busy to be playing on the computer all day.

Lots of sandy kisses,

Jess xxx

# July 2004

This month I was exactly 1 and a half years old. Mummy and Daddy gave me a lovely tricycle. If I hold on tight and keep my feet clear of the pedals I go really fast (if they push me of course). I didn't realise riding a tricycle was so easy. I must be a natural or something! I did enquire as to whether I could enter the Tour de France, but apparently, they don't have a category for '3-wheels and a trailer'... which is a shame. Oh well, there is always next year.

I rolled over for the first time this month, although allegedly I was on a slope, so gravity was partly responsible for my achievement. I only did it because I was worried Mummy was going to make herself dizzy as she keeps rolling around on the floor in some kind of bizarre demonstration. Thankfully she stopped when I told her SHE was a 'good girl' and then I showed how it should be done.

I had to visit my stylist earlier this month as my hair was completely out of control. I couldn't decide between a complete restyle, layers or perhaps lowlights. But in the end, I settled for a trim and a fringe cut in. If I say so myself, it makes me look quite a bit older. I could probably pass as nearly 2 years old!

I have also discovered I can draw. I did a picture and a collage at nursery, so Mummy brought me paper and crayons. I was hoping for watercolours or oils. Crayons are not the best medium for an artist, so I'll just have to do the best with what I'm given! I am pleased with my drawings so far, although no one has actually guessed what I have drawn. To be honest, if it isn't completely obvious then I'm not about to tell them!

I have lots of toys to play with, so I'd better get on!

Lots of slobbery kisses,

Jess xxx

# August 2004

I took Mummy and Daddy to a massive indoor shopping centre this month (they'd been good) and I let them buy me a big foam alphabet mat. It's in my room and it's really cool. It also doubles up as a crash mat when I'm having a particular flopsy day. I suppose it beats wearing a crash helmet and elbow pads.

As it has been warm, I've been in my paddling pool in the garden. I even tried skinny-dipping, which was fun, although Mummy insisted on keeping her costume on. She's always such a spoil sport. I have been watching the Olympics this month and it has inspired me to train harder at swimming. Mind you, I am having trouble mastering tumble turns in my paddling pool and it really isn't deep enough for diving, water polo or synchronised swimming. I think I'm going to need a bigger pool.

I've also gone on some lovely picnics and I've been to the beach and everything. I feel quite well travelled for someone who hasn't been outside of East Anglia! Daddy and I went paddling in the sea at the beginning of the month. It is not exactly the Caribbean on the East coast, but we still had a nice time. That was until a big wave splashed me right up my bottom. And I wasn't even wearing my swimming knickers.

Despite the factor 30 suntan lotion, I've actually managed to acquire a bit of a suntan, although it could be rust after our 'summer' holiday in Norfolk! Don't tell the hell visitor though, as she'll probably be cross. They are anti anything fun.

I have decided I am now big enough to move out of my cot with bars, because I feel like I'm in the zoo! That and the fact I'm allegedly too heavy to lift over the bars and down into a cot! A drawback of liking food too much. So, I now have to sleep in a big-girl cot-bed with a special moveable side panel in case I have the urge to roll clean out of bed. I think they must think I'm stupid or something!

Lots of wet kisses,

Jess xxx

# September 2004

I've been to a local hospital to meet two really lovely genetics consultants from GOSH. They stripped me off down to my nappy and had a good look at me. Apparently at that point, without even asking ME, they came to the conclusion I liked my food. You can tell they must be very clever or something. Anyway, they are going to ask my GOSH neurology consultant to run a few more tests as they have some possible ideas of why I'm so flopsy. The geneticists said they wanted to see me again, which is understandable. I assume they didn't mean medically?!

Talking of food, I went to the International Trifle Festival and ate 2 bowls of trifle. I didn't want to be rude and not eat any. However, I couldn't quite bring myself to try Daddy's dodgy entry!!

I have had my hair cut again. What a relief, it was driving me mad, and Mummy and Daddy had started to grumble about it too! It grows so fast. And for some weird reason, it seems to grow perpendicular to my head, rather than downwards, which is just plain odd. Anyway, the stylist clearly knew what was needed and sorted it out for me.

I made a few staggering discoveries this month which shocked me as much as anyone. I found if I lay on my front and do a cunning manoeuvre with my arms and bottom I actually move backwards. Not fast or anything but I covered over 5 feet in less than 15 minutes. For me that is pretty fast!! I was even facing a different direction when I got where I was going. I also discovered that I can get from a sitting position to lying on my front, via the box splits. A feat possible when you are super bendy and flexible. I just don't understand why people grimace when they see me do it. I think it is quite a cunning technique that might even catch on! Must go - I have to practice my new moves.

Lots of trifle-flavoured kisses,

Jess xxx

# October 2004

At the beginning of the month I went to Centre Parcs (again!) with Mummy, Daddy, my boyfriend Harry and his folks. I was even allowed to share a room with Harry, which was not as romantic as I had originally envisaged as I may have unintentionally woken him up several times in my midnight attempts to find my dummy. I went swimming loads and had a wonderful time in the different pools, and it was all great fun. The only downside was it was suggested I go on a bike seat on the back of Daddy's bike. It wasn't long before I made it quite clear there was, no way on earth I was staying on that thing for more than 2 minutes. So instead, they got me this nice trailer with a roof, that I could sit very comfortably in and watch the world go by. Much more ME.

I also joined a gym club this month. There are only a few of us that go to it and it's not a 'normal' gym club. We do stuff which looks remarkably like physio but it's called 'gym' and it is supposed to be fun. I'm still not completely convinced they are pulling a fast one here and making me do extra physio. If I do stay, I may even invest in the club leotard - now won't I look smart / cute / ridiculous (delete as appropriate). The only thing is, they really have no idea how exhausting physio is for me.

I also have been to see the consultant again and I was exceptionally good this time. It was quite a productive session and lots was discussed. Mummy had it in her head that I could be walking within the next year, but the consultant put her right - it is okay now if I don't walk until I'm at least 3 years old, because the consultant said so. Phew, the pressure is finally off!

I also saw a new eye person and he was much nicer than the bug-eyed monster. He said I could have new glasses and I think this will be my 6th pair, but I have to admit I am starting to lose count!

Lots of pool water kisses,

Jess xxx

# November 2004

At the beginning of the month I saw fireworks for the very first time. Daddy went into the back garden and let a few off (fireworks that is) while I watched from the warmth and safety of the dining room - I'm not silly! I really liked the twinkly sparkly pretty ones. I would quite happily give the bangy ones a miss next year.

This month I went to gym club 3 times and now I have got the hang of it I am starting to really enjoy it. Not only that but I actually look the part, being all gymnastic in my new blue leotard.

I finally got my 6th pair of glasses at the beginning of the month after a bit of a hoo hah with the other ones being out of stock. They assumed I'd happily wait until March for my new pair!!! I could have got through loads of pairs of glasses by then!

In November, I also had my feet properly measured at The Grange as they want me to have some special Piedro boots. I have ordered a pink pair which look really nice on the internet, but I'm not holding my breath on actually getting the colour I want, as apparently, they've never ordered pink boots before. I always knew I was a trendsetter.

We all allegedly went on holiday at the end of the month. Mummy and Daddy went to Paris while I went to stay with Granny and then Nanny! I'm pretty sure I drew the short straw again.

I have also noticed the weather is getting a bit chilly. It seems to be the perfect opportunity for both Mummy and Daddy to put me in ridiculous combinations of hats with ears, mittens, and coats, and where nothing ever matches. I think I am a fashion victim and I feel I should make it known that I do not choose these outfits myself!!!

Lots of extra wet kisses,

Jess xxx

# December 2004

I discovered another new trick. If I am lying face down and the wind is in the right direction and luck is on my side, I can actually get from my front to a sitting position. I use, as you would expect, not the most conventional of techniques, but the main thing is it seems to work. Now if I combine that with the backwards shuffle which I can do while laying on my front, it means I am no longer always found in exactly the same place I'm left... although I'm never far from it!

I had a great but tiring Christmas. I went to see the real Father Christmas at the farm and that was brilliant. He told me, if I had been a good girl all year I'd get some presents on Christmas morning. Well, I must have been outstanding, as I was lucky enough to get absolutely loads of great presents and almost no dodgy ones this time!

As it is Christmas, I did a pretty good impression of an angel in the Christmas carol service at the local church, complete with dress, wings and halo. I think it is because being an angel comes so naturally!!

In this day and age everyone needs a computer and I am no longer an exception to this. I now have a new V-tech laptop to write the monthly journal on, rather than having to borrow someone else's. But it takes a lot of very serious concentrating when it comes to the typing.

I had great hopes of seeing in the New Year properly, but my plans were foiled after a tiring day out at the zoo meant I couldn't keep awake past 8:30pm. However, thanks to the neighbour's fireworks I did technically get to see midnight!!

Lots of angelic kisses,

Jess xxx

# January 2005

A highlight of the month was of course my 2nd birthday. I was very lucky and got some super fab pressies. It was a shame though as I really wasn't feeling myself. I'm not sure who I was. I just didn't feel cheery. Mind you, I put a particularly brave face on the whole thing.

I had a hearing assessment back in hospital, the day after my birthday (Happy Birthday, me!) and to shock and surprise everyone, I PASSED! Me - pass a medical test. I was amazed. Unfortunately, I can no longer blame my cloth-ears for the lack of talking, so at the end of the month I had to see the Speech Therapist. That went really well and the Speech Therapist was nice. In fact, all we did was play and chat. It's the easiest therapy I have ever done! I'm now looking forward to learning sign language. Whatever that is.

The biggest bummer of the month has to be the dreaded eye operation to correct my squint. I quite liked looking at my nose, but apparently, it's not the done thing. Thankfully, we only had to go to a hospital about 10 miles away, but even then, we were all up just after 5am. We didn't actually NEED to get up quite that early but you know what it's like, I couldn't sleep and it didn't seem fair that Mummy and Daddy should lie in, so we all got up. The operation went well, allegedly. I just dread to think what it would have been like if it hadn't! Daddy was a bit concerned as the surgeon had hands like a builder, so it didn't exactly instil confidence in any of us. Anyway, we will know whether the operation really was a success when I see the grouchy old consultant in a few weeks' time. I have to admit, if it isn't a success, I'll poke HIM in the eye and see how he feels. I am however pleased to tell you that I was awarded a bravery certificate, which I feel was well and truly deserved.

Lots of slobbery kisses,
Jess xxx

# February 2005

At the beginning of February, I went out to a nice restaurant for Uncle Billy's birthday and I was especially good. I just wish I could have said the same for the others! The food was really scrummy-licious. So much so, that before we left I made it my mission to try almost everyone's dinner. Just on our table of course. I thought it would have been greedy to work my way around the whole restaurant!

I've discovered finger painting, and it is brilliant fun. Unfortunately, I didn't have enough paper to meet my artistic needs. So, in a creative moment I had to improvise and decorate my legs and mat with paint. I looked very colourful. I couldn't have been too naughty though, as I was allowed to have a lovely bubbly bath afterwards.

I have been back to see the grouchy consultant and he was happy that my eye op was a success. The weird thing is, I've been told not to wear glasses for 3 weeks and then they will retest my eyes. Well, we didn't see that one coming... with or without glasses!

Gym club has been going well and I've been really enjoying it. Although I am convinced it is secretly physiotherapy in a leotard.

I have had another major haircut. The hair situation was yet again getting out of control, so something drastic had to be done. I look like some kind of mad professor when it gets too long, as I have these crazy tight blonde curls.

I'm officially the first person in the area to actually have pink Piedro boots on the NHS. Yahoooo. They are really cute. Just like me. They are a lovely colour too. They look just like normal boots, except these ones are made out of wood or something. Or that is what it feels like anyway. Let's hope they break in a bit sometime soon, otherwise I may just paint the boxes pink and wear them instead. They'd be just as comfy.

This month I have also been trying hard to learn sign language, but it's not as easy as it looks. All the signs look really similar to each other. I have managed to master the sign for 'book', and now I just use it for whatever I want. It sort of works, but we'll have to wait and see. If nothing else, it is giving me the incentive to learn to talk! I'm not sure that is the intention, but you know me, why do what is expected when you can do something entirely original.

Lots of paint-y kisses,

Jess xxx

# March 2005

The real big excitement of the month is if I persuade someone to hold me round my middle ... I can walk!!!!!! It's EXCELLENT. I've been on loads of expeditions. I've been up the stairs, down the stairs, in the kitchen and through the cupboards, up the stairs, down the stairs, in the garden, up the stairs, down the stairs and then usually at that point I'm told to sit down and play. Well, this makes me really cross because I still haven't finished exploring. Parents just do not understand the dedication and determination of a true adventurer.

I'm still not wearing glasses. Partly due to my trial period to strengthen my eyes being increased and partly because, well to be honest... I've lost them!

Mummy and Daddy had a couple of days off work this month and we went swimming, out for pub meals, to Pizza Hut, and to Monkey Puzzle (a play area where Mummy and Daddy end up getting more exercise than I do, as they carry me around the place!) I had a lovely time, anyway.

Last month I was having trouble with sign language. Well, I must be bi-lingual or a genius or something because it has clicked. I now have about 10 signs that I regularly use and most are the conventional 'Makaton' signs, although some have been 'Jess-ed' a little.

I also have been to a bird and butterfly place for the first time and I took Mummy with me. Daddy wouldn't come with us as he's a big sissy when it comes to anything that flies. Anyway, we both had a great time and saw some lovely butterflies and even some wallabies. I'm not exactly sure why wallabies were in a bird sanctuary, but sometimes you just daren't ask!

Lots of slobbery kisses,

Jess xxx

# There's one more angel in heaven

When you are 2 years old, the last thing you would expect is for one of your friends to die. But that happened to me. Not once… but twice, in as many months.

I had a 'special needs gym club' friend. A happy, friendly, almost angelic little boy. We often joked about me being his girlfriend. We were obviously not serious. Harry is MY boyfriend. Anyway, one Saturday morning we sat on the gym mats, side by side, being as gymnastic as we each could manage. By the Tuesday, just 72 hours later, my friend was dead. Meningitis. We were dumbstruck by the suddenness of it all. It made life seem so precious. Tragic. There really was one more angel in heaven that day.

If that wasn't enough to contend with, I was paired up with a super little girl at the local Children's Developmental Centre for our weekly physiotherapy and occupational therapy sessions. We were put together as we were almost the same age, had very similar symptoms and abilities and we were both undiagnosed. In fact, my friend was slightly more able than me, and she was progressing well. One day we get a phone call saying there will be no physiotherapy that week as my friend, since the session the previous week, had died unexpectedly. What freaked out both Mummy and Daddy was that the Development Centre refused to say what my friend had died of. So, Mummy and Daddy were left to speculate whether it was due to her condition, and whether I had the same condition and hence the same fate. For a week, Mummy slept on my bedroom floor. Listening to me sleep. Watching my every move. It was a bit freaky if the truth be told. Anyway, after about a week, Daddy reasoned with the Developmental Centre and eventually, after much persuasion and in the interest of both parents' sanity, we eventually found out why my friend had died so prematurely. Meningitis. AGAIN. This is nuts. Although both Mummy and

Daddy were strangely relieved, they were now also concerned and sceptical about just how rare this disease really is. For weeks, every spot and pimple I had was examined closely under a glass and I was almost literally wrapped in cotton wool. Eventually time passed and we all became that bit more relaxed and settled again.

It took a lot, lot longer before any of us forgot those two very special little people.

# April 2005

This month I went to what I thought was a routine check-up at hospital (with Mummy and Granny) to see the GOSH geneticist. It started well and the consultant was absolutely lovely / funny / gorgeous depending on whose point of view you got. The GOSH man decided it would be worth doing a few more tests, THAT afternoon! Thankfully the EEG couldn't be done at that particular hospital so it'll have to wait until next month. I did though have my hand x-rayed to check for bone age and they also wanted to do some blood tests. Well, they would have had more chance getting it from a stone!! I prefer my blood to stay where it is and despite obvious and repeated bribery of dummies, chocolate and balloons I was having none of it. Eventually however, the doctors won, but only because they joined forces and worked in pairs!

I've also done absolutely loads of walking. Every chance I get and as soon as I have a 'willing' volunteer to hold me up... away I go. The only thing is, I always get that feeling someone is following me - I'm sure it must be just my imagination!!

I am now getting better at using cutlery, but with co-ordination like mine it can be a slow and very frustrating process. This was until I discovered a much faster and reasonably successful technique to eating. Not that unlike a cat. Direct out of a bowl, head first.

This month was very exciting as I got my first set of wheels. It is a walking frame on castors. A bit like a Zimmer frame, but much smaller and more heavy duty. It is not exactly a Porsche or anything and it doesn't go as fast, but it is quite literally a step in the right direction. Or it would be if I could make it go forwards!! My preferred direction at the moment is reverse. Apparently going backwards to start with is quite normal. This in itself is unusual, as I rarely do anything that is expected!

Lots of slobbery kisses,

Jess xxx

# May 2005

Yet another busy month.

I had an EEG. EEG stands for something very long and complicated but basically it is trying to find out why I gaze into space sometimes. Well they didn't need to stick 30 electrodes to my head and then wire me into a computer to find out that I'm just daydreaming about what's for tea.

I've been thinking about all the different tests I've had so far and they are amounting to quite an impressive list. They include: - an EMG, an ECG, 2 EEG's, 3 blood tests (and a 4th one booked for next month), a hearing test, 2 x-rays, an MRI scan, an eye operation, countless eye tests and a head to toe examination every time I see a consultant. I must be the most looked at 2-year-old around... I'm assuming it's because I'm drop dead gorgeous and with my parenting they just can't work out how!

I pretended to be a piggy at the farm today. Daddy unfairly suggested that it was the most apt animal for me to be! Cheek. He's one to talk.

This month I went to another birthday party and had a fabulous time. I did loads of painting and sticking and drawing and most of the time it was on the paper. Parties are fab.

I sent Mummy, Daddy and Nanny on a 'Makaton' sign language course and they did quite well. They even came back with certificates. Now I just need to be able to understand what they are going on about!

I also had the paddling pool out at the end of the month and I went skinny-dipping. I got Daddy so wet he had to strip down to his boxer shorts!! Not a pretty site. It would have put me off my food if I was a picky kind of person. Thankfully, it takes more than that to put me off eating.

Lots of hugs and kisses,

Jess xxx

# June 2005

Well, the most exciting thing that happened this month by far was my first trip abroad. I went in a big aeroplane all the way to Spain. Finally, I got to leave East Anglia (with the exception of my trip to GOSH in London). The flight was excellent fun, and take-off was quite similar actually to being in a car with Mummy driving! The weather there was very nice and I was pleased I managed to still get a tan despite wearing Harry's sun suit the whole time.

I played in the sand lots, although I had to share my bucket and spade with Mummy and Daddy. Not only did they insist on playing, but they were trying to make bigger and better sandcastles than me. I nearly had to confiscate the bucket at one point it got so competitive! Where did I get them from?

In addition to going on holiday I have done absolutely loads of other stuff. I went and saw my stylist and had my hair cut... again! It does have this habit of keep growing. I saw the bug-eyed monster and got the 'all clear' for another 3 months not to have to wear glasses!!! Yahoo! Apparently, my eyes are so good now, I don't even need to wear them for driving. The only problem with that is I can't reach the pedals.

I had a blood test at the beginning of the month, which was as awful as expected, so as a special treat I went to the bird sanctuary place to look at the butterflies. Even Daddy came too this time... well Mummy said if I was brave enough to have a blood test, then Daddy should try and be just as brave too.

There was a parents' evening at nursery and Mummy and Daddy heard how good I am there! Obviously.

I have also been given a lovely chair with a tray on it, from The Grange, which I really like. You can do loads of stuff in it like: - drawing, eating or watching TV... or even all 3 at once! Got to go...

Lots of sloppy kisses,

Jess xxx

# Research

Mummy has got this bee in her bonnet about getting me a diagnosis. (I hate to digress so soon but the thought of Mummy in a bonnet has quite cheered me up as she would look absolutely ridiculous.) Where was I? Yeah, Mummy thinks I need a label, like "I have x". Obviously "x" is not a condition otherwise she would have succeeded already. Anyhow, I think she has had enough of people seeing I can't walk and casually dropping into conversation that they are curious as to what is wrong. My poor old mother, like some village idiot replies, "well, I don't know!" As if "oh, I hadn't noticed she couldn't walk, do you reckon there's a problem?" So, Mummy is on a mission. A while back she actually thought she'd had cracked it (or was it 'cracked-up', I do forget!) when she found a syndrome called 'Angelman'. I think she must have been taken by the name, as I am most definitely an angel, man. Mummy then even had the audacity to contact Great Ormond Street Hospital (GOSH) to make sure they had tested me for Angelman Syndrome. Strangely enough they had considered this over a year earlier, tested for it, found the results were negative but kept it on the 'possible' list just in case. I think Mummy was a bit disappointed in some respects. She had said she hadn't actually liked the sound of the condition very much but thought that at least the mystery would be solved. I really don't know what she expected though. All those top people up at GOSH, with years and years of studying behind them and years and years of experience, could be outwitted by a manic Mummy surfing the internet for a few (hundred) hours. It was hardly surprising that they were one (or more like ten) steps ahead of her. Anyway, call it stubbornness, stupidity or plain bloody mindedness, but this minor setback has not deterred her in the slightest, in fact I think she is now quite determined to solve this riddle. Well, let her get on with it, rather her than me!

# July 2005

This month I turned two and a half. I was quite bewildered because I had a birthday cake with, would you believe it... two and a half candles! I'm not sure how common it is to celebrate a 'half' birthday, but when I had cake and presents I decided not to argue the point.

I was very excited this month to hear the 2012 Olympics is coming to London, although it is such a long way off. Even longer to wait than Christmas. Since this announcement, I've been trying to decide which event to compete in. Me, Daddy and Uncle Billy Bobs tried synchronised swimming in the 'sea' (even though Mummy is convinced the water there is radioactive due to a relatively nearby Nuclear power station). We practised hard, although Daddy cheated by keeping one foot on the bottom.

One big achievement this month is that I have learnt to bottom shuffle. It is moving around on the floor on your bum. Not any great distance or anything you understand, as it is not as easy as it looks. I also only move when money is involved ... well I have to make it worth my while you know! I made this discovery when Granny volunteered to count the takings from church fete. Well, I'd never seen so much money in my life and the urge to move became irresistible. I even managed to wedge a couple of pound coins up my nappy, although they were discovered before I made away with them.

I went to the beach with Daddy, Nanny and Grandad and we made some sandcastles. Not in quite the same league as the Costa Blanca but very nice all the same. In fact, I enjoyed myself so much, I decided to go without a lunchtime nap - unlike some of my relatives! Also, after much borrowing of my boyfriends' blue sun suit, I now have a lovely pink sun suit of my own. It isn't the world's most flattering outfit, but it does the job.

Lots of sandy hugs and kisses,
Jess xxx

# August 2005

I'm starting to get the hang of bottom shuffling to the extent that I can now actually move without any form of bribery, although I do go faster when chocolate is involved.

I have also been trying to learn to count, but I just don't get it... however, it is fun when Mummy tries to help by putting a hula-hoop on each finger. If this continues I may pretend I can't count for some time!

I do a lot of exercises now. I have to keep in shape you know to maintain my figure. If I say so myself, I do show off a little bit and even my gym coach is impressed with my flexibility some weeks. On the subject, gym club is going well and I've even learnt to play badminton there! I'm just not sure why.

This month I got really excited about my new uniform for nursery (well, just a t-shirt and matching hat really) and thought I looked very smart. I have showed absolutely everyone my new outfit, however the people at nursery reckon they have seen something strangely similar before!

One breakthrough, in more ways than one, is that I got my last 2 teeth this month. Yahoo, I finally have a full and complete set. No more hot flushes and grumpiness... well not for a long, long while anyway.

I have had quite a busy month. I went to the bird sanctuary place yet again, but this time Mummy accidentally let a butterfly almost escape and we had to get a keeper to re-catch it and everything! It was the most exciting fun I've had in ages. I've been to the zoo... but we went on the same day as everyone else! Mind you, I know my way around the zoo so well now, that I managed to miss most of the crowds. Anyway, must go, I need to help wash the car!

Lots of soapy hugs and kisses,

Jess xxx

# September 2005

This month the strangest thing happened. Both Mummy and Auntie Piglet went running!!!! Thankfully not at the same time, as that would have been just plain scary. But they both plodded along for miles (and in Auntie Piglet's case, miles and miles AND miles!) all to raise money for GOSH. You never know, GOSH may be so overwhelmed with all this money that they get some inspiration out of the blue and give my wobbliness a name. I was thinking something along the lines of 'cuteness-itus syndrome' but apparently, there is no such thing!?

The local County Council Educational department have finally decided to 'band' me. I was graded an E (it only goes up to F, but they reserve that one for the real wallies!) I was wondering what 'E' stands for and came up with some possible suggestions... however, the County Council didn't like any of them!

I've had a major hair cut this month as I started to look like a mop head. Amazingly my stylist was able to sort me out in no time, just in readiness for my week away at the end of the month.

Centre Parcs (again... will I ever go somewhere different?!) was good but busy. Loads of swimming, which was great fun. I even tried out the slide in the toddler pool, but then was hugely embarrassed when Daddy did his Baywatch impression and clambered up the slide to rescue me after an untimely flopsy moment. I'm just hoping no-one saw! I also did dancing and painting classes (but not at the same time!) and had my face painted to look like a pink rabbit. I hasten to say that was Mummy's idea, NOT mine! Anyway, got to unpack all my things.

Lots of hugs and bunny kisses,
Jess xxx

# October 2005

I have test driven a new 'bike' this month. It's lucky it isn't a walker because I HATE walkers now. Although the more I look at it, the more it looks strangely familiar. Anyway, I got on so well with the one on loan, that they said I could have my own 'bike'. The only problem is it'll take weeks to order. It will be really hard to be that patient. Once it arrives I'll probably jazz it up with a nice bell or something.

I now can do the box splits on command. It is my latest party trick, although at the moment I can only do it lying down with the careful assistance of my favourite teddy, pooh bear.

I have had a go on a real on a swing. Now it may not seem much to you, considering I'm nearly 3, but this was my first ever go on a real swing. It is a bit embarrassing really, but I had a bit of a swing-phobia until this month and then I suddenly summoned the courage from nowhere and shocked everyone by asking to go on it. It was rather good and I went quite high, although I kept a close eye on where the chain fixes to the frame, as it still looks like a bit of a dodgy design to me.

I have also started to learn to stand at gym club and can do 1.5 'bananas'!! (that equates to about 1 second). Anyway, it's very tricky when the floor is so wobbly ... or is it me that wobbles?

Being Halloween at the end of the month, me and Mummy decided to make a pumpkin head. It was good fun at first, but then I felt sorry for the pumpkin and fed all the scooped-out insides back through his mouth with a spoon! I'm sure it'll recover in time.

Anyway, time for a lie down!

Lots of hugs and pumpkin covered kisses,

Jess xxx

# November 2005

Well, winter has arrived and thankfully my parents were more on the ball than usual as they had bought me new hat and mittens. This was a blessing, as the ones from last year were cutting off the circulation to my ears. And I am very fond of ears as you know. They had also ordered a new pair of Piedro boots, which arrived earlier this month. They are to replace my pink wooden ones. I liked my pink ones, but these new ones are jolly jazzy – they are red boots and my physio persuaded me to have them. They're quite the fashion statement you know! My new and improved winter clothing all arrived just in the nick of time, as I actually witnessed several flakes of snow!

At the end of the month I saw Father Christmas. It went well until he told me that in a month's time when I'm asleep and it's all dark, he was going to come to my house and into my bedroom to bring me presents. I wasn't entirely sure this sounded like such a good idea and told him as such!! However, things did improve when he gave me a nice present.

Me and Mummy had quite a clear out this month and I discovered my old armbands. It was such an exciting discovery for me that I had to wear them, there and then, over my pyjamas while playing in my bedroom. Well, with global warming and everything you can't be too over cautious. Anyway, I think Mummy and Daddy felt sorry for me and actually took me swimming the next day. I had a nice time, although was a taken by surprise by a handsome little toddler grappling with my leg trying to help me walk.

A big improvement that got my physio all excited (she IS easily pleased!!) is that I learnt to roll... fast!! It is quite an effective method of getting around, except when you stop you have to wait for the room to stop moving too!!!

Lots of hugs and dizzy kisses,

Jess xxx

# Discovering Brainwave

Thanks to an article in December in a national newspaper, and possibly even more thankful that Nanny actually reads the papers, it came to light that there is a charity in Somerset that help children just like me to literally get on their feet. There are no guarantees or promises or anything you understand, but they do give you something that no one else has managed to provide so far... hope. So, because of this I (with a bit of help from Daddy) applied to go and see the nice people involved, to see what they could do. Unfortunately, it appears that half the nation read the same article and flopsy people like me are coming out of the woodwork like nobody's business. The good news is, that although the charity has been completely inundated by enquiries they will be able to see me for the initial 2-day assessment in May. As a result of this I will then have to do a daily exercise program. Apart from my gym club, I don't really get much in the way of a structured physio sessions anymore and Mummy and Daddy are keen that I get as much exercise as possible. I have noticed they have not got quite the same philosophy for themselves, although allegedly I am getting a bit heavy now to lug around and their defence is that is plenty of exercise in itself. However, it is at the thought of all this exercise that I wonder if it is all such a good idea, until I remember that I am so desperate to get on my feet that I will try almost anything. Anyway, with all that training I'll probably be representing Britain in something or another by the end of the year, so watch this space. Meanwhile I think I should make the most of not having to train at the moment, so if you don't mind, I think I'll have a lie down!

After sending off the confirmation and deposit to say I would definitely be coming down to Somerset, I got this almighty pang of guilt. It suddenly occurred to me that the Children's Centre that I go to may not actually like this idea as much I do... in fact they may not like it at all. Then I got to thinking. I have only seen my physio a handful of times over the last nine months. According to the Paediatric Consultant I am supposed to be having weekly physio sessions. Putting this in perspective makes me not feel anywhere near so bad. It is not even my physio's fault. She's in fact quite lovely. It's the NHS - they just don't have the time and resource to give everyone everything they need. Mind you, they do get all funny if you try and go private, so it's a real no win situation. Anyway, I have now been able to justify to myself that going behind the backs of the Children's Centre is a good idea and at least my conscience is eased, all be it briefly.

# December 2005

My favourite thing is now Christmas. Although, I insisted on putting my stocking up in the living room and not in my bedroom, after the unsettling encounter with Santa last month. Despite that, I discovered that Father Christmas was really nice, as he gave me a whole load of lovely presents.

In the end, it actually took me 5 days to open all my presents!! I'm still really very slow at the unwrapping bit, despite all the practice.

Anyway, I was really lucky... I only got one dodgy present this year and I managed to hide that one at Nanny's. I just hope she doesn't find it!

As I'm almost 3 years old now, I've been to visit 2 primary schools with Mummy & Daddy this month and we will see another 2 in the New Year. They were quite nice and one even had a swimming pool, so that one got my vote!!

At the very end of the month I made a bit of a break-through with my... well, there is some dispute as to what this thing is actually called. The physio calls it a 'walker', Mummy & Daddy think it's a 'bike' and I clarified the whole issue by explaining it is quite clearly... a horse!! Anyway, I rather like my new horse although, like a typical pony, it can be a bit tricky to control. I'm sure though, if I talk to it nicely, it'll be fine.

We finally saw some snow just before New Year and Daddy threw together a makeshift sledge (disguised as a plastic box). Being really floppy, I fall off a conventional sledge. With a bit of help from Mummy, I was dragged half way around the town in near blizzard conditions. It was fabulous fun and we threw snowballs, made a snowman and everything. It is amazing what you can do with one whole inch of snow!!!

Lots of hugs and cold wet kisses,

Jess xxx

# New Year's Eve 2005 'CBeebies Live'

The timing of my theatre visit was not quite as clever as Mummy and Daddy had first hoped, when it became clear it was going to be on the same day as a tube strike and just 12 hours after the most snowfall we had had all year. Despite this, 'CBeebies Live' was most definitely too much of an attraction to give up on lightly, so we wrapped up in our new winter woollies and headed for London. On the train on the way up there, me and Mummy could not take our eyes of a young (being the operative word!) man sitting across the aisle from us. Partly as he was rather good looking, but mainly because he was an absolute dead ringer for Will Young. Phewie! I, at least tried to be subtle, but Mummy was quite embarrassing and people kept falling over her tongue and bumping into her nosey nose. Really quite embarrassing. Once in London we were confident that we had loads of time for a leisurely lunch so off we went to a burger bar. Not exactly my cup of tea, but Daddy was paying so it's best not to argue. So, there I am taking my time and the pair of them (my parents I mean) start getting all fidgety and keep looking at their watches and huffing. Before I knew what was going on I was manhandled back into my pushchair with a chip in each hand and whisked away to the taxi rank. This was just my 3rd time being in a London taxi. The other twice were to and from GOSH, so it was nice to be in the big smoke in a more social capacity. Well, I really don't know what all the fuss was about, as we got to the theatre with over 10 minutes to spare. However, they were both still twitchy. I do wonder sometimes where my laid-back gene comes from. Daddy grabs the pushchair as we leave the taxi and Mummy practically throws me up into a fireman's lift (I'm pretty heavy now!) and we race up to the Circle where both the buggy park and our seats are. Well, after just minimal pushing, shoving and I'm sure a few words I'm not familiar with being cursed under people's breaths, we arrive at our seats, 2 minutes to curtain up. See, what did I tell them... loads of time. Well, obviously, Mummy agrees with me, as at this point she announces to half the theatre that she could do with powdering her nose. So, like a loony, Mummy disappears off into the distance. It is only on her return it is clear there are a lot of people who arrived even later than us. I guess trying to seat hundreds of under-fives is quite a tall order. So, the theatre then generously announces that there will be a delay and there is now 3 whole minutes to curtain up. Well, with this announcement Daddy jumps up and decides it is his turn to skip to the loo, and off he goes. What a palaver! I hope they didn't keep doing this every time an announcement is made, it is rather wearing. Daddy reappears and drops into seat just as '1 minute to curtain up' comes over the speakers. It is at this point that Mummy, bless her, has just noticed that every single child in the theatre seems to have a flashing fibre optic toy, with the obvious exception of me. Well, in her eyes this is clearly a disaster, so she gives Daddy the challenge of 'get one of those, you have 50 seconds!' Like a starter at the blocks he is off, which is remarkable when you look at him as he is not exactly built like an athlete. Anyway, I shouldn't be too harsh on him as an incredible 45 seconds later he is back with a flashing thing clutched in his hand. Exhausted he flops in his seat just as the curtain goes up. See - what did I tell them? Loads of time.

The show was fab! I saw the Tweenies' and Postman Pat and Boo and... well, everyone. It was a great show, out only slightly marred by the unnecessary accusation that I was the cause of a disgusting smell that was wafting around the theatre. You'll be pleased to know however that I was able to prove my innocence during an impromptu nappy change in the interval. Daddy laughed, Mummy cried. I sang, I danced, I hit the woman in the row in front with my flashing toy and I sang some more. Eventually all the fun and excitement of the show was over and it was time to make our way home. Considering the aforementioned tube strike, I felt we were exceptionally lucky to actually get a tube back to the mainline station and we got home without any accidents, incidents or excitement. What a way to spend New Year's Eve. Not one of us was able to see in the New Year. We didn't even get close. Oh well, there's always next year.

# Visiting Schools

In December 2005, there was a meeting between Mummy and lots of my specialists to talk about me! I'm glad I didn't go as apparently, they just sat around a table drinking coffee - yuck. I at least got to play at nursery while they talked and talked and talked. Good grief, I know I'm a girl, but 6 women in a room meant it was never going to be a short meeting. I'm sure the interesting topic of conversation (me) was partly to blame for the extra-long meeting.

Anyway, the outcome of that meeting meant that I was dragged around a load of schools over the coming weeks and then (really exciting) I went to the local Council offices to apply for a Blue Badge. The good news was that I didn't have to demonstrate that I couldn't stand, although I think Mummy was ready to give them a demo if they wanted one. And then I was told my application was approved and to expect my badge through in the next couple of weeks. I was quite pleased with this. I was then astounded when the badge actually arrived home 2 days later with my photo in it and everything. Very impressive. I won't be rude about the Council ever again.

The schools... well, that was quite an eye opener. We were recommended to look at 4 special schools and because we are all (me and Mummy and Daddy) well behaved, that is exactly what we did! I had to take my parents with me, partly so they could do all the talking and secondly because I'm not at all good at driving - can't see over the steering wheel. It was amazing how different they all were.

Before I visited these schools, I was kind of undecided whether to actually go to a special school or risk being the only one with their own set of wheels (by this I mean a pushchair or possibly a wheelchair) at a mainstream school. My other big worry about going to mainstream is that although I know what I'm saying, I appear to be in the minority. So, with that all against me I was concerned that my good looks and charming personality were just not going to be enough to get me through mainstream. Now I've seen the special schools I know I was right!

One of these schools we visited said that because I am banded an 'E' by the local County Council, they wouldn't be able to take me. I was too severe to go there. To be honest I was quite taken aback. I'm not particularly stupid or daft or anything, just a bit wobbly on the legs (well to be honest, a bit wobbly everywhere!) and a bit behind my peers. I was prepared not to be accepted freely into a mainstream school, but to be too much of a problem for a special school was... well frankly quite a shock.

The good news is that the other schools I saw were more than happy to have me. What I really loved about these schools was that they had: - walking frames, special chairs (like the one at home), somewhere to order my Piedro boots, Makaton sign language, nappy changing facilities, a speech therapist and a physiotherapist. This was all completely normal to them. It was just amazing to be like the other people around me. To be wearing the same boots, doing the same sign language and facing similar problems to overcome. For the first time in my life I felt completely NORMAL!!!!

So, that is it. I have decided I'm going to one of those 2 schools I liked. I'll just have to convince Mummy and Daddy that we'll need to move a little closer, otherwise we'll spend forever in the car - but somehow I don't think they'll mind moving for little 'ole me.

# January 2006

I had a birthday this month and I am quite nearly very old, at 3 whole years. I had brilliant fun at my gym party with all my friends. We played in and under the parachute and we danced and ate and... well, we did all the things I like doing. And to top it all, I even had presents too!

It was all very good timing really, as I had a rather unexpected growth spurt just before Christmas and my title of 'best dressed toddler' was under threat. Thankfully lots of lovely clothes meant that my wardrobe is now back to full capacity!

I also had a rocking horse for my birthday. He's called clip clop. I could have sworn that the horses I have seen before were much taller. But I suppose at least my feet nearly touch the floor and it is nowhere near so far to fall.

Daddy was more excited than normal this month as my blue badge arrived which means we can park the car pretty much anywhere for free. The only downside is that Daddy is now trying to hire both me and my badge out to anyone who would like free parking. I must warn you though, I'm not a cheap date! Once you've lugged me and my pushchair in and out of the car, I've eaten 4 cookies, had lunch at Pizza Hut, been brought a new outfit and perhaps a book as well, it may have just been cheaper, and easier to pay for parking!

Lots of hugs & cookie kisses,

Jess xxx

# From the not very terrible two's, to the very frustrated three's

I am started to get a bit frustrated nowadays you know. I have been dead patient these last couple of years, but I'm getting fed up now. It doesn't seem to matter how hard I try, I'm not actually getting anywhere - mobility wise, I mean. I can roll, but to be quite honest it is not exactly ideal. And if I've just eaten or am out at the zoo or something, it is quite an inconvenient form of travel. I have been having a bash at crawling but unless I get a willing volunteer to support my body weight, then that is currently a non-starter. The walker is good fun and I can now do a few steps in it by myself, however it is going to take much, much, much, more practice and I have learnt that I need to avoid shingle at all costs. The walker is most definitely one of those things that is more tricky than it looks. Oh, I can bum shuffle too, but pretty slowly and it should now come with a health warning after I lost my balance on the kitchen floor and toppled forwards straight onto my head. You'd have hoped that I would learn, but I have managed to do that, not once, not even twice - but three times now. I am rather concerned that I may be forced to wear a crash helmet next time I'm anywhere near the kitchen. So, you can see I have tried a few options, and I am still trying. It's just... well, I'm not going anywhere fast, in more ways than one. Meanwhile my friends are going to ballet, gymnastics and learning to ski of all things. It's not that I'm jealous or anything... oh, what the hell... I am REALLY jealous. There's just not a lot I can do about it. I kind have missed out on being a really terrible two, or so I claim anyway, but I am quite happy to admit I am most definitely a very frustrated three!

# February 2006

I have been quite creative this month, painting with Mummy and cooking with Daddy. I had a new paintbrush, pots and a plastic apron which needed trying out, and I think Mummy wanted a nice painting or something. I however was already decided that I wanted to do hand and foot prints. Excellent fun, although just the tiniest bit messy, even if I say so myself. You've heard of the 'Naked Chef', well I am the 'Naked Artist'! When I paint, I wear nothing but a nappy and a painting apron. I'm not sure if it is because I look dead cute like that, or whether my extra-neat Mummy is going for damage limitation.

Now, when I'm cooking with Daddy, I am anything but naked. You will only see me in all the appropriate attire - fully clothed, apron and of course a chef's hat. I made some rather tasty biscuits. Unfortunately, there weren't that many chocolate chips in them. I kind of accidentally ate a few while I was cooking. The recipe should really allow for the odd taster, or two, or three.

This month I have had a scratchy eye and Daddy found I had a bit of a bump inside my eyelid. YUCK! I puggled with it quite a lot but that didn't seem to solve the problem, so me and Mummy waited for ages and ages to see a nurse. She didn't know what it was, so gave me some really awful gunky ointment. Anyway, as luck would have it, I had an appointment to see the bug-eyed monster, and as eyes are her area she had at look at my funny lump. She then even got the grouchy old consultant to have a look too. I am quite popular sometimes. To cut a long story, medium length, he diagnosed it as a cyst and gave me some new and improved eye drops, which are just as horrid as the old lot. I never really wanted a cyst. I would have much rather had a sister... but that seems a tad unlikely.

S i g h ! Me and my teddy bears need a nap now.

Lots of hugs and ointment-y kisses,

Jess xxx

# March 2006

The cyst has gone - it has apparently dispersed, gone a.w.o.l., lost at sea... a bit disgusting if you think about it, but as long as it doesn't turn up again, I don't care where it is.

I've been doing a bit more modelling at a professional photographers', and even though I was under the weather, I still had a rather successful photo shoot. I may well have found my calling.

We have now got a hot tub - well that is what it should be called. Mummy and Daddy call it a hydrotherapy pool (I think they want to blame their extravagance on me!!!) I just call it a pool - but when you are not very big at all, it does actually double up as a small swimming pool and it's a whole lot warmer too.

I have had an assessment this month at Wheelchair Services for what I thought was going to be for a nice new and improved big buggy, instead of my off-the-shelf, run of the mill, pushchair for tiny people. Well unless I am mistaken, it seemed to be a bit of a waste of time. We are allegedly going back to test drive two of their recommended pushchairs, but they look really basic to me, so I may be taking my own cushion and umbrella!

I've seen the speech therapist again and she is pleased with my progress. And so, she should, as I proudly managed 4 words in a row the other day, which appear to have been 100% understood. I can say loads more than that, but usually I get a blank look from people as if I am speaking in a different language... and sometimes I do wonder whether I am!

Not much else to report other than I've been a bit poorly this month, but once I'd shared it with Mummy and Daddy I did start to feel a whole lot better!

Lots of hugs and germy kisses,

Jess xxx

# April 2006

This Easter children everywhere were sampling the delights of chocolate. I on the other hand discovered beer!! Non-alcoholic I should probably add before I swiftly get put into care. Even so, it was beer all the same. It is rather nice too, and I was kind enough to let Uncle Billy have a sip.

I think Mummy and Daddy sold our house this month. They keep telling me there's nothing to worry about, but it is making me a bit nervous. If that wasn't bad enough, I could have sworn I had loads more toys in my bedroom than I have now... Mummy is forever throwing things in boxes and taping them shut. I hope I see them all again!

At the end of April, we (me, Mummy and Daddy) travelled all the way to sunny Somerset. They say "it's a long way to Tipperary", well trust me; it is much, much further to Somerset. Thank goodness Daddy treated me to a portable DVD player. That way, on the journey I was able to watch Balamory, Postman Pat, Balamory and then Balamory! I could really do with another Balamory DVD, as one is just not enough. I may be a fan, but it is starting to get a tad repetitive, even for me.

We did some strange but nice things in Somerset. I went on a 'choo choo' steam train, which was great fun, and then I bottom shuffled half way across Minehead beach with my bucket and spade. That may sound like a nice way to spend a Bank Holiday, but I should point out I was in a thick jumper and winter coat... not what I would call beach weather! The reason I'm braving this typical English weather is to go to my 2-day assessment at Brainwave at the beginning of May. I'll update you on how it goes next month.

Lots of hugs and kisses,

Jess xxx

# May 2006

Day 1
| | |
|---|---|
| 8:45am | Arrived at Brainwave |
| 9:00 – 9:30am | Music Therapy |
| 9:45 – 11:30am | Background, and current status |
| 12:00 – 1:15pm | Physical assessment |
| 1:15 – 2:00pm | Lunch |
| 2:00 – 3:00pm | Hydrotherapy session |
| 3:10 – 4:20pm | Program summary and round up. |

Day 2
| | |
|---|---|
| 9:20am | Arrived at Brainwave |
| 9:30 – 10:50am | Physio program |
| 11:20 – 12:00am | Physio program |
| 12:00 – 2:00pm | Lunch |
| 2:00 – 3:00pm | Hydrotherapy session |
| 3:10 – 4:00pm | Physio program completed |
| 4:00 – 4:30pm | DVD, equipment and fundraising |

Well, the weather in Somerset is still strangely cold and windy for May, but I am not here to get a tan. The month started with my assessment at Brainwave in Bridgwater. My first session was music therapy and I had a go at playing a guitar. I then met the therapists and we did lots of playing, kneeling, and rolling and... clapping! I worked so hard and had so much fun I kind of lost track of what was going on. When we were finished, I found myself standing there, leaning against a wall... no one holding me!... in just a t-shirt, nappy and Piedro boots. Apparently, I looked quite gorgeous.

It was decided that I am too floppy and weak from my shoulders to my bum (pretty much all of me!) and the plan is to increase my strength and balance enough so I can crawl.

Then after a spot of lunch I had a session in the hydrotherapy pool, where I had a ride on a 'horsey-woggle'. You had to really be there for that one! Swimming was fun and they even came up with some exercises I can do in the hot tub at home. Unfortunately, this means the hot tub has now been renamed (again!!!) the 'hydrotherapy pool'.

So, that was one day down, one day to go.

The next day started with a very hard and long session and we went through all 18 exercises in my program. Once with the therapist doing it and then Mummy and Daddy both had a go. They were rubbish but thankfully I was rather good, so between us we almost looked like we knew what we were doing. Then it was a short break and time to have all the exercises videoed. Well, I was totally pooped. I managed about the first 6 exercises and then I just couldn't carry on. As I had worked so hard I was given a 2-hour lunch then another session in the pool before I had to finish off my exercises.

They were really pleased with me - said I had loads of potential and want me to come back again in October to see how I'm getting on. So, I am now on a mission to crawl, I'm just not exactly sure how I'm going to do it yet. I want to show them they are right to have every faith in me.

On the way back from Somerset, we all stopped at LEGOLAND. We had great fun... that is once me and Mummy had revived Daddy. This was necessary after he found out how much the entry fee was to get in! AND they lied about my age! Disgraceful. I drove a boat, a jeep and went on loads of rides. I'm quite the thrill seeker really, although I did pass on the roller coaster. I'm adventurous - not stupid!

On the subject of not being daft, I think my parents had some hair-brained scheme that I would actually carry on doing the exercises we did at Brainwave once we got home. Well I wasn't born yesterday and there was no way I was going to stand, kneel OR crawl for that nonsense. However, despite my strike, I keep finding myself in a familiar exercising position right in the middle of playing. They are definitely up to something.

They should really give me a break as I'm falling to bits at the moment!! I've been really tired and grouchy... and not only has my silly cyst come back, but I've somehow managed to get a whole thigh full of eczema. So, life right now is a barrel load of ointment!!

It looks like we may have had some success at last at getting a new pushchair. It resorted to Mummy and Daddy going in force, and they were most definitely on a mission. We found a nice one, and Daddy approved once he realised it had suspension and quick-release wheels. Apparently, these things are important to boys. Me and Mummy just noticed it was a nice shade of blue with the smallest shopping basket in the world! Well, you can't have everything. It apparently handles well too, so I put pooh bear in for a quick spin. However, I found the handles were a tad high for me.

Lots of hugs and kisses,

Jess xxx

# There was a little girl, with a little curl ....

Well, the saying goes: -

'There was a little girl, with a little curl, right in the middle of her forehead. When she was good she was very, very good. But, when she was bad she was horrid.'

Allegedly, I am she. I personally find that very hard to believe. Not the 'very, very good' bit obviously, I couldn't describe myself better. But 'horrid!' ……… me?! ……. Never! Misunderstood perhaps, but horrid is a bit harsh. I think I had better prepare my defence.

My pet hate at the moment is shopping. Really, really, r e a l l y boring. Mummy and Daddy seem to be forever buying things. One relatively recent thing is looking around houses and bungalows as we are hoping to move home soon. Well, if they have gone to the trouble of bringing me along to view a house, then I assume they are after my valued opinion. So, why is it when I clearly express a preference in a particular property, do they completely ignore me? I am more than happy to live in the Jam factory and I most definitely told them as much too. Why don't they listen? Parents can be so annoying.

We have also been out looking for a new bed for me. The cot bed is getting a bit small and I am forever getting uncovered in the night. This means I wake up at some unreasonable hour (apparently) with feet like blocks of ice. And as I can't cover myself back up I have to call for assistance. Although help does come, albeit eventually, Mummy and Daddy never seem that pleased to see me. So, I am hoping a big bed with a big duvet will mean we all get a good night sleep.

So, we are bed shopping, and again I find the perfect bed for me. It is a bunk bed with steps and I naturally want the top bunk. Probably not an unreasonable request for an active 5-year-old – but a 3-year-old that can't walk – it may be a bit of an ambitious request. Strangely enough, at first I was the only one who thought the bunk bed idea was a good one. That was until Daddy came up with a very cunning plan. The top bunk has wooden sides to stop small children plummeting the 5 feet to the ground in the middle of the night. Which apart from anything else, would be incredibly noisy. And, the bunk supposedly separates into 2 individual single beds. What if (Daddy thinks) we put the bed with the sides on the ground, and we'll store the other bed for a rainy day. Or even better, for a day when I don't need sides on my bed. So, the deed was done. We buy one complete bunk bed, but with just one mattress. That took a bit of explaining to the sales assistant, but we got there in the end. Now this sounds like an event free shopping trip – well, not quite. While Mummy and Daddy pondered on the endless options and combinations of beds put before them in the shop, bearing in mind they are both notorious for not being able to make a quick decision, I sat nicely in the children's corner on this gorgeous miniature armchair playing with a bead game. Completely happy. I even made several references to the very nice chair, in the hope that if I dropped enough hints, I perhaps could take it home with me. Mummy even picked up on the subtle suggestions and asked if they sell the chairs. I think she was quite taken with it too. But apparently, no. It's a bed shop. They don't sell chairs. So, when it came time to go, I decided the only logical option was to take the chair with me. This unfortunately was not what Mummy and Daddy had in mind. And after I was prized out of my most favourite chair, I was literally carried kicking and screaming "CHAIR!!!!!!!!!!!!!!!!!" the full length of the shop and all the way back to the car. Parents – AGHH! They really make you scream. And loudly too. And then to top it all, they keep trying to pacify me by saying they had actually bought the bunk bed I wanted. However, when I got home the old one was still there. I think I have been hoodwinked and this '14 days delivery' nonsense is just them trying to buy time. They can't fool me.

# June 2006

A lot has happened this month.

In May, I thought I was falling to bits. Well, now it's official. I AM!!! My cyst has come back with a vengeance and now looks disgusting, eczema keeps flaring up on my hand AND I managed to come down with the poxy chicken (also known as the chicken pox) AGAIN!!! And I did this somewhere en-route between home and arriving at the holiday cottage on the Isle of Wight. Thankfully I only had it mildly this time, but it was still completely bizarre timing. This holiday on the 'Island of White', was definitely the main event of the month. And at last we finally saw some good weather in the UK. I went to the beach, ate ice cream, and swam in the sea and everything. Apart from being a bit under the weather, it was a pretty good holiday.

I have 2 new catch phrases. "Oh dear" and "did it". Both have come in hugely useful. The first because I am majorly clumsy, but I mostly get that from Mummy. And "did it" has been used a lot as I have had a rather successful few weeks regarding my progress. I am absolutely definitely, 100% sure of it, almost certain that I am getting stronger and more steady. I attempted to crawl on holiday and moved about 30cms (one foot in old 'money') on all fours with no assistance. I'm also walking a bit better, and Mummy and Daddy have progressed to holding my hands when I walk, rather than my tummy, so I'm starting to look more like a toddler and less like a wally. Better late than never!

I also got a big girl bed this month. We agreed on a bunk bed of all things. I'm sleeping in the top bunk as it has nice wooden sides so I don't fall out accidentally in the middle of the night. The bottom bunk is not where it would usually be (i.e. under the top bunk!); it is in the garage ready for a time when I am less likely to plummet onto the floor with no warning. Could be a long wait!

We have also celebrated 'Happy half Christmas' (also known as, June-mas) on the 25th of this month. As some of our family and friends had a really pooy Christmas last year, it was decided only right and fitting that they should have another Christmas. So, in true crazy style, the tree and decorations went up, and we had presents, turkey, crackers, Christmas pudding and well pretty much everything Christmassy!! It went well enough that there was talk of it being a more regular feature. Because of the additional Christmas however, it was decided that I wouldn't have a half-birthday party this year. So instead, I had a couple of extra presents to make up for it. One main one is a truck that people can pull me around in and which has been rather catchily named the 'boat car truck brrumm'.

It makes a very pleasant change from the stupid old pushchair and it carries loads more too. Talking of pushchairs, I am still waiting for my new one from Wheelchair Services. I was only referred there last September, so if it does actually arrive next month that would be pretty speedy for them!

Night, night. Lots of hugs and kisses,

Jess xxx

# July 2006

Unlike June, this has been a reasonably event free month. Well apart from Mummy launching herself down the stairs as fast as gravity would take her AND with me on board for the ride. You will be pleased to know that I wasn't hurt much, but that is mostly due to the soft landing I had. Mummy on the other hand had to go one step further (or she would have done if she could have walked) and was carted off in a 'naw naw' (ambulance). So, quite an exciting day after all. Well for me anyway.

Still no pushchair!!! I have been reliably informed it will arrive next month, although I won't believe it now till I see it!! Sometimes I feel I want to bite someone. I went for my initial assessment in March, 6 whole months after I was originally referred, and if I'm lucky they MIGHT get me a new buggy for August. Glad I'm not in a rush! AGHH.

Oh yeah, I suppose one big thing is that Mummy and Daddy did actually sell the house officially and for real this month. Contracts have been exchanged and everything, and we are moving to a bungalow in August. The only disappointing thing is the new house doesn't have stairs. Not any. And I have only just recently discovered quite how entertaining they can be!

In preparation for the move, all 3 of us have been packing. I've done CDs, DVDs and videos. However, I cannot completely or even remotely guarantee that every disc or tape is actually in the right case, or even in a case at all for that matter. Oh well, I'm sure no-one cares.

Phewie, what a warm month! I don't like it really hot and just my luck it has been the hottest July on record. This has meant I have spent a lot of time in the pool and sporting my favourite pink swim suit... so I suppose it hasn't been that bad after all!

Lots of kisses,

Jess xxx

# August 2006

Well - the journal has been going for 3 whole years exactly this month! And I now feel decidedly older and wiser because of it all too. What started as a one-off idea to keep people posted has almost got out of hand and become quite the regular feature. Never mind, I will just have to add 'novelist' to my never-ending list of achievements!

It has been a month for new things. First the new house and then more excitingly... new shoes. I believed I was on a roll for a while (as good things so often come in threes) and I thought I could actually get my new pushchair from Wheelchair Services too. PAH. Well my luck ran right out at that point, although I am scheduled to go and collect it in September. That would have been just 11 short months since I was originally referred. And people moan about the NHS! I can't think why.

It's official. I have well and truly got the hang of my yellow bike (walker). I can now go fast (for me), reverse it and spin it in circles. I am tempted to take my advanced driving test - if for no other reason than to keep my insurance premiums down. It can be quite costly being an accident-prone under-4! And at the rate I'm going, I may need to get 3rd Party too, as people do get in my way and I don't have brakes!

Oh... I forgot to mention. I really wanted a blue and yellow bedroom. Well, as luck would have it, my new room in the 'house with no stairs' is just that. And, once I decorated it with my pooh bear stickers it felt quite like home. I'm so settled in fact, that I have decided I might even stay there.

Lots of sloppy wet kisses,

Jess xxx

# September 2006

What a month! Where do I start??

Well, you had better be sitting down for this one... I actually, really and truly, no word of a lie, finally got my new blue pushchair from Wheelchair Services. After a minor hiccough, where Daddy was trying to assemble it all back to front and upside down, it did eventually turn out to be a rather good chair and what's more, I really like it. One downside is, it only just fits in the boot of the big car. It could have been worse though... it might not have fitted at all!

Oh yes, I have a new playhouse in the garden of the new bungalow. It is lovely. It is wooden and due to popular request now has blue carpet and matching blue curtains. I could live there. I even tried asking for my bed to be brought out there, but Mummy drew the line at that one.

Taking of drawing, I entered the local Flower Show with some of my arts and crafts. I entered six whole classes, including some rather yummy looking decorated biscuits. I don't know who was more astounded, as not only did I win a prize for every single thing I entered, but I also got the 3rd Best Exhibit in the Children's section for my handprints made to look like a flower. Chuffed or what! I never knew I was quite that talented, and nor did anyone else it transpires either!

One hot and sunny Sunday this month (there weren't many!) we all went off to the beach and had a lovely picnic. Mummy kept gibbering on about the tide, but me and Daddy were having far too much fun eating and playing to listen to that nonsense. Daddy kept reassuring us both that the tide never comes up as high as where we were sitting, and that we'd be fine. Well, that's the last time we ever trust him! We ended up scaling up a cliff face to safety, as all other exits had already been cut off by the tide. Another 5 minutes and we'd have needed air sea rescue. Oh well, it would have probably been quite a dull trip to the beach without the odd bit of danger thrown in for fun!

Now - what else has happened...?

I had my routine 3-month eye check-up at the opticians at hospital (it's the ophthalmologist, if you want to be technical!). They decided it was about time they checked my long-sightedness again. Well, it didn't go too well. They discovered I have astigmatism - it's quite common (my eye apparently isn't actually round!!!) and it also looks like my eyesight is still actually as shocking as ever! So, before I left the hospital I had to choose a new pair of glasses. I've gone for blue ones, just like Mummy's. I thought they would at least be a bit more lenient with me this time as I looked the part, dressed in my nurse's uniform (complete with hat and stethoscope... and everything!), but it didn't help one bit. I picked up the glasses the following week and so far, I quite like them, although they give me a bit of a headache sometimes. ugh!

You'd think that would be enough excitement for one month, but it keeps on going >>>>>

I had an accident-prone couple of days in the middle of the month. Mummy tried to assemble the new pushchair (with me helping) and I got my finger trapped in the footrest. Thankfully Granny was in attendance and was able to swiftly produce an ice pack. So, that wasn't too bad in the end.

I then managed to land flat on my face at nursery, causing a grazed chin and a fat lip. I looked like I'd been in a boxing ring!

The 'Evel Knevil' stunt of the month however, was diving headfirst off Daddy's bed (Mummy was in my bed - don't ask... it's a long story!) landing precariously on my head, on the radiator valve. OUCH!!! It may have been 3 o'clock in the morning but I was not turning down the volume for anyone. Mummy and Daddy however stayed strangely calm. That was until I started throwing up. And then we were off to A&E sooner than you can say "concussion." It's even funnier now when you realise neither of them knew where the nearest A&E Department was (considering we'd only just moved) and we ended up having to follow the signposts - just to add that bit more excitement to our early morning dash!! The good news is, there is no lasting damage and we were all back home later that morning.

I like to keep my parents on their toes... I'd hate for things to get too dull!!

I have had quite a drastic and well-needed haircut and look rather gorgeous as a result. But I guess that goes without saying!

I've been doing a bit of gardening this month and I was quite well kitted out, although I'm not sure the Bob the Builder hat is technically part of the gardening set. It was fun digging and I even weeded a perfectly healthy bush of its blossom. Well, I didn't like the stupid flowers on it in the first place!

I also this month, went along to the Trifle Festival again. Purely in the spirit of raising money for the church you understand, I managed to force down three whole bowls of trifle this time. It was tough, but someone had to do it! Talking of spirit, I can't guarantee they were all alcohol free either. It is just lucky I didn't have to drive home!

Well the month ended as chaotically as it started. I had a medical for my statutory assessment (they are working out how much care I'll need at school!). First the car wouldn't start and Daddy had to come home from work to give us a jump-start, then with minutes to spare we screech into one Clinic only to find the doctor is in a different, albeit nearby, town... they forgot to tell us the appointment had been moved! That meant a mad dash to where the assessment was now to be held, and we just arrived in the nick of time!

Nothing is ever easy!

Lots of stressful hugs and kisses,

Jess xxx

# October 2006

I've been to Brainwave again and despite not technically sticking to the program letter for letter, I had actually done some serious work since I last saw them, and they were suitably impressed with my improvement. Which was quite a relief as I did think I might get the tiniest bit of a telling off for refusing to do all my exercises every single day. Or, possibly more truthfully... refusing to do any exercises most days. Anyhow, I have a new program of exercises to rebel against, so that will make a nice change for all concerned.

We stayed in the lovely Brainwave bungalow this time, which was a real home from home - so much so, I was very nearly tempted to stay. And Mummy was very nearly tempted to leave me there!

Hopefully that is the last time we do that 450mile round trip, as Brainwave are kindly opening a new centre much closer to our new home, which is great. It does mean though that I won't get to go to any more places like LEGOLAND and the Living Rainforest (or any other attraction strewn along the M4 for that matter), on our way to and from the 5-monthly checks. Oh well, you can't win them all.

My new hobby is photography. My best one so far, I call a 'portrait of pooh'. However, you can just about see my feet in one corner of the picture, but apart from that it is practically a work of art. And I took it with absolutely no help whatsoever. My talents seem almost endless!

I have also been to The Grange this month. I hadn't been for ages and ages and ages and ages. Mummy rather selfishly was on crutches when I was last supposed to go, and she wimped out of taking me. However, it was worth the wait. I have a new walker!! I still have the old one thankfully - it would have been a shame to give that one back just as I got the hang of it, but this one makes me look less like a muppet and better still, it is blue. I am absolutely determined to walk with this damn thing if it kills me!

I suppose the big event of the month was my second (I am

keeping count) eye operation. It was nearly a non-event as Daddy, would you believe it, started driving us to the wrong hospital! It wasn't until me and Mummy put him straight did we actually end up at the right place - and just in time too. In a desperate bid to then take my mind off the fact I hadn't eaten or drunk anything all day, I got dressed up in my ballet shoes and skirt. I have discovered I am a ballet dancer you know. Anyway, I did some ballet to pass the time and before I knew it, it was my turn to go into theatre. Gulp! Apparently, I am the first person there to have had an operation in pyjamas AND a ballet outfit! Well I do like to be different... as you very well know.

After the operation, I felt really grim and cried pink tears, and was not at all like a ballerina should be. Later that day, thankfully, I started to feel a little bit more like my usual self. Let's just hope it was all worthwhile.

I have a trial run at 'Gymbabes' coming up soon so I had better go and limber up and be all-athletic - I don't want to look a wally.

Hugs and kisses,

Jess xxx

# Post Brainwave mission

Since visiting Brainwave for the second time, Mummy has been on a bit of a 'mission'. They came up with the useful suggestion that if I put up a bit of resistance against doing my new program of exercises, we should supplement the physio with something less tedious and dull. I'm not sure they were their exact words, but you get the drift.

I did hydrotherapy again while I was in Somerset and it was discussed that I join a hydrotherapy group near home. Well after making Mummy search the Internet for ages, it was decided that I could have the choice of a number of centres, as long as I was a dog!! It appears canine hydrotherapy is as common as muck. Hydrotherapy for someone like me… well, we are clearly asking too much. Mummy did find one that is about a half hour drive from home at a hospital, but that is technically just for adults. Obviously, children like me don't need help. However, after contacting my occupational therapist, a few strings were pulled and I am now on the waiting list. The only problem is the only session available is a day when both Mummy and Daddy work, so I am going to have to talk really nicely to Nanny.

It was also suggested, as a supplement to my physiotherapy and exercises, I should join Tumble Tots. Well I did try when I was about a year old and they said come back when I'm crawling… problem is, I'm nearly 4 and I am still not crawling. So, I never did go back. This was all recounted to the people at Brainwave, and they suggested giving it another go but this time mention that my therapist has personally recommended I start Tumble Tots and was there anything they can do to help. After a bit of too-ing and fro-ing it was agreed I join Gymbabes. The pre-walking equivalent of Tumble Tots. The only downside is I'll be there at almost 4 years old and the next oldest child will be pushing 18 months. I'm going to look like the giant in 'Gulliver's Travels'. Let's hope the locals are more friendly!!

# The peasants are revolting

I feel a mutiny is happening all around me and the peasants (also known as 'parents') are revolting!

I definitely used to be in charge but the tides are turning and things appear to be changing. Rumour has it, I have had it easy so far, as it was decided I had enough on my plate what with; operations, glasses, physiotherapy, speech therapy, hydrotherapy, occupational therapy, cognitive therapy, any-other-kind-of–therapy, and visiting educational psychologists and consultants. It appears my 'get out of jail card free' has expired and I am no longer getting my way. Dummies are being rationed, Mummy no longer sits in the back of the car with me, bedtime IS bedtime, and milk isn't always dispensed in a bottle.

Well, I just thought people should know - I will not be taking this lying down, I will probably be sitting. And I am, as I write, assembling my troops (teddy, eek-eek, oof-oof, dolly AND pooh) for a full-fledged retaliation until normality is resumed and I get my way.

You have been warned.

# Visiting Schools... nearly a year on

Well I was right. A year ago, if I had to go to school THEN, one of those special schools would have been just perfect. Now things have changed. I've changed. I'm not exactly running about or anything rash, but since then I've learnt to bottom shuffle, I can manoeuvre my walking frame with ease, and I'm a bit easier to understand too. I'm not so sure I want to go to special school any more.

Now we have moved house, me, Mummy and Daddy made the executive decision to look at a couple of mainstream schools. We thought we might as well, as one school was now only 6 doors away! We were actually ready for a hostile and unwelcoming reception, as to be honest; I will be more trouble than your average 4-year-old starting school. Well, thank goodness, we were pleasantly surprised. According to my physio however, we were lucky, as that is not usually the greeting you get. Thankfully all seems fine. The two schools we went around, both within a mile from home, were more than happy to have me. One has a swimming pool and the other already has a child in a wheelchair (so I wouldn't be the only one with their own transport in that school). It all looks very positive. Now we have just got to make a decision. It'll be tough as I now want to go to mainstream, but it will mean I will probably be the slowest and least able in my class. At least I should have a 1 to 1 carer with me while I'm there – assuming the statement process continues as well as it started.

Aghhh... I wasn't expecting to actually make a decision so soon! The form from the local County Council has already arrived, wanting to know my top 3 choices of schools, in order. So, Mummy, Daddy and me are going to have to agree what to do, and quickly!

It's done. After several rounds of paper / scissors / stone, we have decided on the biggest primary school in the area (as allegedly you are more likely to get the help and care you need!) and it is the one already dealing with children just like me, so I won't be the 'odd one out'. It has a lovely open plan feel with loads of space and I am a bit excited now, so I hope I get in.

We have even devised a long-term plan if I start to struggle and get too left behind, unfortunately it is dependent on me walking and improving my current County banding from an 'E' to a 'C'. But IF everything falls into place, plan B is a lovely special school only about 10 miles away. We also have a plan C (aren't we ever so organized), which is a special school that will take me if I say banded as an 'E', and this too is only about 10 miles away. These, in special school terms, are practically next-door.

Our second and third choice of mainstream schools that we put on the form, were hopefully just a technicality, as Mummy wrote a very convincing letter to go with the school application form begging, pleading and insisting (or in Mummy's terms, 'putting together a fool-proof case') that my first choice is the only logically place to send me and that they would be barking mad to send me anywhere else. She may have actually used those exact words... you can never tell when Mummy gets on a roll. Anyway, what's more, since I have found out the uniform is blue gingham, and that is my most favourite colour right now, it would be rude NOT to let me go there. So hopefully it's a done deal... we'll just need to wait and see.

Aghhh... I wasn't expecting to actually see the proposed 'statement' before Christmas. Or if you refer to it by the Council's catchy title, 'The Statement of Special Educational Needs'. This is a document that gets put together by the Local Authority using input from parents and key workers (like the physio, nursery, doctor, and speech therapist etc. ....). The idea is that all my needs (over and above that of a regular child who actually walks through the school gates) should be documented in the 'statement' so I get the extra care I need. Or as we discovered, what actually happens, is the Council elaborate and under sell any difficulties you do have, meaning your 'proposed statement' arrives so woefully inadequate that our kitchen door will now have to be replaced... it's a long story... you don't want to know, but Mummy did lose her temper! So, while everyone, including me, spends the Christmas break unwrapping presents and eating too much, Mummy goes on a mission that would have frightened anyone. Her mission is to take on the local County Council at their own game, whether they like it or not. And it appears 'not' was most definitely their initial response. With troops in position and tactics afoot, Mummy and Daddy went to see the Local Authority Educational people and they took with them a secret weapon... Grandad! Between the 3 of them, they didn't say what actually went on behind closed doors for over an hour, (I am hoping it didn't involve the torture of a Council official), but 'the good, the bad and the ugly' (I'm not sure who's who!!!) won the show down, to the extent that I will now have full time one-to-one care while I am at primary school. At least to begin with anyway >>> HORAHH!

So, we are hoping that is yet another problem sorted. I don't know what it is with all my problems, accidents and the like, but it is more chaotic sometimes than a chocolate fountain at a playgroup.

Or was that the dream I had last night?

# November 2006

I've been to my trial at "Gymbabes" (Tumbletots for babies) and I got on fine despite being twice the size of the other children - or should I say... midgets! I have been put into the pre-walking class due to my ability (or more accurately, lack of). I'm sure the others must think I am some kind of giant. Oh well, as long as they are friendly and don't tie me to the ground with ropes, I really don't care.

I have had a bit of a girlie transformation this month, with the resistance and horror of both parents. I made my request quite clear that I would like to start wearing skirts in the day and nighties in bed. And being the obedient pair they are, I am now adequately kitted out at being a real girl. My new dress sense has been well received so far and I have had nothing but compliments... mind you, I'd expect no less!!!

Mummy and Daddy have been redecorating the kitchen/diner/family room (whatever you want to call the place we cook and eat!) and being the helpful person I am, I have had a hand in; wallpaper stripping, plumbing and even painting. Except with the latter I wasn't technically entrusted to actually use paint!

One exciting thing is I have dabbled in 'cruising' and I did it without any help. This (for the uneducated bunch out there) is walking while leaning on furniture. for support, and not (as Daddy thought) donning your lifejacket and jumping on-board a yacht. It is a big milestone and because of this I don't want to do it very often because it always seems to get the audience too excited!

Oh, I should probably tell you - I've now officially applied to go to a mainstream school near home, so fingers crossed.

Hugs and kisses,

Jess xxx

# Supplementary to November's Journal

Well that'll teach me to be organised and write the journal before the month is out! I thought it was such a non-event of a month, but it appears I may have tempted fate.

In the short space of about two months I have managed to go to hospital THREE times (excluding all the normal appointments). Once, when I fell out of Daddy's bed and landed on my head (I'm not actually sure where Mummy sleeps anymore. Again, for my eye operation. And then yet again, at the very end of November. My 'piece de resistance'. Where shall I start?

Well, I was at nursery and we were all outside playing. It was a bit chilly, being almost December, so I had my nice thick winter coat and hat on. I was zooming around the playground on my yellow bike (walker). I stopped briefly to talk to my best friend and key worker, and to get my breath back. I then went to start off again and pushed back on one foot. But rather than roll elegantly backwards, the whole thing toppled back with me strapped in. CRACK. Before I knew what was going on, I was suspended part mid-air (as I was strapped in so nicely you see) and my head went back and hit the concrete. OWWWWWWWWWW

Oh - that hurt, but I don't feel too bad. Phew. That was lucky. I had a lovely cuddle and a wet flannel on the back of my head and went indoors with the others to play some games. The next thing I knew... I was strapped to a bed in hospital! Perhaps Mummy better fill in the gaps...

Jessie was playing nicely at nursery and appeared to have recovered well from the fall. Then, with little warning she went pale and limp and started crying. From that point on they got even less sense out of her than normal. The nursery desperately then tried phoning Daddy, but as he was on a course, all the phones were switched off, so they made the call to phone 999. It was just after this they finally got hold of me, Mummy. I deserted work like the Marie Celeste and made my way to nursery, possibly a tad faster than I would normally. However, before I had even got to nursery, I found out the paramedics had arrived and had made the decision to take Jess straight to hospital. Jess and her key worker were strapped to the bed of the ambulance and zoomed off with blue flashing lights. They even used the sirens to get through some of the traffic. Meanwhile, I have to divert from en-route to nursery, to en-route to hospital, and with the speed of a mother with her baby in distress I actually got to the hospital before the ambulance! When she was carried out of the back of the ambulance, she was so limp and confused she didn't recognise either me or her favourite teddy - I don't know which was more shocking. The next several hours are all of the same... Jess crying, going pale, going pink, crying, going pale, while constantly being monitored and not once really opening her eyes or saying anything. It got scarier when she went really quiet and very grey. Thank God that didn't last too long, although it felt like hours at the time. Doctors kept coming and going and the consensus of opinion was that she would get transferred to another hospital and admitted overnight once they did the CT scan. So, off we go to the x-ray unit and Jess gets all strapped down to the bed... then suddenly, for the first time in hours and hours she says something... "out bed... new house". In her few choice words, she had said it all - 'get me out of here, I want to go home'! From then on things started to improve. I'll hand you back over to Jess to tell you the rest ......

Mummy and Daddy were there to rescue me from the big scary machine and took me back to a grey room with a big white bed for a cuddle and a drink. The funniest thing was, my key worker and another lovely lady from nursery were there too. How funny. Then I remembered the big 'naw naw' (ambulance) and that they were with me then. Everything hurts, especially my head and shoulder, but it is nice to see so many familiar and friendly faces. We all chatted, and it was decided I could go home, but under strict instructions that if I did go funny again then I was to be admitted straight into hospital. Well, that was incentive enough to get better, and get better fast. So off we went home.

"No more now" ... I've had enough.

# December 2006

Daddy has enlisted a plumber this month and got the washing machine moved out of the kitchen and fully plumbed into the utility room. Normally not a topic I would care two hoots about, but I took interest this time as I helped. At least that is what I called it... Daddy and the plumber called it something else.

Being that time of year, I was actively involved in the Nursery Christmas carol concert. I did most of the actions and even some of the words, and when the applause was not quite at maximum level, I joined in to ensure it was.

I went to see the real Thomas the Tank Engine train just before Christmas. It is a lot bigger and a lot noisier in real life compared to the TV, but at least we did get to go for a ride, which was fun.

I also got to meet Father Christmas... twice! The first time at nursery. I never knew he lived in the staff room; otherwise I would have visited him sooner. And then a couple of days later he was at the same train station as me, visiting Thomas. Quite a coincidence I thought, bumping into him twice in one week. His beard had grown a lot in that time - must be all the fresh air he gets.

I asked for a car for Christmas, so Mummy painted a big cardboard box and drew wheels on it. Not quite what I had in mind. I hope Father Christmas is more on my wavelength.

Christmas was an obvious highlight of the month. I am, I think, beginning to understand the whole Father Christmas thing. To the extent that I know he wears a nice red bobble hat and he has given me a present every time I have met him. In preparation of his official arrival this year, I helped put out a mince pie and a drink for him on Christmas Eve and we then lined up our stockings along the hearth. I even practised my pretend sleeping, but apparently it wasn't good enough to fool anyone and especially not Father Christmas. So, under the threat he would pass me by, I did actually go to bed and go to sleep... almost on time.

It was good fun this year opening presents; now I have finally got the hang of it. The timing was fortunate too as I had one parcel even bigger than me! It was a red car. And with a bit of persuasion, Grandad filled the boot full of chocolate!! Staying on the transport theme, I was also lucky enough to get a lovely new yellow bike, complete with an 'ooter.

Christmas seemed to be over so fast... but thankfully someone pointed out, it is only a few weeks until my birthday!!

I did have one fun first this month. I went to the cinema. It was dark and noisy but fun. Me and Mummy had to hide in the scary bits and were only coaxed out with the promise of chocolate. Needless to say, that worked well for the pair of us and we were then able to watch the rest of the film. The movie was called 'Happy Feet' and at times my feet were more ecstatic than happy, as I clapped and danced in my seat to the great music.

Well, the year has come to an end and yet again I never actually got to stay up and see the New Year in properly, although at 12:03am, thanks to neighbouring fireworks, me, Mummy and Daddy did get together for hot drinks and cuddles, which was nice.

Hugs and milky kisses,

Jess xxx

# January 2007

Happy Birthday to me. This month I was 4. And on the very same day Pop Pop was... erh... was... well, he was more than 20, and that is as far as I can count. For arguments sake, let's just say, Pop Pop was old!

We both had loads of super presents, although I think I got more, and mine were much nicer too. One star present I got was a piano, complete with microphone. I can be quite the entertainer you know, once I get started. One of my other favourite presents was a hair styling kit, and I have been practising on any willing victims / clients / family (delete as appropriate)! Because my actual birthday fell on a nursery day, I had my party a few days later. In celebration of both events, (actual birthday and actual party) I managed to wangle two Pooh Bear birthday cakes. The only downside was, the second time around my cake didn't half look familiar!

My party was great fun and I think I enjoyed it even more than last year. All my friends seemed to have a nice time too and at the end everyone took home a helium balloon. I let go of mine accidentally before I had even got to the car. It was last seen heading north.

I have now officially started my hydrotherapy course, but as it is on a nursery day (not exactly convenient) I go with Nanny and Grandad. We've only had a couple of lessons, but Nanny seems to be picking it up quite fast. So far so good.

Apparently, a fight has been going on, on my behalf I hasten to add, but I have been entirely oblivious to it all. If you don't have to get involved with the Local Authorities, then my advice is, keep well clear. Mummy, Daddy and Grandad however couldn't resist the urge to take the Council on when it became clear that they weren't actually planning to give me the full time 1 to 1 care we all assumed I'd have when I go to school. They obviously thought I was perfectly capable of getting to lunch and to the playground and goodness knows where else, without any help at all. The reality is, that if someone puts me in a chair, there are only 2 possible places I will be hours later (assuming someone doesn't come and give me a hand). The first is clearly still in the chair. However, due to a combination of hopelessly clumsy and unusually inquisitive, it would more likely be the second option, which is on the floor, after doing an unceremonious head first dive straight out of said chair. Anyway, after much arm twisting, fool- proof logic and what I understand was just the tiniest bit of torture, we finally got our way. We even have it in writing now that I will now get the maximum number of hours help possible when I start school. YAHOOOOO!

The only other really exciting thing that happened this month is my 'batman' clothes arrived. Well, that is what I call it. Mummy and Daddy keep talking about an outfit called 'Theratogs' which can help wobbly people walk. Anyway, don't know what that has got to do with me, all I know is I have a shiny new, slightly snug outfit to add to my dressing up box.

Watch this space, I'll either love it or hate it. Daddy already has his money on the latter!

Now get me out of these damn clothes!!

Hugs and kisses,

Jess xxx

# Careers

I know I'm too young to be thinking or worrying about careers, but suggestions have already been made about what I might do when I am older... and not just recently either.

The most common theme is a musician or dancer of some sort, and on that note (pardon the pun) the most specific prediction is 'concert pianist'. 'Model' has also been mentioned after doing some rather successful photo shoots. And, I have been told I'm an 'angel' too; however, I don't think that technically counts as a career.

I on the other hand have come up with two potential careers all on my own. I am considering either being a hairdresser or nurse – as I am practically part-trained in both professions already. I had a hairdryer, tongs, hair clips and everything in a set for my birthday. I have practised on myself, on Mummy and on Granny. So far, I have been quite pleased with the results. The main downside is I'm not allowed scissors, so it is more styling than hairdressing at the moment, although it's still fun. Being a nurse however seems almost a natural choice, for three reasons: I have the medical kit; I have the outfit; and I've had enough experience on the receiving end of nurses and doctors to know what to do with most of the equipment. I already know how to use a stethoscope (although I can't pronounce it), I take blood pressure and temperature, I apply bandages and plasters and can administer both medicine and ointment (pretend obviously... I AM only 4!!). I am really quite the experienced all-round medic. In fact, I am certain I'm destined to work for the NHS, because I always ensure I get back all my medical supplies before I discharge my patient. That way I can re-use them for the next casualty. And I have a feeling that is actually standard NHS practise.

# February 2007

Boy, did we have snow. I mean, we REALLY had some good snow. It even lasted a couple of days and was several inches deep. This typically coincided with me having a chest infection and being on antibiotics. So, my actual time outside was cut short. I did try to argue that I would happily take my chances with a bout of pneumonia, just to spend another 10 minutes outdoors, but I was over-ruled. Mummy did however kindly make me a snowman, and I was allowed to dress it in hat and scarf. However, I think she regretted mowing the lawn just days earlier, as it was the greenest snowman I have ever seen. Mind you... I haven't actually seen that many snowmen.

Me and teddy have had to be educated from home for 2 consecutive weeks, as I had to miss nursery. The first was the aforementioned chest infection... there was talk of trying to send me, but the barking cough and streaming nose did seem to give it away.

The following week I had what can only be described as an infestation... of bees! Well, that is what I thought I had. Granny was the source of expertise in this area, thanks to years of working in primary education, and she can spot a nit at a hundred paces. However, the description didn't quite match what Mummy and Daddy saw. In their words... 'these aren't nits, these critters are running about the patch.' And they appeared to be having quite a party, as there were loads of them. It seemed funny, until we all had to be de-loused and the novelty quickly wore right off. Ughhhh.

The most spectacular thing that has happened this month is I stood, all by myself, for about 3 whole seconds. If I hadn't got quite so excited about the event, I may have lasted for 4 seconds, but the astonishment of said achievement got the better of me and I tried to clap, bow and curtsey all at once and then the balance was gone. Oh well, perhaps next time I will be able to contain my excitement!

Almost as exciting but not quite in the same league, was I

went to get my feet measured and after a whole year they have finally grown! In celebration of the occasion I have now got some fabulous new green 'Crocs' wellies and some green lace up boots (Miss Hoolie boots), which have got flowers on. I like green at the moment, but that is because I sometimes only answer to "Miss Hoolie." For those of you not avid followers of Balamory, Miss Hoolie always, and I mean ALWAYS wears green... head to toe... and everything in between. I got new glasses this month and I was allowed to choose them all by myself. Considering I AM only 4, I think I made quite a sensible and wise choice. In practise, leaving the decision to me could potentially have been quite amusing at best. Anyway, being the daring type, I have ditched my old blue glasses and gone for lilac. In fact, you may (if you are very astute) just about be able to tell the difference.

I can't quite decide if my family are mad or just plain hardy. Nanny, Grandad and Daddy thought we'd have a nice day out and go to the beach... in February!! I hope this craziness isn't hereditary, I am weird enough already.

Before I go, I have some popular new phrases - "can't do it", "too tired" and "not fair"! Apparently, I'm more normal than I ever realised!

Hugs and kisses,

Jess xxx

# Calling cards needed

I think I am going to need to get some of those cardboard, credit card sized, calling cards made up. As it is official. We have all finally had enough of it. Some people are just plain interfering, me thinks.

We go out as a family, with me, aged 4 years old, in my enormous 'Wheelchair Services' pushchair. Problem is, unless you are particularly observant, you would think it was just a basic pushchair. Other than it being a bit bigger than a standard pushchair, it is not obviously 'special needs' or anything. We actually have had people stop us and call me lazy, and reprimand my Mummy for not making me walk! People tut, and stare and mutter at why such a large child is still being wheeled around in a pushchair. At that age!

If I had a calling card, it would say something along these lines:

---

No, I'm not lazy. I can't walk.
No, I don't know why.
Yes, we have tried to find out.
Now, mind your own business.
And, if you wouldn't mind,
hold the door open for us on your way out,
as this pushchair is pretty tricky to
get through doors on your own!

---

# March 2007

During the month, I test-drove a new walker. I got on so well with it, and my Occupational Therapist was so impressed with me, that she said they would order me one right away. Now, quite unlike the fiasco I had with my pushchair, the walker was home within the week. I was absolutely staggered!! Now, you may recall I had a bit of an accident in my last walker in the playground at nursery. Apparently, it was due to a combination of me outgrowing the frame and it being used outside when it was an indoor only walker. We never knew any of this, until it was all too late. Anyway, we are now assured that this big, stable, and very purple outdoor walker is practically indestructible. Mind you, they did say that about the Titanic and they haven't accounted for me being at the helm!

I have a new bedroom. Me and the computer swapped rooms in what was a mutually amicable arrangement. I'm pleased with my little girl room, newly decorated in lilac with blue carpet and blue table and chairs. I was even allowed to choose both my new bedding (lilac with castles and houses) and my new curtains (big colourful spots.)

I even did a lovely co-ordinating painting at nursery and Mummy framed it and Daddy then hung it on the wall. I'm chuffed. In fact, I like my new room SO much; I even ask to go to bed, even if it isn't time!

I have been on a slide in a playground, and it was almost as big as I am tall. I'm in training for the thrill seeking, adrenaline packed rides that I may just encounter when I go to Disney World later this year. I hope they're all this exciting!

Just when I thought the whole decorating the bedroom thing was done and dusted, we started pulling the living room to bits - literally. I quite like pulling the wallpaper off, although it is hard work sometimes. Thankfully by the end of the month that room was practically habitable as well. Let's hope that's the end of decorating for a while.

I have been really enjoying my educational pre-school

visits. It happens at home and a nice lady comes and helps me with work and stuff to get me ready for starting school. As I will be a bit behind the others, I think they've decided the more prepared I am the better. Unlike the other help I'm supposed to get, like physio and speech therapy, I actually do get to do this every week (rather than every couple of months!!) It's good fun too. I've just started working on a real laptop, but you have to be really careful your mouse doesn't get all carried away in the excitement.

Well, I actually got to see a GOSH consultant this month - what good that did me I'll never know. They are supposed to be one of the best groups of children's doctors in the world and all they can come up with is "well, we've never seen anyone quite like her - she's unique". Obviously good in some respects as there are a lot of people out there I don't want to be like. But it just seems ridiculous they don't have the foggiest what is wrong! Can I really be the only one like me?

This month I learnt to clean my glasses... on the bottom of my t-shirt just like Mummy does it! I'm getting very grown up.

Oh, I finally finished my hydrotherapy sessions. They weren't as good as the ones in Somerset, but at least the pool is deeper than the hot tub. I did cause havoc though by refusing out-right to go in the electronic hoist. This meant Nanny and Grandad had to take NHS Health & Safety into their own hands to keep the peace!

Hugs and kisses,
Jess xxx

# April 2007

This month we went to Brainwave again, and thanks to the new centre opening, we were there in no time. Quite a difference from the 5 hours it took the last time we went. This meant the day started that much better as we arrived practically alert and refreshed. The day went rather well considering we hadn't actually been doing the exercises in the structured format that we had been given them in. When we ran through the current exercise program it became clear, with the exception of two particularly tricky moves, that we had been incorporating all the remaining exercises into our usual daily routine. Without realising it, we had adapted each exercise to become functional. This, apparently, is not a bad thing - so we had all been feeling guilty failures for nothing! In fact, when they reviewed my progress it was rated as 'Excellent'. I now have a whole new list of exercises that we can again incorporate into our normal daily lives. And as before, we'll try to forget they are even 'exercises' - as we are all agreed, that word, rather than conjure up a picture of fun and excitement, actually puts the fear of God into all of us!

We celebrated Easter this month. I had an Easter egg hunt at both the new house and at Granny's and by the time I had finished, my Easter egg bag was overflowing. So far, I have been taking my time with my eggies by slowly savouring each one. At this rate, they will last for ages - that is if Daddy keeps his sticky hands off of them. He has been looking at my chocolate collection a little too fondly for my liking.

I have recently been trying to explain to my rather simple parents that the sun is too bright and could they possibly do something about it. They originally and rather pathetically said that there wasn't much they could do about the sun. That was until one of them (I don't know who - as they are both now taking credit for the idea) came up with the suggestion of... prescription sunglasses. Not exactly rocket science on the ideas front, but useful none the less. Anyway, after a couple of visits to the nice glasses man, and nearly £20 later, I now have some lovely new proper big girl sunglasses. All being well, assuming I don't actually lose them, scratch them to bits, change prescription or break off an arm, they will be decidedly perfect for the summer ahead and our holiday in September. I look dead cool in them too.

On Easter Monday I went for my first ever 'walk'. I have indirectly been involved in similar round-the-block post roast dinner type jaunts, but previously I have been a mere passenger in my pushchair. This time things were different. Daddy got out my purple bike (walker) and I quite literally walked alongside everyone else. I was chuffed and the others were clearly quite proud too. It was hard work and I was grateful of the regular stops to take photos* of the auspicious occasion and to talk to the locals. On the way back, Pop Pop helped by giving me a push for some of the way and I quite literally put my feet up.

Talking of which, I have currently got my feet up showing off my new slippers. I was so pleased with them (helped by the fact that these are only the second pair of slippers I have ever had... I am quite hard done by!) that I insisted on wearing them in bed and quite happily fell asleep with them on. What I don't understand though is the 'slipper fairy' must have paid me a visit in the night or something, as when I awoke they were neatly by the side of my bed and most definitely not where I had left them.

I have been doing some dressing up - which I love. And I have discovered I am a princess, or I think I am... which is close enough.

Hugs and princess kisses,
Jess xxx
*see book cover

# May 2007

May has been quite a sickly month for me. I blame global warming. Summer in April, followed by April showers in May. I don't know if I'm coming or going. I picked up this really grim sickness bug at nursery. The good news is it only lasted 24 hours. The bad news is I managed to get through 5 changes of nightwear and 3 changes of bedding... not all of it in my own bed even! Then, within a week I caught a cold with a lovely chesty cough, which helps with the sympathy vote of course. It's official; I have spent almost the entire month smelling of Vicks vapour rub.

Broccoli. You either love it or hate it. I hate it. Unfortunately, I was rumbled at nursery the other week when my key worker found I had stuffed my pockets full of the stuff. Out of sight, out of mind, was my motto. As long as I didn't actually have to eat any.

It was only last month I got my sunglasses and I tempted fate by thinking they'd be great as long as I didn't lose them or break them. What I hadn't factored in was the possibility that Mummy would stand on them. Then in an attempt to mend them, Daddy broke them completely. In Daddy's defence, he has managed to transfer the lenses, which are thankfully still intact, into my old blue glasses. They don't look anywhere near as nice, not helped by the teeth marks in the arms of the glasses - but I wasn't exactly expecting them to be recycled!

I had a good trip to The Grange this month for a physio session. Physio is a bit like buses... you don't get any for absolutely ages and then you get 2 sessions within a month. Mustn't grumble. Anyway, I worked really hard and they were thankfully suitably impressed with my progress. There was however some concern over my feet. Apparently, you should put the soles of your feet on the floor. I however often prefer the 'angled so they are facing in completely opposite directions' approach. This has resulted in me being referred to a 'foot man'.

Then, within a couple of days of that Podiatrist referral, I get 2 more referrals. This is a personal best for me. 3 referrals in 4 days... and it spanned a weekend! I am starting to lose count, but including these new people I will now see, I think I am under 16 different specialists!! From Neurology to Cognitive Therapy and back! Anyway - back to these other 2 referrals. The first relates to my so far unsuccessful attempts at potty training. I'm not stupid, but I just don't get it at all. I sit there but nothing happens. So now there is a debate that there may be something wrong, and as a result I have to see an incontinence advisor to see if she can help. The final referral came about because I viewed my new school with my physio (I told you I saw her twice in a month!!) and apparently, school are not allowed to lift me in and out of my pushchair. In fact, they are not allowed to lift me at all. So, that leaves us with two options. The first is Mummy or Daddy lifts me out of the pushchair when I'm dropped off at school each morning and then lift me back into the pushchair when I'm collected. This does mean however, I'm not allowed my pushchair at all during the day, so wheeling me around the patch could prove tricky. The second option is to get a wheelchair. This is fine because you can get in and out of it without any lifting, apparently. It has therefore been agreed. I'm to be referred back to Wheelchair Services to get a wheelchair for September. That's only 3 months away. No chance. It took them 11 months to get me a pushchair. I'll be at least 5 when I see that... if not older! Watch this space!!

Hugs and germy kisses,

Jess xxx

# June 2007

Everyone keeps on having birthdays, except me. This month it started with Nanny, then Granny, Daddy and to top it all Mummy. If that wasn't enough, there was Father's Day thrown in for good measure. Now that's a lot of wrapping, card writing and shopping in one month, and for such a small person too. I would have felt quite deprived usually with everyone getting pressies but me, but thankfully a visit from Auntie Piglet meant 'Happy April, May and June' spoilages, which more than made up for it!

I think in a bid to compensate further, me and Mummy bought the rest of my school uniform. I now have P.E. kit. Lord only knows what I will actually do in it, but I guess we'll have to just wait and see.

Last month I mentioned I was going to be referred back to the grouchy old Wheelchair Services people for a wheelchair. Well things have a habit of surprising you sometimes. Mummy, allegedly, was on the radio promoting Brainwave. I only know this as Mummy told me. Me and Daddy missed it; we had more exciting things to do. Well, apparently, the whole shenanigans of me needing a wheelchair in the next couple of months was mentioned on air and how it was more likely pigs would fly than we'd actually get a wheelchair in time to start school. Well, no sooner than you could shout, "duck, pig overhead" a charity agreed to buy me one. Well, knock me down with a feather (don't try it - you might just succeed). So, we've been looking at pictures of wheelchairs and I have found two: a pink one; and one that has wheels that look like pooh bear. I want either one of those. So, please cross everything for me. I am going to try a few out early next month, which should be fun. I have already had a quick go in my friend's wheelchair from gym club. Her one was really nice, very comfy and blue.

I have decided I quite like being different, except for all the tests and operations, and therapy and stuff, it is almost good fun sometimes.

I took part in my first ever sports day at nursery this month. I'm not sure if they have had them previously, as I've been there for 4 years now and never been to one before. I have however, about this time of year, for no obvious reason, been taken out of nursery, just for the day and gone to the zoo or something for a special treat. I'm assuming this is all very coincidental?! Anyhow, this year things were different. This year I have my purple bike (walker). I was given clear instructions of "keep your feet up" while my special needs teacher, and best-est friend, pushed me up and down the course with egg and spoons, and balls. I do think I actually won a couple of races and I was awarded a lovely rosette for my efforts too. And so was my helper.

Well, my first ever pair of prescription sunglasses that I got the other month were clearly destined for disaster. Mummy trod on them a couple of weeks after I had them and when I went back to the ophthalmologist (optician man) earlier this month, my prescription had changed! So, I now have 2 new pairs of glasses. Pink normal ones and purple sunglasses. Hopefully this pair will be good for my big holiday in September.

I decided to leave home on Mummy's birthday. I packed the laundry basket with the essentials - my handbag, a potty and a pair of wellies and dragged it as far as the kitchen. Then there was talk of going to the cinema, so I thought I'd leave the 'great escape' until at least after the film. Anyway, when I got home, someone had unpacked for me. It'll just have to wait for another day now.

Hugs and kisses,

Jess... Tom, Dick and Harry! xxx

# July 2007

After some initial set-backs early on, July finally turned out to be a very wet, yet productive month.

I had 3 trial sessions at 'big school'. The first 2 were only for an hour or so, but on the 3rd one I stayed all morning and for lunch too. I even wore my school uniform, because most of the other children did too. I think I managed to achieve the somewhat tricky balance between: smart, cute and downright gorgeous.

My book bag was nearly as big as me - and me and Mummy between us did a grand job of filling it up. I had to take a mid-morning snack, a drink, and I packed sunglasses, school hat, and sun cream for playtime (I'm forever hopeful that we will get a summer!) and also nappies for "just in case(s)". I'm glad I only had to pack for a morning at school. I'll need a suitcase to get me through a whole day!

The wheelchair trial was exactly that. A trial. The first appointment was cancelled just hours before we were due to go. I then had to wait 2 whole weeks before it could be rescheduled. This time me and Daddy were in the waiting room half an hour, before it was cancelled again. Thankfully they managed to reschedule it for later the same week and 3rd time lucky we got the physio, me, Daddy, a wheelchair man and a real live wheelchair all in the same room at the same time. Shame the only chair he had with him was suitable for a 10-year-old. At least we got the gist and we finally had some good advice about the sort of chair I need. I chose the sparkly front wheels that looked quite jazzy and big 'push along' back wheels. We will have to see what magic can be done in the spoke guard department. I have left that with Mummy and Daddy and I'm sure they won't let me down. The wheelchair man measured pretty much all of me and because I am on the small side of tiny, they are going to have to custom-build me a chair. Typically, and unsurprisingly, they don't appear to supply cushions or seats that small in a colour other than black. Not exactly my 1st, 2nd or 3rd choice!

At least I did get to choose the frame colour. I'll go for... purple. No, pink. Purple. Oh crumbs, it'll have to be pink. That's it. I've decided, it is absolutely certainly and quite definitely, is going to be purple. NO, I mean PINK!!! Well, I think I finally got that sorted.

I have started reading the 'Woolworths' catalogue when I'm in the car. It has lots of pictures of toys and things. I found a must have, can't live without, please can I have it "pink princess playhouse". It's LOVELY! I showed Daddy the picture and in a typical boring grown-up fashion, he pointed out that I had a perfectly decent brown (ugh!) wooden playhouse in the garden. In fact, he added, it is exactly the same as the picture, except it isn't pink. At that very moment I actually witnessed Daddy come up with a cunning plan. Me and Daddy plotted together and when Mummy got home we went out to the boring brown playhouse. Daddy handed me the catalogue, on the right page and everything, and I showed Mummy the picture. Then in my best well-rehearsed voice I said, "I know. Good idea. Mummy, you paint my playhouse pink". Although no promises were made, I am impressed to report that by the end of the weekend my new and greatly improved pink playhouse took pride of place in the garden. Even me and Daddy helped a bit too.

I found out at the end of last month that I need a special chair at school. Not a wheelchair (that is in hand), but a chair that goes up and down so I can write on the board, sit at the desks and reach anything in between. It's also on wheels so I can be pushed about the place too. It's called a 'wombat' chair, but I prefer my more catchy 'does what it says on the tin' title of the "up down chair." I really hated it at first, but once Daddy had cleaned it and washed the seats and got a big girl seat belt rather than baby straps... I started to like it a bit. Then Mummy pushed me round and up and down the new house and I discovered it is actually rather fun!

I have seen the orthotics specialist this month and he felt all round my feet and pulled them all over the place. He kept telling me to relax. Well I decided I'm not having any of that, and I fought back. They talked about splints and other strange contraptions, but it was decided I needed 'heel cups', which are funny things you put in your shoes. To do that though I had to have both feet put in a plaster cast for a couple of minutes and they'll make me my own set from that. I chose the pink butterflies design but I'm going to have to wait a whole month for them.

I had a bike assessment this month too. It was a bit like the wheelchair thing but with tricycles. Because I can't ride a 'normal' bike without damaging myself, the bike and anyone around me, I was given the chance to 'test drive' a special needs trike. I was even able to pedal it forwards and backwards with no help whatsoever. And this time I have decided I'll go for the purple one. Definitely purple. Absolutely, no hesitation. Purple.

Only one slight tiny hitch - it is apparently nearly £1,000 and according to Mummy (she's good with figures), my £20 birthday money won't quite cover it.

I'm crossing everything at the moment in the hope that I can have both a colourful wheelchair and a special trike. I'll just have to wait and see.

Lots of hugs and kisses,

Jess xxx

# August 2007

I saw the neurologist from GOSH (Great Ormond Street Hospital) and she has got a couple of ideas that she wants to check out regarding getting me a diagnosis. Unfortunately, this means a trip up to London for another MRI - but this time they want to specifically look at the back of my head and my spine. I don't know what they expect to find, but at least they are still looking... I guess!! I'm looking forward to going on a train again more than actually going back into hospital. In fact, I dislike the idea so much of going to hospital that I am considering doing a runner. The problem is, with bottom shuffling you don't exactly go anywhere fast enough. Thankfully due to a long waiting list, I won't be going to GOSH until October, so I'm hoping they'll forget all about it by then.

My newest and most favouritest present ever is my Stephanie 'Lazy Town' outfit. I would wear it every day of the week if I could. In fact, I tried, but on the 4th consecutive day it was nursery and Mummy and Daddy finally put their foot down. Although I did manage to wangle taking my 'Stephanie' musical bag instead!

I have now got my pretty heel cups. I could have sworn I chose butterfly ones, but I seem to have got ones with bunnies on instead. Mustn't grumble. They're not too bad. Anyway, once they are in my shoes you can't see the pattern. Be it bunnies or butterflies.

One bit of rotten luck was the heel cups don't fit in any other shoes I've got, other than my special red Piedro boots. Not even my nice new blue Clarks school boots. So, here's the dilemma. Start school in my new blue boots but with no heel cups, or wear my bright red Piedro boots with the new heel cups inside? I did ask for new Piedro boots that wouldn't clash horribly with my school uniform, but they won't issue me with a new pair until I've grown out of the old ones. Last time it took a year for me to go up half a size... so, I reckon the dilemma will haunt me for a while.

I had my last ever day at nursery this month. I'd been

there over 4 years and it seems weird to be leaving. But I suppose when you are a big girl like me, the obvious move is to leave all these silly babies behind and go to big school. As a special treat on my last day, I took party bags and cake and was allowed to wear my 'Stephanie' outfit complete with pink wig.

Well I suppose the top most exciting and astounding thing that happened all month, and it waited for the penultimate day, was the arrival of my wheelchair. Now, need I remind you, we only actually ordered this wheelchair last month and it is here already! With 2 whole days' spare before I start school too. Thank goodness we went a different route this time, and thank heavens for the charity buying it... because without them, I would no doubt still be at the very end of the mother of all NHS waiting lists.

My pink wheelchair is pretty. But not only that, Mummy and Daddy have done some magic by getting some super spoke guards too. They did mutter about them coming all the way from the other side of the big pond and them costing a fortune. I can't see what the fuss is about. The big pond is just down the road. I know. Me and Mummy fed the ducks there last week. The most amazing thing of all though, is I am a complete natural. I went in it as soon as I got home and with no help or instructions I moved it backwards and forwards. And after a few minutes I even turned a corner in it. I think it would be an understatement to say my parents were utterly amazed at my hidden talents and I was suitably praised with copious amounts of chocolate cake and cream! Must go - want more cake!

Lots of hugs and cakey kisses,

Jess xxx

# September 2007

This month I started a proper, big, grown-up mainstream school. I was super excited about going too - and rightly so, as it was great fun and I met my really nice teacher and helpers. Then after about 3 days I had pretty much done as much schooling as I had planned and decided I actually didn't want to go back. Unfortunately, Daddy didn't take this as an adequate excuse and he took me regardless, kicking and screaming... literally.

After that I decided it was too much effort to put up a fight, so I went quietly. Thankfully I didn't have to go much longer as Mummy had rather cunningly booked our summer holiday to coincide with my first term at school. And she is supposed to be the clever one in the family! There is no hope for the rest of us! In her defence, originally (when the holiday was booked) it was agreed that I would not start school until the October half-term. But due to a problem with one-to-one funding, that got changed to me starting at the beginning of September with everyone else. Thankfully the Headteacher was fully aware of all this too-ing and fro-ing, so we did get special permission to go away on holiday. But it was quite funny at the time.

Which leads me nicely on to the other main event of the month - my holiday to Disney World in Florida with my whole family. There were 8 of us in total! Now, I was continually warned it would be a long journey to get there, but I quite seriously under-estimated just how long it would take. It felt like years! Eventually we did arrive safe and sound and after a relatively good night's sleep, considering, we were off to explore the world of Disney. It didn't take long before I discovered my absolute all-time favourite thing to do, is find a larger than life character - and if at all possible, give them a larger than life hug!

Mind you, it only took a few days and I was off exploring the roller coasters and things that go around and around and up and down (in the kiddie section of course) and riding each one as many times as my adult company would allow, before they felt sick!

We went to loads of parks, but I have absolutely no idea (and I don't even care) what any of them are called, I just want to know (a) is there a 'big girl ride' there and (b) when can I see Minnie Mouse (again).

I did other stuff too. I went to a couple of water parks and some of the rides I had to go down by myself. Which was handy as I could tell Granny had no intention of joining me! I also went on an airboat across a huge lake. While the others looked out for alligators, I was more preoccupied with the fact that I had been made up to look like Snow White that morning, and the wind and rain were playing havoc with my hair and outfit! You could tell Auntie Piglet had gone off doing her own thing by this point, as you never saw this kind of disorganisation when she was around!

The wheelchair was not only comfy around the parks, but also worked as a 'fast pass' onto most rides and some character viewings too, and I also seemed to be getting preferential treatment in the free sticker and pin badge department as well. I'm not complaining. Sooner or later this lack of walking must bring the odd advantage. So, WHEN can I see Minnie again??

Lots of hugs and kisses,

Jess (princess on wheels) xxx

# October 2007

As always, life is never quiet. What a month. Where do I start?!

Within a week of getting back from holiday, barely over the jet lag, I had an appointment with the incontinence consultant at hospital. Completely unexpectedly, he actually talked a lot of sense and told me things I never knew. Apparently, because I spend most of my life on my bottom, cute that it may be, it means my insides are unlikely to function properly. I even had my tummy x-rayed and it was decent enough to actually prove the point. Shame no one bothered to mention it before. So, I am on a special medicine to see if that helps with the problem and I'm going back in 3 months to see if things have improved.

A couple of days later I did my first ever guest appearance at an inter-county Darts Championship. There I met the lovely people who raised the money that paid for my jazzy wheelchair. I even had my photo taken with some important people and I could be in the next edition of 'Darts World'. Not many 4 year olds have managed that, I reckon.

Then, a couple of days after that, I was in the school Harvest Festival Service in the church next door to school. And despite teasing Daddy, by practising the harvest song inter-dispersed with words from my toilet song, I sang the correct words beautifully, complete with actions.

Less than a week later, I was hoodwinked into going up to Great Ormond Street Hospital (GOSH) for a number of tests. I went on the pretence that I could go on the train and get some new stickers. I would have usually complained about being starved for a whole day, but I was so on my guard as to what was going to happen, that hunger was the least of my worries. I had, I believe, almost every orifice swabbed (I've been here before, I thought!) It wasn't exactly fun, although some did tickle! I had a muscle test thing, which meant linking my leg up to the National Grid, or similar, so they could record the speed of my muscle reactions. The consultant was looking at the 'after shock' where the message is supposed to run (walk or bottom shuffle) from my foot, up to my spinal cord (or something) and back. Usually there is a pattern to this bizarre process. It was almost interesting to hear that with me, there seems to be no pattern whatsoever. I reckon it depends which impulse I send. Some would stop and ask directions while others would stop for lunch. I guess?

After that I had to have a sleep. Mickey Mouse was a sport and agreed to put the smelly (gas) mask on first. He fell asleep in no time and with no fuss either. So, as he was so brave I agreed to have a go. It wasn't so bad.

Problems did start however when I woke up. UGHH. I felt groggy and woolly and sick and blurry and sick (again). I had a sore back, where they had done a lumbar puncture and a sore and bandaged hand from a number of blood tests. Thankfully the brain scan left no lasting impression (well not on me anyway!). Eventually, and over an hour after my bedtime, I was finally discharged from hospital. Shame it was nearly 2 hours travelling to then get back home. I never knew that time of day existed and I am not that bothered if I don't ever see it again. I was so tired, I appeared to have lost any control of my arms and they stayed in the air like I was surrendering. Actually, I WAS surrendering!

It wasn't until late the next day, and only once my bandage was removed, that my most poorly arm ventured out of my dressing gown sleeve. Until then I was like a one-armed bandit.

Less than a week after that (I told you my life is hectic!), me, Mummy and Nanny went to Brainwave again. They made me work really hard and my poor little knees were pink and sore by the time they had finished, from all the kneeling and crawling (with help of course - I'm not THAT clever yet). Anyway, that is another set of exercises that I need to feign tiredness or boredom so I can go do something more exciting instead.

Talking of exciting, Mummy made it her mission to find cosy toes (like babies have in pushchairs) to keep their toes cosy, obviously, but big enough to fit a great big grown up school girl like myself. It was almost Mission Impossible, or so I have been told hundreds of times, but after much playing on the internet, Mummy found somewhere that does wheelchair clothes for adults and children, just like me. And some are almost jazzy.

I now have a proper poncho, with a bit that goes over the back of the wheelchair, to stop water running down my back and onto my seat. I've got waterproof cosy toes too. Thankfully, because Mummy (and not Daddy) chose them, they co-ordinate beautifully with the wheelchair. And not by chance either, I bet.

Well to finish on a really high note after everything else that went on in the month, there was a letter waiting for me when I got back from holiday. I do get letters quite often, but they are usually 'inviting' me to a hospital appointment or similar. So, there was no immediate excitement about receiving this letter as you may imagine. But this one was different. It said that I am one of only two runners-up in the whole country for the Right Start magazine 'Child of the Year 2007 Award'. For that I won £50 in Verbaudet vouchers, with which I have chosen a lovely selection of pink things, AND I have won a 10-day holiday in Europe, and I'm allowed to take Mummy and Daddy with me too. They are putting an article about me in the local paper too. I knew I would be famous one day. I just don't know why!

Oh well, I better go, I am on 'Exercise Avoidance Tactics' at the moment, which I think I may abbreviate to 'EAT'?! Talking of which, I fancy a smackerel of something.

Lots of hugs and kisses,

Jess xxx

# November 2007

This month would have been considerably busier if I hadn't been poorly sick and we kept having to cancel parties at the last minute due to me coughing and spluttering all over the place. The stupid cough also means I'm not sleeping at all well. In fact, I haven't slept well for most of the month. But this can be alleviated if you believe in the motto "a problem shared is a problem halved". So, I gave Mummy and Daddy a few germs and got them up every night, at least two or three times a night. We have also started playing musical beds. I am not sure if there is a true purpose to it all, or whether it is just to alleviate the middle of the night tedium. Either way, we never seem to wake up in the bed we first went to sleep in! Although it hasn't been a busy month, it has felt like a very long one!

Me and Mummy did get to go to 'Wheelchair Services' as they wanted to review my special pushchair and check it was still the right size. Well it took ages to get there in rush hour traffic and then Mummy said loads of rude words parking the car. Within 5 minutes we were back in the car fighting to get to school. They can be as much fun as broccoli. Sometimes.

On a more positive note, I have come home from school on two consecutive Fridays with certificates for 'Special Achievement Award' and 'Star of the Week'. I take this to mean I am probably settling in okay. That or my recent celebrity (darts) guest appearances and pictures in the paper are becoming common knowledge. I have made sure my holiday I won is now booked. I don't know where the South of France is, but I do know we are staying somewhere right on a beach with a huge pool. Well, that's me sorted.

I've been out with the parents and grandparents for a pub lunch. All, behaved as well as could be expected, which made a nice change.

And at the end of the month I shaved Daddy's moustache off, which was really funny. Once we had stopped laughing we told him to grow it back straight away. He looked utterly

ridiculous.
    Lots of hugs and kisses,
    Jess xxx

# December 2007

Well, a month that includes Christmas was bound to be busy, hectic and exciting - and that pretty much sums up my month.

I saw the incontinence consultant and he is happy with my progress. But he wants to keep me on my current medication for the foreseeable future. Apparently loads of kids in wheelchairs are on it. It kind of goes with the territory really. Anyway, I've had quite a few potty successes in the last few weeks. Quite a milestone for me really. Mummy and Daddy put it all down to the medicine. But I know it's because of my new potty song that I made up. It goes... "wee wee, poo poo, bum bum". Frankly, I find it hysterical, and if nothing else at least I now have a bit of a giggle while on the potty.

Being the festive season, I took part in the school nativity play. I was a carol singer. I only made 2 of the 3 performances - it was the pressure! That and I was too exhausted to keep going. I hear the show managed to go on without me on the last night.

I was barely well enough in time to go on the school Xmas outing to the panto. I took Nanny and we both had a brilliant time. "He's behind you!!"

I went to see the real, the one and only, Father Christmas at the farm, a couple of days before Christmas. He was, as always lovely and we had quite a chat. He even let me touch his fluffy beard. I had rehearsed in the car that I would ask for a handbag (just in case of stage fright you know). Anyway, when I got there, and in the excitement of it all, I accidentally asked for a dolls house. He seemed fine with that as long as I would leave him out a chocolate off of the Christmas tree on Christmas Eve. Good plan to me - so a done deal.

Father Christmas came up trumps and I got both a handbag (well actually 4 in total!!) AND a dollies house.

I got loads of lovely presents - to the extent it took me 2 days to open them all. Problem was - some I just had to play with right away. We had a complete houseful over Xmas. So much so, that people were sleeping on my bedroom floor and even on the drive! Having everyone at home was rather lovely, and they were all rewarded with special hugs.

You would have thought I would have had enough excitement for one year, but I took a rapid and rather scarily impressive downward turn on the very last day of the year and managed my all-time hottest temperature of 102.5 degrees! I knew I felt really hot and confused and sleepy and got confirmation of my exact temperature when Mummy spoke to someone called 'NHS Direct'!?

Anyway, I did manage to get both a chest infection and antibiotics before the year was out, and now I have to make the fastest recovery in history, as my birthday party is early next month. And as I'll still be on 'antibionics' - I will have to lay off the beer too!

Lots of hugs and banana flavoured medicine kisses,
Jess xxx

# January 2008

Well, as you know, the year started with me being poorly. But due to a cunning combination of antibiotics and giving most of my germs to Mummy, I was well enough to enjoy my birthday party. I had about 20 friends there - which is also as far as I can count - so any more would have been wasted on me! We had a crafty party. This meant making things like hats and masks and doing painting and stuff. Good old-fashioned messy fun. It was nice to have all my school friends there. Me and my best friend did a painting together. And after all the making, sticking and colouring, we had tea and then I went home to unwrap loads and loads of birthday presents.

I thought that was good fun. Then the next day I had another party with the grandparents. Not quite as messy as the previous day, which is surprising as Mummy and Granny were there, but I had another party tea and even more presents.

Being 5 is much better than I had anticipated.

Then a couple of days after that, it was really and truly my actual birthday. So, I took mini cakes to school and me, Mummy and Daddy had a party tea and my last few presents.

The excitement then didn't even stop there. The day after my birthday I got new glasses. These are purple, rather than pink frames with purple arms and they are a slightly different shape too. However, you'd do well to tell them apart. I chose these all by myself, and despite lots of encouragement to go for a jazzy pair, I decided to stay sensible. Well I am 5!

My Statement (which is technically known as the 'Statement of Special Educational Needs') had its annual review mid-month. This time I was invited too, along with the SaLT (Speech and Language Therapist), my 1 to 1 teachers, my real class teacher, the SENCO lady (Special Educational Needs Co-ordinator) and Mummy and Daddy. The only bit I really took notice of though was the shortbread biscuits, and amongst the chomping and crumbs, the sum-up implied that there were no planned changes to my Statement for next year - which is great. I really, really like my two 1 to 1 teachers, and it would literally be a showstopper if they weren't allowed to help me out.

I had my first proper appointment at the new (well, new to me) Children's Development Centre. It is my new catchment centre since we moved, but we stayed under The Grange until I started school, allegedly to make the transition easier. Frankly it's been a complete disaster. Now I have finally been to the centre and seen someone, they seem to be quite helpful and friendly... and dare I say it... good! Time will tell, obviously, and we are still fighting for both a potty chair for home and new boots. In fact, we started fighting for these about 3 months ago, and seem to be going around in never ending circles. I know Mummy has got bored with it, as she's threatening to buy me real shoes from a proper shoe shop instead!

Just one last thing - now I'm 5 I thought it would be really helpful to offer to drive now and again. What I don't get is neither parent will actually take me up on the offer - even if I cry loudly. Why are they so stubborn and annoying?

Lots of hugs and teary kisses,
Jess xxx


Mummy has insisted she help write a bit. I have no idea why, or what about, but it will no doubt be dull - so you can (like me) skip this bit... I won't tell... and no-one will ever know! I'll hand you over - good luck!

# The unexpected trip to GOSH

Right - my chance at last to finally download the latest news and information that I have in my head, before it explodes!!

Jess went for tests back in October last year. Brain scan, lumbar puncture, blood tests and stuff. Believe it or not, we knew the results would take about 3 months and it was actually closer to 4 months, but we're used to waiting now. And usually, no news is good news. Right?

Anyway, what usually happens is they send a letter through saying, all test results are now complete, they've all come back negative (i.e. fine) and we'd like to see you all again in 12 to 18 months. This time we got a letter saying - all test results are now complete, please come in person to GOSH (Great Ormond Street Hospital) to talk to the consultant and don't bring Jess with you.

Curious and a bit worrying. I did then phone them (twice) and asked if it really was necessary for us to do the 4-5 hour round trip. But they insisted on this case they would like to talk through the results with us. Curious ... and frankly a bit more worrying.

Anyway, as it is with these things, we had about 4 weeks' notice before the meeting, so enough time to try and rationalise it all. And in the interests of keeping our sanity, we tried to convince ourselves that they would want to discharge Jess from GOSH. Not a completely unexpected move, as we've been through over 4 years of tests and still we are none the wiser. So, we went with that in mind.

The people there, as always, were lovely and made us comfortable and reassured us that this is quite normal to get together for a 'chat' now and again to make sure how everything was going.

Now the good news was that all the test results came back normal. That is, except the brain scan. There is, apparently, a bit at the very bottom and back of your head called the cerebellum. This, it seems, controls quite a lot, including: sensory perception (how you feel things, physically), learning, gait (the way you walk, if you can walk!), processing of language (understanding), muscle tone (floppiness), muscle strength, eye movements, body and limb movements, coordination, posture, balance and position of body in space. Anyway, that bit of her brain has not grown at all in the 4 years since her last scan. In the words of the consultant, 'this is potentially worrying'. It shouldn't get smaller in proportion to the rest of the brain and they don't know why it has. Because they don't know the 'why', they don't know what is actually going on. The plan is that in about 2-3 years, Jess is to go back to GOSH and have another brain scan. They will then be able to compare the then 3 scans and see if there is a trend or pattern. At that point they will be in a much better position to say what is going on. Until then she has been 'labelled' with a "Cerebellum Disorder". It isn't a diagnosis as such as there are many Cerebellum Disorders, but it narrows the field of what may be wrong.

Here comes the confusing bit - if you are still with me. Usually you would expect this to show as a loss of skills or some kind of regression. However, on a positive note, Jess is still progressing - albeit exceptionally slowly. Apparently, the lack of brain growth has been masked by the fact she is at an age when progression is typically exceptional. And what it has done to Jess is reduce the rate of progress from an avalanche to a trickle. If, however, she was at an age where development and progression was relatively static - we would have probably seen her get worse. (If you understood that bit, you did better than most!)

So, we now have to wait a couple of years to find out more.

What we have been told is if the cerebellum does get smaller, it is an indication that Jess has a progressive disorder. This means she will start to deteriorate and never recover.

There is no cure.

But we have to move on. For her, if nothing else, things have to carry on as normal - as this is still just a worst-case scenario. The only problem is it is slightly closer to home than it ever has been before.

So, to sum up - A bit of her brain has not grown in at least 4 years when it should have. And if it continues to stay the same - she'll stay the same. If it gets bigger - she'll progress faster. And if it gets smaller, then she'll get worse.

So, it's back to a waiting game. Again.

While we were there we made the most of a world-famous hospital and a top neurological consultant and asked as many questions as we could muster considering the previous information was still flying around our heads.

Anyway, the summary of the responses was:

- the eyesight problems are directly linked to the cerebellum thing.
- the incontinence problems are probably linked too.
- if she isn't walking by the age of 7 years, she probably won't.
- however, in their opinion they think she is unlikely to ever walk independently (i.e. without a frame).
- the fact that she is a midget is curiously interesting, but is nothing to do with the whole cerebellum thing. In fact, she will now be referred to a growth specialist (her height has shifted from the 91st percentile at 1 year old (i.e. she was a huge baby), to less than the 2nd percentile aged 5. In fact, she is the smallest in her class and the height of a 3.5-year-old.)

So, that's that. No real diagnosis as such. And as before she could get better, stay the same or worsen. So, in that respect nothing new to report.

We'll just have to wait and see what the future holds.

# February 2008

Not so much to tell you this month.

Auntie Pig-lit and friends came down to see me this month and brought me pressies... as always! We had fun and went out for lunch and everything. But I didn't want them to go. And despite lots of 'pleases', they still went back to their own house. Sigh.

Thankfully, I was suitably distracted from the whole 'missing Pig-lit' shenanigans as we went on holiday during half term to Centre Parcs (oh no, not again!) It was nicknamed the 'hungry holiday' as I was constantly starving and ended up eating every couple of hours. I don't know whether it was all that swimming, fresh air, riding down flumes or if I am finally about to grow... either way, if there was food about - I'd eat it!

It was a good holiday with only one tiny mishap involving the flume in the toddler pool. Daddy wasn't allowed to come down the flume as apparently, it is for under 8 year olds. I was sure no one would notice, but he was insistent he could not pass as an 8-year-old anymore. Anyway, I got stuck in the tube, part way round, and I had just started to bottom shuffle myself to freedom when a big girl (she must have been nearly 8 years old) came whizzing down the slide and we both popped out the bottom in a tangled mess. Well, if you ask me that was a bit too much excitement for one day and you will not be finding me riding any more flumes 'all by myself' for a long while.

I also did other stuff like gluing, sticking, feeding ducks, horse and carriage rides and face painting, but the best bit was going down the big slides really fast with Daddy.

I have learnt a new and fun thing to do at school. Spellings. I have been practising a lot and although I think I'm getting there, I seem to be driving everyone around me a bit crazy with my chanting.

I'll share with you my favourite 'spellings':

P - I - N   = "pin"

D - A - D = "Daddy"

M - A - T = "pin"

M - U - M = "pig"

So, as you can see - I've pretty much sussed this spelling malarkey.

I had a real Physio session in the new Development Centre after school one day. AND I'm going back next month. It was rather good. However, it was all a bit de ja vous, as the majority of the exercises they suggested, I've already been doing for months... thanks to Brainwave! Well, at least it looks like they were good exercises. It also looks promising that I may get referred, so I may finally get my new boots and all the other stuff I need at the moment. I won't hold my breath as I know what the NHS is like. However, to keep you on your toes, they just occasionally have a habit of surprising you!

I have 2 new catchy catch phrases.

The first is essential in the mornings when Daddy insists on getting me dressed into my school uniform while I am trying to play toys. This is when I usually say... "go away, you're annoying me".

The second is when Mummy inevitably does something stupid. Like picking up chocolate hob nobs in the supermarket when we went in for yoghurt. At times like that, only one comment will suffice... "you silly nah-nah wally".

At the very end of the month, due to the imminent 'Mother's Day', Daddy taught me all about keeping a secret. Me and Daddy wrapped up a present and as soon as Mummy came in I couldn't contain myself a moment longer... "Mummy, bought you present. A DVD. It's hiding in the spare room".

I don't know what I did wrong. I kept the secret to myself for what literally seemed ages... but now Daddy says he won't tell me any more secrets.

Oh bum.

Lots of hugs and kisses,

Jess xxx

# March 2008

One exciting first this month, was going ice-skating. I had been watching it on TV and practising hard in the living room at home, but it isn't quite the same as actually being out there on the ice. Nanny and Daddy pushed me around the rink and they found it quite a hot and tiring experience. I couldn't see the problem. In fact, it is decidedly cold on the ice rink, and although it was exciting, it was relatively laid back (for me anyway) as sports go. Meanwhile Grandad and Mummy were in charge of photos and spectating.

Uncle Billy Bob's came down to stay for a few days this month and we played really nicely together. We did dancing, had an Easter Egg Hunt and Uncle Billy built the biggest snowman I had ever seen, with me, Mummy and Daddy all helping a little bit. I always knew there was a good reason for us to move, and on Easter Sunday I discovered what it was. SNOW. And lots of it. I thought it was supposed to snow at Christmas, not Easter. The weather meant that the Easter Egg Hunt had to be done indoors, but it more than made up for it, as we did sledging, had snow ball fights and built snowmen. Jolly good fun. I'm looking forward to next Easter now.

Not much else happened. Still haven't even got an appointment for my new Piedro boots, so I am wearing pink Clark's shoes to school at the moment. They match beautifully with the wheelchair... if nothing else!

Lots of hugs and snowy kisses,

Jess xxx

# April 2008

I have reached, achieved and conquered another milestone – or in other words, I did something new... once. Don't expect me to do it again. I got from sitting on the floor to standing up – all by myself. Well, with quite a bit of help and support from the sofa, as well as a reasonable amount of bribery. I had got from sitting to kneeling with minimal fuss or bother. Then I asked Mummy to help me up. She seized the moment and said that if I stood up without her help I could have 3, yes THREE stickers. Well that kind of incentive doesn't exactly come around very often. So, a considerable amount of effort and determination was then required to avoid missing out. Anyway, I DID IT!

My school 'Easter Holidays' were technically a lie. This is partly because the break from school didn't actually coincide with Easter and then to compound the issue, I didn't go on holiday either. I will rename my break as the 'grandparent fortnight'. I took it upon myself to 'play toys', go swimming, play shops/hairdressers, do baking and anything really that wore the grandparents to a frazzle. A good time seemed to be had by all.

I went back to Brainwave and although we went with a very real intention this time to make it my last visit (as we haven't actually been doing the exercises at home) a combination of unexpected factors meant that we booked to go back in October before we had even got home. Brainwave came up with some ingenious ways to make some of the exercises into games. And it seems to fool me every time. Also, I was a star for a couple of visitors who may provide potential sponsorship to Brainwave... in fact, I was so fabulous, they may be even part sponsoring me! This would be great as it apparently isn't exactly cheap to go there. Without Brainwave, I would definitely be worse off... by 3 stickers, for starters!

Well, I have actually done a bit of growing. It must have been all that eating I did in Centre Parcs back in February. I am about 2cms taller (an inch in old money) and my feet have grown too. It took a year last time to go up half a shoe size and in the last 3 months my feet have grown a whole shoe size. This means I got yet another pair of shoes before my appointment with the orthotics man.

I did a 'welly walk' at school. It was good fun and we all got really wet. We would have got a good deal wetter, but thankfully it stopped pouring with rain just in time. I did 5 laps in my walker and only ran over a handful of people accidentally. The rest I did on purpose.

I finally got my orthotics appointment months after I had grown out of my Piedro boots. I have been to this kind of appointment many, many times before, just not at this particular Children's Centre. I was so prepared in fact, that I had even decided in advance what colour my next pair of boots would be – purple. Because of this, I was then utterly baffled when the lovely specialist looked at my feet and told me that my old boots and heel cups were not giving anywhere near enough support and that I would need ankle splints. Catchily called DAFO's (Dynamic Ankle & Foot Orthosis). If I have these, I won't have to wear boots any more. The only downside was that I had to have my feet put in plaster, temporarily (of course), so some splints could be custom made. This time I have chosen a Tweety Pie design. I think that should make them look pretty.

I did another guest appearance for the Darts people at another inter-county match. It was tiring but fun, and they are the loveliest people you could ever meet. It was like being famous this time. Everyone knew me. I guess that is what being special is all about.

Lots of hugs and kisses,

Jess xxx

# May 2008

I wished and wished for a purple trike. I suppose a wish THAT big actually takes a while to materialise. But this month it happened. And it is great. I can cycle it all by myself. I can go forwards and backwards. However, turning is still a bit tricky. I like to go up and down. And down and up the road outside the 'new house'. However, this cycling lark can be a bit tiring sometimes.

I have met my new 1 to 1 that I am going to have at school. She is starting after half term, which is really soon. She seems ever so nice and I'm sure we'll get on just fine.

Talking of school - I did my first 'show and tell'. I was really proud to take in my pot plant that Granny had bought me for my playhouse. I told everyone all about it and even answered questions.

I suppose a major thing this month was going on the holiday that I had won. I took Mummy and Daddy with me for 9 nights in the South of France. I wanted somewhere nice and warm, but not too hot, that had a pool and a beach. This seemed such a great plan at the time. We should have guessed it was never going to go to plan when we were at Stansted airport. We were in the middle of our leisurely lunch when we realised we had minutes before the gate closed. This meant we had to go, right there and then, to avoid missing the flight. I was wheeled off with spaghetti still hanging out of my mouth, shouting "Don't go yet. Finish my lumpch first". When we got to France, we got lost finding the campsite. Mummy was navigator so she should get the blame. By the time we arrived, the shop had just shut and we were all starving hungry. So, understandably, I was a tad grumpy. That night it started to rain. In a caravan, rain sounds pretty loud. A bit like sleeping in an upturned bucket. Not that I've ever tried it, you understand. Anyway, it rained. And rained. Then we had thunder and lightning and... hail! Before we knew it, there were floods everywhere. To add insult to injury, it was cold too. I had rather selectively packed my new summer dresses, my 'big girl' sandals and my sunglasses. What I actually needed was my wellies, a coat and well actually a boat would have come in quite useful. I even got Mummy and Daddy wading knee deep though waterlogged pathways, carrying me in my wheelchair, just so I could get to the beach. It sounds dreadful. And at times it was! The 'Day after Tomorrow' type storm at 3:30am one morning was by the far the worst thing I have ever witnessed (weather wise anyway). It was made only slightly more bearable by the entertainment of Mummy hysterically running around the caravan like some kind of lunatic.

The holiday wasn't a complete right off though. We had a couple of warm, dry days and we even went in the sea – which was on the freezing side of chilly. My favourite bits were making sandcastles, or stone castles (depending which kind of beach we are on) and playing 'hunt the ball' after I had buried it in the sand. I also liked going to the shops on the wet days as I got new things. The best one was a new Disney Princess sleeping bag. I even got to sleep in it in the caravan. Mummy and Daddy were jealous as it got really cold at night. Finally, and despite it being a bit of a cheat on a caravanning holiday, I enjoyed watching films on our newly purchased portable DVD player. By the end of the holiday I became quite the expert on 'High School Musical'. I'm off to practise my moves and singing.

Lots of hugs and kisses,

Jess xxx

# June 2008

I took part in my first ever school Sports Day. We did 2 races each. I did a dressing up relay where my 1 to 1 pushed me in my wheelchair and my bestest friend helped me get dressed. I think we came 4th in that one, thanks to my 1 to 1 speeding across the line. I did a bottom shuffle and walk relay. I obviously did the bit nearest the ground as it is less far to fall. It was quite good fun and I was almost tired afterwards.

I got my new Tweety Pie splints this month. And despite them being a bit uncomfortable, I have worn them absolutely loads already. The weird thing is, I had to get Mummy to buy me special shoes to fit over the top of them. I was an '8F' in just my socks. But with splints on, I'm a '10-off-the-chart-but-H-will-have-to-do'! So, there is no mistaking which shoes are which. That and the fact that the only style that would actually fit 'off-the-chart-but-H-will-have-to-do', were trainers. The only pair they had in that size had pink flashy lights. Oh well, not exactly a real hardship after all.

Daddy had a big birthday this month. I went to one of his parties which was good fun. His other party sounded a bit babyish to me, considering what a big girl I am now, so I didn't go.

Being so grown up, I decided that I was ready to finally give up dummies as well as milk before bed. I did it all by myself. Mummy and Daddy had been trying for ages to get me to do that, but I wasn't letting them get the credit. It's me that has to do the whole cold turkey thing. Anyway, I waited until they had lost the will to push it any further, and then I gave it all up, all by myself. While I was on a roll, I also announced that I will no longer be needing help from anyone. Not Daddy, Mummy or teachers. I am officially a big girl.

Lots of hugs and milk-free kisses,

Jess xxx

# July 2008

A busy month with lots of nice things going on. A particular highlight for me was the end of the school term. And boy, was I ready for it too. School is okay while I'm there. I have a nice time and lots of nice friends. But frankly, if I had to choose between school and 'playing toys' at home, school would never actually get a look in.

I have been treated to lots of days out this month. Two visits to the theatre and one to the cinema. All very musical – which is right up my street. The first was probably my favourite (and according to Daddy, the most expensive). I went to London to see 'High School Musical' (HSM). Really good fun. I did lots of singing and clapping and came away wearing a new HSM t-shirt, lanyard and pin badges. It was instead of a half birthday present and it was well worth it.

I also went to see 'Lazy Town Live' at the theatre. I went dressed as Stephanie, complete with pink dress, bangles, leg warmers, pink wig with hair band, pink bag and my Lazy Town mobile phone. It would be an understatement to say I looked the part. It was a really good show and I joined in with both the singing and dancing.

Me and Mummy then had a girlie day while Daddy went out on his boat. We did shopping for knickers and accessories and went to see a big girl film at the cinema. Mamma Mia. Brilliant. Lots more singing and dancing.

At the end of the month we had a short family holiday to LEGOLAND. It was my first time staying in a hotel. I don't really understand hotels. I never did find the kitchen or living room. Anyway, LEGOLAND was brilliant fun. My most favourite thing was the roller coaster. I went on it 4 times. I must go. I want to go and build some stuff out of Lego. But I have to share my bricks with Daddy and Grandad.

Lots of hugs and kisses,
Jess xxx

# August 2008

As it was the school summer holidays, I enjoyed not being at school. However, I didn't actually go on holiday.

My 'holidays' started with 2 weeks at Granny and Pop Pop's. Mummy did point out that I was not actually returned after the first week totally intact. Instead, I came home with a bit of me in a box! My first ever tooth fell out, so I brought it home for the tooth fairy. It apparently doesn't visit Granny's. I reckoned they banned the tooth fairy there in case she made away with any false teeth in the night!!! Ha, ha, ha. I asked Daddy about the tooth fairy and what happens when you put your tooth under the pillow. He seemed reasonably well informed and told me all about the tooth fairy and how she brings me money in exchange for my old tooth. This seemed quite a good deal. So, I enquired into the going rate for said tooth, just in case I could potentially make a career out of it. Well, to my shock, Daddy had no idea. Thankfully a text to Tooth Fairy Headquarters answered the question, and I was pleased to find 2 coins (2x £1 coins) under my pillow the next morning. Unfortunately, the other teeth are not quite so valuable, apparently, so I'll only be getting one coin in future. Oh bum.

While I was at Granny's, we went to the hospital for an appointment, which was okay as I got a sticker. The nice incontinence man seemed pleased with me too, so I don't have to go back and see him again for months and months. Which is great.

I went to see the Panda film too. And I made sure that Granny was fully aware of where the pick and mix was before we found our seats.

We also went to a photo shoot at Brainwave. I've been told many a time before that I am a natural model. I just can't help it. I like posing when a camera comes out.

I did lots of swimming in an outdoor pool with Granny. Not exactly what you would call a modern-day leisure pool. In fact, it is not what you would even call heated. But hey ho –

these country folk do tend to be quite hardy. Anyway, despite the freezing water, I am proud to announce that I got 4 swimming badges. Frankly, I deserve at least 2 for getting in the pool. My piece de resistance though was my 5-meters in armbands badge, which I am especially proud of.

In fact, I made so much progress in the swimming department, that Mummy has signed me up to start a real course of big girl swimming lessons. And they are in a heated indoor pool too. Luxury!

After my fortnight at grannies, I had a week at home with Daddy. He took me to appointments too. First the physio and then the bug-eyed monster. The highlight there is that I got to choose a new pair of glasses. And as always, they are a very sensible pair.

It's a shame my summer holidays aren't a holiday from all these appointments too. Last count I think I was still on about 16 specialists/consultants, all of which are referrals of some kind or another. And as far as I'm concerned, that is 16 too many.

They are:

1 Paediatric Consultant

2 Physiotherapist

3 Speech Therapist

4 Occupational Therapist

5 Orthotics (feet!)

6 Social Services OT

7 Consultant/surgeon Ophthalmologist (eyes)

8 Another Ophthalmologist aka the bug-eyed monster (eyes)

9 Refractologist – or something like that (eyes)

10    Brainwave Cognitive therapist

11    Wheelchair services

12    Incontinence advisor

13    School SENCO (Special Educational Needs Co-ordinator)

14    Council Educational advisor

15    Geneticist at GOSH

16    Neurologist at GOSH

One good thing was, I did get to have my very first proper pair of big girl school shoes. Before, because of the splints and boots and heel cups and everything else, I have never actually had a proper pair of school shoes. However, we found a shoe shop that actually stock nice shoes wide enough to fit over my splints. And to make it even more exciting, the shop is also next door to the build-a-bear workshop. So, it is impossible now to get new shoes without needing a new outfit / handbag / shoes / all three!! (delete as appropriate) for my bear. Finally – some good luck has come my way. Now with the new bear outfits and proper shoes I am almost excited about going back to school.

One of the most fun things I did with Daddy, was go camping in the garden. I slept outside for 4 whole nights, although I did start to lose count a bit as the first couple of attempts weren't exactly successful. However, by the end of the week I had really got the hang of packing my suitcase each night, complete with midnight snacks, ready for another adventure.

Another highlight was going to Alton Water with Daddy, Nanny and Grandad. We cycled around the reservoir. Grandad supplied the entertainment by falling off his bike with the start still in sight. I reckon the beer at lunchtime made his bike all wobbly. I however managed to successfully stay on my bike. Helped by the fact that it had 3 wheels. That and the fact that Daddy was steering... and pedalling.

Auntie Piglet came down to see me again in the summer holidays. As usual I had a selection of lovely pressies. In particular, I had a pink 'trolley' bag, which I now take with me almost everywhere I go.

Mummy and Daddy have been really boring this month by doing lots of decorating and making a mess. The only upside to all of this, is that we also keep buying lots of new things. And some are for my new bedroom.

When they haven't been pulling up floorboards and knocking down bits of wall, they have been doing something even worse. Watching the Olympics. I hate the 'lympics. And it seemed to follow me wherever I went too. No matter who I visited, there it was, the 'lympics. I never really saw the appeal at all.

However, Mummy did tell me all about a special 'lympics that is starting next month. And in that they do stuff like wheelchair basketball. Now THAT sounds like it may well be worth watching. I would like to be able to do that kind of thing. So, I may tune in and see what it's all about, just so I know what I should be training for.

The last week of the holidays I stayed with Nanny and Grandad. One of my favourite bits was going to the beach. Now Nanny is quite hardy, so going to the beach could happen at any time of the year, in any weather. This visit was special as it almost felt like summer. And this year summer only lasted a week, and that bit of sun didn't happen all at once.

At the end of the holidays I was invited to go to the 'Police 4x4 fun day' held at the farm, along with lots of other special people from the area. It was a brilliant day and I met some lovely firemen and had my photo taken with them. And I went in their fire engine too. Well, I AM my mother's daughter! I also went off-roading in a 4x4 too. Well, I AM my father's daughter! At the end of the day they gave me a goody bag full of exciting things, and I got to go on the top deck of a privately hired double decker bus on the way home too. I made friends with other boys and girls and even tried on a police constables hat. It was a really good day. I hope they invite me back next year too.

Lots of hugs and kisses,

Jess xxx

# September 2008

I suppose an important thing this month, was that I went back to school. But this time I was a big girl. I'm in Class 4, but year 1. Work that one out!  Now I'm big, I have suggested that I should be the one that drives to school. No-one has taken me up on the offer, yet.

I went to the Brainwave fun day, which was a fun day. I got some prizes and balloons and sweets. So as far as I was concerned, it was a rather successful afternoon.

I started my new swimming lessons at the beginning of the month. It's a bit like gym club, where there are lots of people like me there. Not all cute, blonde and with a fabulous swimsuit... I mean everyone has their own individual challenge. Some can't see, some have trouble talking quietly... and there is me. One of the teachers has a wheelchair too, which I thought was really cool. I did some lovely swimming in my armbands and woggle, to the extent that I somewhat impressed the head swimming coach. In fact, within a couple of lessons I was compared to a Paralympian who started swimming at the club at about the same age as me. I don't want to go to the 'lympics though, as the pool looks quite a bit bigger than the baby pool that I am currently 'training' in, and I'd be exhausted by the time I'd done a length. That and the fact I understand you are not allowed armbands in the 'lympics. I don't swim so well without my armbands.

Mummy entered a lot of my creations, mostly chosen by me, into the local Flower Show again. On a par with previous years I was awarded a prize for every single entry. Some of which were helped by no-one else bothering to enter some of the classes. Anyway, whatever, I still had the 2nd highest number of points in the children section and had several pounds of prize money too.

Probably the highlight of the month was moving into my new, very pink, and greatly improved, Jessie-friendly bedroom.

My mattress is now on the floor, so I can get into bed 'all by myself'. I have 2 new toy boxes designed so I can open them, and then empty them, without any help. With my old toy boxes, I always needed help to open the lid and then I could never reach my toys inside. This way I no longer have to wait (and wait, and wait) for someone to come and rescue me. Because my bedroom is bigger, there is also room for my dolly's house too. I can even reach my main light switch now, as it has been lowered. This is really MY room. With all this new super accessible stuff, I hate ever leaving it. I've even had breakfast, lumpch and tea at my new desk, just so I can stay!

Love & hugs,

Jess x

# October 2008

This month started, as they so often do, with a number of boring appointments. Nothing new or enlightening to share. I did go to Brainwave again though, and this time, for the first time ever, my 1 to 1 school teacher came along too. I worked really, really hard and they seemed pleased with my progress, which is always remarkable considering I only do a few exercises a week. The problem is, at home when it comes to exercising, I am either too tired to try hard, or there is something much more interesting I could be doing instead.

I took Daddy to see Mamma Mia. It was my third trip, but I still sang along. I also went to the cinema with Mummy and Auntie Piglet to see High School Musical 3. It was good fun and Auntie Piglet almost enjoyed it. I'm sure once I have both the DVD and CD, I'll be singing all the new songs!

An exciting moment at school this month was me getting a Head teacher award. I wrote 4 two-letter words and they were legible too. They were quite big though – I only just got each word on an A4 sheet of paper. It's lucky I don't hand write the journal, otherwise it would be like war and peace each month. I know the writing thing doesn't sound particularly spectacular or anything, especially as I'll be 6 in a couple of months, but this is a really big thing for me. I really struggle with my pen control. It seems like pens and pencils have a mind of their own. I'm hoping I may finally be getting to grips with writing.

Going to Disneyland Paris has got to be THE most exciting thing I have done all year. We went with Auntie Piglet and Uncle Lamby and stayed in a Mickey Mouse hotel. We had great fun. My favouritest bits were doing roller coasters and meeting the characters... I think I cuddled 19 different ones, but I did start to lose count. Some roller coasters were so scary they made me wee a little bit. And I bet I wasn't the only one! That didn't however stop me going back on them another couple of times!

I have also learnt a couple of French words, which was a

bit impressive. I'm not exactly bilingual or anything, but I think my foreign vocabulary almost matched that of anyone else I holidayed with!

Anyway, I'm going to go and look at my holiday pictures... I have loads!

Love & hugs from

Minnie Mouse and Jess x


Sorry – Mummy interfering again!

# Everyone is a doctor

It appears that despite years of extensive tests, the best doctors and consultants in the land are still struggling to find a diagnosis to explain Jessie's inability to walk independently and consequently, we are none the wiser on a prognosis of what the future might hold.

This however does not stop the numerous opinions of other people that we are constantly being bombarded with.

Several unhelpful people have actually suggested that they would have made Jess walk by now if she was their child. I still find that a remarkably arrogant and ridiculous thing to say. But then you begin to doubt your own sanity about whether you have done enough. What if, I often think. I am full of self-doubt at the best of times, without anyone else's help to make it worse.

Then the other extreme is the 'she'll be fine, she'll walk one day' camp. I just want to shout in retort, "HOW THE HELL DO YOU KNOW??" I am fully aware it is a gesture to placate me, a voice of unwavering optimism, but all it does it infuriate me. Clearly, she is not fine – at least not physically. And we are all determined to ensure she will achieve her absolute potential, whatever that may be, and we will not let any disability hold her back. But at the same time, you also need some degree of realism to stay sane. Why does everyone else think they know better than the doctors?

# November 2008

I saw 2 separate firework displays. The first Daddy did in the back garden, which were pretty and not very noisy. I was very excited watching them; however, Mummy didn't seem quite so impressed. The other was a really, really big display that lots of people went to, but we watched from the warmth and comfort of the living room with Nanny and Grandad. It was a great display and the fireworks were pretty and noisy and I think for the first time ever, good fun!

We got a little bit of snow this month. Not enough to do anything with, but I kept an eye on it while it was snowing and watched it make my playhouse go all white. It was gone by the time I was dressed, so I'm hoping the next lot will last a little longer.

I have noticed some people say some really funny things. People keep saying that they 'Love me to bits'. But, I'm not broken! I don't understand.

I had a walker trial this month. It happened because Daddy had noticed someone else had a different type of walker to me, and thought that might be good fun. The next time I went to physio, Mummy suggested that I at least get a chance to try one out. So, I did! Apparently, I was quite the natural when I had a go and the physio was so impressed she said she'd order two, one for home and one for school. And, the icing on the cake (which is always the best bit as far as I'm concerned), is not only are they ordering two walkers... hopefully... they are going to order two pink ones!!!

I did another one of my guest appearances at the Darts County Championships. Lots of smiling, shaking hands, photos and general socialising. It is a bit like being the queen sometimes. Probably why I'm often mistaken as a princess.

I had an exciting invite from Father Christmas in the post, asking if I'll come and visit just before Christmas and help make toys. I can't wait!

I've been having swimming lessons every Saturday evening for the last couple of months and have been trying really hard. When I started, back in September, I was in armbands, had a woggle and needed a helping hand. I enjoyed swimming but I seemed to be just as wobbly in the water as I was on land! Over the last month, the armbands went and I have been swimming with just woggles and floats. Well, at my last lesson we all had a go at real swimming... no armbands, no float, and no woggle. Mummy held my head and I did kicking on my back. And then in a rather spontaneous, unrehearsed and unexpected moment... Mummy let go! And I sank. Then we tried again, but this time I was ready for it when Mummy let go a second time. And I swam. ALL BY MYSELF. Not for long, but I did it. I got new goggles and I think they helped a little. In my excitement, I decided to show my teacher and then Daddy. Each time I managed a little bit further and a little bit better. By the time the lesson was over, the furthest I had managed was about two whole metres on my own. It is ground breaking amazing progress in my little world. And we are all so excited.

Love & armband-free hugs,

Jess x

# December 2008

Probably a big highlight of the month, and one of the best things that has happened all year was me, Mummy and Daddy going to Lapland (Lapland UK), as invited by Santa Claus himself. It was absolutely fabulous. We drove for long enough for me to just about watch all of Mamma Mia in the car. When we got there, we had to go into a big tent that was 'passport control' which was run by elves! We were given one passport to allow the 3 of us to 'travel' to Lapland. Then they took us to a secret woodland tunnel. It was nice and we saw more elves inside. They showed us which way to go and the woodland trail turned into a snowy, fir lined trail and when we popped out the other side of the secret passageway, it was snowing. Snow was on the trees and everything. We were in Lapland!!! We helped out in Santa's toy shop and made rocking horses. I decorated gingerbread men with the help of Mother Christmas. I listened to lovely Christmas stories. I wrote a letter and posted it and I went ice skating in my wheelchair with Daddy pushing. I met big cuddly reindeer and real ones too. But possibly best of all, I got to meet the very jolly Father Christmas himself. He was really lovely. I was given a toy husky and Mummy and Daddy were given a story book to read to me on Xmas eve (which they did). I'm so glad I was invited to go. I just hope I'm lucky enough to go again.

I've had a constant cough and ear ache this month and had to have a dose of yellow medicine to get me through Christmas. This meant I had to lay off the booze, again – which was a shame. Despite this, I managed to take part in all three school performances and I went to the panto with Mummy in the last week of term.

I did manage to lose one of my front teeth early in the month. However, I was determined the other one didn't fall out before Christmas as there were serious threats of a certain song being sung ("all I want for Christmas is my 2 front teeth"). Despite the other tooth wobbling furiously all over Christmas, it was still present and correct come the end of the year.

Christmas was really hectic but great fun. Absolutely loads of great presents, and loads (and loads) of family at my house too. I did a headcount check and I think there were 12 of us. And they all stayed the night (or two!) as well. We played lots of games, but a favourite of mine was a new Wii game that Mummy and Daddy got, which meant I was able to practically perfect down-hill skiing over the Christmas holidays. This created some very entertaining and sometimes rather competitive moments. Especially when it was discovered that my sitting down approach to skiing was more successful than the stupid stand up method. Occasionally, spending your life on your bottom, does have its benefits.

I'm going to be rock star. Simple as that. I got some Christmas money and have bought an electric guitar (a pink toy one, obviously). I absolutely love playing it. But more importantly, with my matching sunglasses, I seriously look the part.

Love & big squishy hugs,

Jess x

# January 2009

Back to school after Christmas, but it wasn't too long before it was my birthday and this year I was 6 whole years old. I had a High School Musical birthday party. The best bit was lunch – but isn't it always! It was also Pop Pop's birthday the same day too. Which was strange. He had a birthday the same day as me last year. And the year before, if I remember correctly. Anyway, I got some good presents, lots of clothes and some Build-a-bear vouchers. So, me and Mummy had a whale of a time buying a new bear and everything a bear could ever wish for, from pushchair to sleeping bag. Great fun. And I've played teddies and camping loads since. Talking of camping, me and Daddy even went camping in my bedroom one Friday night. It was quite an adventure until I realised Daddy's improvised duvet-bed, looked considerably more warm and cosy than my sleeping bag. Nothing a quick bed swap couldn't sort out. And after that I was much happier. We even had a midnight feast too.

The New Year meant it was back to gym club and swimming after weeks and weeks off. Frankly I hadn't missed gym at all and quite clearly stated that I didn't want to go ever, ever, ever again. It's too hard work. Makes me feel yuck. However, despite what I thought was a crystal-clear message, I was taken to gym twice this month. Once there, I yet again made my feelings quite clear, tears and everything. We even left the lesson early on our last visit. So, I'm hoping I'll not be going back again. I think I might hide my leotard so I can't.

We had a trip up to GOSH this month. We went prepared for the worst, with overnight bags, toothbrushes and everything, and we were in and out of the clinic within the hour and home in time for tea. Not especially eventful. I'm going back later this year and again in January 2010. But if it was like this visit, then there's nothing to worry about.

Auntie Piglet and Uncle Lamby came down for Piglies birthday. We had a nice time, especially unwrapping presents. But I wore myself to a frazzle playing hide and seek, so much that I couldn't do any kicking or anything in my swimming lesson that night. Talking of swimming, I'm getting quite good. My record now is about 13meters (or 40 foot in old money) swimming on my back, all by myself. I even did it in the big pool. It looked like the 'lympics, as it had lane ropes and people watching and everything!

I got a new pink walker this month at home but I've been a bit too pooped to use it much so far. I have played in it up and down the hallway. It's good but tiring. In fact, I find everything tiring.

I grew out my old splints and I've had to have some temporary new school shoes until I get new splints. I did have my feet put in plaster at an Orthotics appointment this month, so new splints should be ready soon. Although I really like my new flashy, sparkly shoes, not wearing splints make my knees hurt. So, it'll be sort of nice to get the new splints.

Love & huggles,

Jess x

# February 2009

Probably the proudest moment I have had in a long time, came in the form of a nomination by my swimming teacher for me to receive a swimming award. It's from the swimming club I go to for people with disabilities. The initial slight flaw was that the award ceremony coincided with bed time. It mostly just affected me, as I was by far the youngest there. So, it was a challenge to remain on my best behaviour when I was so sleepy, but I think I pulled it off. Anyway, I clapped for the others as they collected their awards and we were especially impressed with one of the swimmers getting a special award for breaking a World Record! I may have been just slightly out of my league.

When they got to me, they announced me as 'winner of the Achievers Award (Beginners)'. Then they said lots of nice things about how I started lessons in September with armbands and woggle and support, and by Christmas I had swum 10m on my back, all by myself, using my own 'mermaid kick' invention. All done with my usual endless determination. At this point, Mummy's bottom lip was quivering and although she'd promised to push me up to the front to collect my award, it being past my bedtime and all, I seized the moment and pushed myself up to the front in my wheelchair, all by myself, just like a big girl would. I only crashed into the wall once, and only then was I given the tiniest bit of help to straighten up. I held the little glass trophy, which is all engraved with my name on, and managed to smile for the photos without dropping it. I liked the big wooden trophy best, but that had to go into the club display cabinet, so I didn't get to keep it for very long. I am apparently going to be famous, as the group picture is due to go on the club website and in the local paper as well.

I've got new glasses. I choose some really jazzy pink glittery ones, thanks to some fashion advice I got from Pop Pop. I like them as they look a bit like mummies and they make me look really grown up too. I could even possibly pass for 6 and a quarter.

I don't know why, but everything seems to hurt, all the time. Particularly my knees, hips and back. I don't know if I'm growing big or just falling apart. Either way, I've had to resort to the trusty pink strawberry-flavoured medicine to get me through each day. I even had to get checked out by the physio, but she couldn't find anything wrong. Well, no more wrong than usual.

I spent half term at Granny and Pop Pop's. A highlight was probably going to see Bolt 3D at the cinema. I had to wear funny magic glasses and then everything kept jumping out of the screen and landing in my lap. Which was weird.

I have a newly acquired skill which involves me getting out of bed, all on my own. It is quite handy sometimes, although my lack of being able to tell the time has meant I keep getting up several hours too early. Which doesn't seem to be going down too well.

Love & early morning hugs,

Jess x

# March 2009

I've been ill. And despite sharing the cough, cold, runny nose and everything with everybody, I still felt rotten for ages. The only thing I wasn't able to share was the spots! Both Mummy and Granny did numerous spot checks and finally came to the conclusion that although it looked remarkably like the Chicken Pox (also known as the Poxy Chicken) I couldn't possibly have it 4 times. The only rational explanation was that this bout of spots, and possibly the previous 3 lots of spots, were all viral infections. Either way, I spent a reasonable amount time not feeling overly well and I even had to have 3 days off school. I tried for 4 days off school (or even more), but apparently, school were missing me. Understandable.

This term I have started playing football and rugby using my wheelchair in P.E. at school. Don't ask me about it. I don't even want to talk about.

I have decided I am going to get married to a handsome boy in my year. He is 6 too. I have been discussing wedding plans with my hairdresser who's also getting married. I've decided Mummy and Granny can be bridesmaids and I want a pink wedding car with pink ribbons. I am going to need a dress, wedding hat and flowers. I've got plenty of time though to get all the arrangements sorted because I have decided I won't get married until next week.

My latest most favourite pastime to do when I get home from that place that must not be mentioned (school) is running. Yep, you heard (or should I say read) that right... I like running!!!! I play on the Wii Fit (also known as the W2 Fit, by some of the over 60's – you know who you are!!) and I've found if I sit on the floor, hold the control tight and move my arms fast, my Mii runs. It's great. I did 2 x 10 minute 'runs' the other day. I was so hot and exhausted I had to take my jumper off!!!

I like creating new Miis too. It is the best way to see what you'd look like with a beard!

An influx of new equipment for me is entirely due to me finally being appointed an Occupational Therapist (OT). I used to have one, but when the last one left I must have gone almost a year without an OT. Well in the space of a week or two, I have had a new walking frame and joystick mouse delivered to school and an up/down (wombat) chair delivered to home. Wonders will never cease.

I have been to the 'Wakey Shakey' club at school twice with my most favourite 1 to 1. It is a wakey-up club because it is early in the morning before lessons have even started. The first day I was there they even did bottom shuffling as the exercise, so I was able to join in. It was particularly funny seeing my 1 to 1 on her bottom.

For the first time ever since I started school, I had a school friend round for 'tea and toys'. It was good fun but surprisingly tiring. We did dressing up, played Wii, played toys and all sorts of stuff. I might even have another friend round really soon, once I have summoned up the energy.

I couldn't wait for Mummy's Day, so I ended up giving Mummy a present and her card a day early. I opened both for her of course. I like to be really helpful. I then got Daddy to put the card back in the envelope so we could do it all again the next day, but with a different present. I bought her a note book and a 'thingummyboggy'. I like unwrapping presents. Especially mine. So, it was handy that I saw both Uncle Billy Bobs and Auntie Piglet this month. This meant, as always, I was spoilt with nice presents as well as something almost as nice, lots and lots of huggles.

I went to some nearby lakes and fed the ducks, whether they liked it or not. Our timing could have been better as they seemed to have already had breakfast, a mid-morning snack and elevenses by the time we arrived. I even tried shouting at them to stop playing toys and come and get their lumpch. I hear the same requests at home! But just like at home, that didn't work either. Oh bum.

We did something really cool this term at that place I don't like to mention (school). We have been learning about 'Carnivals' and we did our very own walking carnival through the village. Everyone had been making costumes, banners and masks at school and learning about different cultures. I was behind a banner that said 'Snow Queen'. I think technically my teacher was the Queen. I guess I was probably the snow princess on wheels. We were really, really lucky with the weather. It kept raining all week, right up to us putting our costumes on. And then just before we went outside, it stopped. And it didn't rain again until we got back. I was pleased. If I had to wear my pink rain coat over my white outfit, I wouldn't have looked much like snow, let alone like a princess!! It was great fun. Loads of people came out to watch us too. Partly because of the noise we made, but also because the police people closed the road so we could walk up the middle of the street. I did lots of waving and smiling. I like doing things like this. It is lucky I'm famous. It suits me. I hope we get to do another carnival next year.

At last, I have finally lost my 4th baby tooth. It has been wibbling and wobbling for 6 months. It is handy really as you are supposed to have 2 front teeth, but for the last few weeks I've had three!!

Anyone want to play hide and seek?? It is one of my favourite things to do. My favourite place to hide is behind the curtains. The living room patio-door curtain that is, not the window curtains – I'd fall off the windowsill!

If you have any 'Starbursts', let me know. I keep them in my coat pocket. For some completely unknown reason though Mummy keeps calling them 'Opal Fruits'. I think she's going mad in her old age! Anyway, I do believe I've run out of sweeties, so I'd better go out and fill my pockets, literally.

See you soon, alligator.

Love & sticky hugs, Jess x

# April 2009

I had a really busy week in the Easter holidays as Mummy and Daddy and me all went away and stayed in a caravan and did lots of different stuff. Most of it was good fun.

One of the best and exiting days out was at a theme park for small people. And when I say small, I mean young, not necessarily short. I went on the roller coaster lots of times, but roller coasters ARE my absolute favourite ride of all time.

I met 'Dora the Explorer' and 'Diego' too, had cuddles, blew kisses and shook hands. As you do.

I went to a Discovery place, did an Easter Egg hunt, played big outdoor instruments and danced and sang with large woodland creatures. They were great, cuddly and funny too. Especially the air-guitar playing fox. You really had to be there!

As our days were busy, it was often nice to get back to the caravan in the evenings. The only problem was, my bedroom was absolutely freezing cold. I don't mean chilly, I mean: vest, pyjamas, socks, jumper, duvet, blanket and I was still freezing cold. So, after the first night we went shopping and I discovered what a hot water bottle looks like. After that it became my new most favourite thing to cuddle in bed. After 4 nights in the caravan we travelled down to see Uncle Billy Bob's, who has a lovely and warm house.

While there, we had an ice cream in the rain and went to a farm where I fed a goat, drove a tractor and saw water buffalo.

Before we came home we went to a Monkey Forest, which we all enjoyed. We got to see really silly monkeys running about the place and it was cool because they weren't in a cage. Well, I suppose technically they were, but then I guess so were we! The 'cage' was huge... you wander through the enclosure and visitors and monkeys roam 'free'.

The month continued to be exceptionally busy even after my weeks' holiday. I had a few days at Nanny and Grandads. While I was there I went swimming, saw Great Grandad, played in the sandpit and went out in 'Nanny's van'. In the fortnight that followed I went to the dentist, had a physio session, went to Great Ormond Street 'Hostipal' (GOSH) and had my hair cut. Life is never quiet.

My trip up to GOSH was particularly exhausting. We had to be on the ward by 7:30am at the latest. And although I am not good at telling the time, I knew this was early. When we left home it was dark and we were apparently on the choo-choo train before 6am. I knew that as Mummy kept saying that it was 5 something! It is amazing though how many people are awake at that time of day. We got to the hospital by 7am and were there even before the outpatient nurses. They soon turned up though. I had a few checks, but just stuff to get me ready for my anaesthetic. I knew I had to go to sleep while I was at hospital as I can't possibly lay still long enough for them to do an MRI, as it apparently will take an hour. I'm not sure why it takes them quite that long to take a picture of my head. With my camera, I could take absolutely loads of pictures in that time, and not all of my head.

I felt really sick after I woke up from my general anaesthetic. But that was not half as bad as when they have to take out the cannula line that was in the back of my hand. I shook, I cried, it hurt. I really, really hate the huge plasters they put on you in hospital. I had 4 big plasters this time, and that was less than normal. Thankfully, once the cannula line was out, they promised not to put another plaster on top to stop the bleeding, so instead I had a lovely big bandage and I was almost happy with that.

Each time I got through something, I took a deep big-girl breath and said "what next?" I know what it is like in hospital. It feels like it is one thing after another. So, although the worst was over, for that day anyway, the only problem now was passing enough checks to be allowed to be discharged. And the last hurdles to overcome before I was allowed home were: to prove I could eat, drink and wee. I really couldn't face eating... to the extent I had 2 sick bowls on my bed ready, just in cases. I tried drinking, but that was quite a struggle too. And there was the wee. That wasn't so tricky.

After what seemed like forever, I was discharged. It was just after 2pm. It felt like we'd been there for days, but it had only been 7 hours.

As a special treat, we went straight from GOSH to 'Hamley's' toy shop. I had never been there before. It is huge. I even got to meet the real 'Bob the Builder' while I was there too. And I got 2 free 'Bob the Builder' hats, a drawing and my nails done. And that was before we bought anything! I couldn't decide what to get as my 'being brave in hospital' prize. In the end, I chose some Hamley's felt tip pens and then I saw the Build-a-bear section. Well, that made it easy for me. I got a High School Musical (HSM) bear with a HSM necklace and a matching HSM cheerleader outfit. I named the bear Megan after my morning 1 to 1 carer. I thought that was a really good name for a bear. And then we decided we had had enough and came home. A small detour via Nanny's, meant we finally got home just in time for bed. I'm tired. What next?

I've been listening to some 'Queen' music. It makes a change from 'Mamma Mia' and HSM. My favourite Queen song is, "We will, we will, yoghurt". Do you know it?

See you soon, alligator.

Love me, hug me, Jess x

# May 2009

Mummy has been worrying about how she is going to manage once I get too heavy to carry around. What a silly billy. I've told her not to worry, as I will walk all by myself if I get too big to be carried. I'm not exactly sure why, but this announcement has seemed to have surprised 'everyboggy'.

I like playing bedtimes, just before real bedtime. It involves putting pillow and blankets in the living room and putting my drink on my bedtime table and pretending to go to bed. Strangely, I absolutely hate really going to bed. I would rather stay up all night drawing, scribbling, watching DVD's and playing toys. Real bedtime is so boring and very overrated.

We were talking about nicknames at school. My 1 to 1 carer calls me 'Pumpkin'. Auntie Piglet calls me 'Pickle'. My friend however has a much better name and is called 'Princess'. Mind you, anything would be better than what I get called at home... it's either 'silly sausage' or 'wally bags'!

I think I won a gold medal at the 'lympics or something, as absolutely everyone was really pleased with me. After several practice attempts to find my (webbed) feet, I swam miles and miles and miles, all by myself. No woggle, no float, no anything and was rightly awarded my 25m badge and certificate. I actually did closer to 50m, but as I had done it in circles it was difficult to measure it exactly, so I was officially awarded my 25m distance badge, hoping the 50m one won't be far behind.

There was a half term this month which meant over a whole week with no school. Yippee. Don't like school. You have to get up too early and it is hard work.

Half term was busy but fun. I went swimming indoors and out. And as the weather was really hot, I also went to the beach twice as well. On the subject of getting wet, I played in the paddling pool a couple of times too and discovered the excitement that is squirting dry people with mega super-duper water pistols. Problem was mine kept running out of water.

I convinced Daddy that camping in the garden would be a really good idea. And, it was. We even had duvets and a TV in the tent. Proper camping, I call that!

I went on my longest ever cycle ride on my big purple trike. I must have cycled nearly half a mile. I went so far, my legs nearly fell off. Well, my knees really hurt anyway.

The month ended well with a trip to the theatre. I got to see High School Musical. But it was a bit de-ja vous. I'm sure I've seen it already. Regardless, it was really good fun.

See you soon, alligator.

Love, hugs and indoor stuff, Jess x

# June 2009

A couple of new things this month. I have started to really get the hang of the camera I had for my birthday. I took a few pictures, all by myself, in the garden. I particularly like the one I did of my play house. I took some of the sky and of the Artex on the ceiling too, but those pictures keep disappearing. If I didn't know better, I would think someone was deleting my artistic photography.

For me though a real highlight has been discovering 'Rainbows'. For those of you not up to date in the scouting organisation, 'Rainbows' is the thing you can now do before you start 'Brownies'. I have been several times already. I've got the uniform, a badge on my t-shirt and everything. I really like going. Some of my school friends go too. We do fun stuff like swimming, drawing, treasure hunts and games. And next month we go on a 'Rainbow Romp'. I don't even know what that is, but it sounds exciting!

I went on a School outing to do some beach combing and to see the lifeboat station. There I tried on the crash helmets that they wear. The beach combing was good fun but I think the best bits were probably lunch and the trip home on the coach. It didn't help as it was one of the wettest days of the month. That didn't appear to dampen Daddy's spirit, who seemed to be in his element 'playing' lifeboats. I guess it doesn't hurt to get friendly with them, he'll never know when he might need them, when he is out and about on his little boat.

Something that caused a lot of excitement at the end of the month was the newly acquired 'Hippocampe'. It is an off-road wheelchair. So, it seemed only fitting to take it for a proper 'test drive'. Me, Mummy, Granny and Pop Pop took it for miles and miles (literally), across fields, over styles and gates, and around reservoirs – collecting feathers along the way. It was quite the expedition. Then the next day Mummy and Daddy took me to the beach. I feel like someone from Star Trek... I've 'boldly gone where no-one (in a wheelchair) has gone before'.

And I think this may be just the beginning of my adventures. You can get a ski to attach to the front wheel, so there is already talk of a skiing holiday. I obviously will be doing the sitting down version, if there is such a thing. Mind you, so will Mummy and Daddy... they may think they'll do 'stand up skiing' but they will be on their bottoms just as much as I will.

See you spoon.

Love & super squashy hugs, Jess x

# July 2009

Sports day was great. I did 2 races. I did a bottom shuffling race, which technically I should have been good at. However, it's difficult to go fast and wave at the crowd. I'm such a crowd pleaser. I said hello to everyone along the way who was watching and kind of accidentally came last.

I also did an egg and spoon race. This one I won, due to a combination of my classmate pushing me really fast, and the egg being blue-tacked to the spoon! Shhh... that was a secret.

I went to a 'Rainbow Romp' and a Rainbows party this month. The 'Romp' was really good fun. We played games, made stuff and had a picnic tea. The party was good too. We played games, made stuff and had a picnic tea. Bit de-ja-vous come to think of it. At the party, we celebrated the really big girls moving up to Brownies and me being enrolled. I have a nice shiny badge to go on my uniform and I believe I am now technically a fully-fledged proper Rainbow, rather than a pretend trainee one.

I went to a big village BBQ. For me the best bit was seeing my friends and 'paddling' in the river in my new Hippocampe.

I went to the theatre and saw the Cirque de something... or something like that. It's a circus, in a theatre. Bit weird, but I liked it. Mind you, I'm used to weird. You should see my family! Talking of which, I'm not completely sure, but I could have sworn one of the circus performers doing the somersaults and headstands in just his knickers was Uncle Billy. If it wasn't him, then I have seen the very same show in my own living room! There were other acts, other than Billy's gymnastic one, and they were really good too. I liked the big clown best, as he gave me a sweetie.

Apparently, it is the end of the school year. I can't really believe it though. Every few days I double check with a 'is it school tomorrow?' and so far, I get the answer I want. But sooner or later I just know my luck will run out.

So far in my holidays, I've got new splints. Good news is they are pink. Bad news is they don't actually fit any of my shoes so I'll need to buy more. Did I say that was bad news, come to think of it, that's pretty good news. So, a win, win on the splints. In fact, it is a win, win, win... because Megan bear got my old splints!

Since school ended, I've been to the cinema, played toys, had a magazine and sweets, been swimming and done baking and drawing... and, that was just the first couple of days! I think it's going to be a busy summer.

Tootles.

Like you to pieces, Jess x

Mummy here, interjecting yet again, I will butt out and leave you to it at some point, I'm sure!

# Que Sera, Sera

With regard to Jess undergoing tests, I had decided enough is enough. But every time we plan to stop the tests, we are left in limbo with what seems to be even more unanswered questions, and that happened yet again.

I thought it was a sign that she had been through enough, when she played with Lego... but rather than making houses or something conventional, she builds hospital beds. Not any normal bed – but the blue hospital beds you get in GOSH.

So, we went for what I hoped were the last ever tests, in March 2009, only to find this isn't the end. We can't stop here either.

Jess had her 3rd Brain scan in March. The 2nd one, done about eighteen months earlier showed her cerebellum had shrunk. But with just 2 scans at that point it wasn't a complete picture. As a result, we agreed to the 3rd scan earlier this year in the hope, that would be that. Unfortunately, this scan showed that not only had the cerebellum got smaller again, but this time they could see the tissue had degenerated and dispersed. It was the worst we had been fearing, a sign of a progressive, degenerative brain disorder. One with no cure and where nothing could be done to slow the deterioration. However, we still have no prognosis, as there are many (rare) things that could cause this atrophy (shrinking). Depending on what was causing the problem, it is possible that we could still get a diagnosis. But much more importantly now for us... a prognosis.

We are left not knowing if and when she will start to regress, although we now know that is a real possibility.

In some respects, we have as many unanswered questions as ever, although we have narrowed down the problem. We are slowly mentally preparing ourselves for the possible outcomes that will determine the future of our tiny family. Meanwhile, life goes on as 'normal', because it has to. She will no doubt be even more spoilt than ever before and we are less likely to wait to do something. We will now seize the moment, as we don't know how long we will all have together.

There are two different approaches to this. The first is denial. I like it there. It is the relatively easy and the 'safe' option. There, I cling to the (anon) poem 'It will all be okay in the end. If it's not okay, it's not the end.' But I'm more realistic and logical than that. I know you don't necessarily get what you want, regardless of how desperate you want it. So instead I will settle for the sentiment which concludes the 'Harry Potter and the Goblet of Fire' book. "what would come, would come... and (we) would have to meet it when it did (does)".

# August 2009

I got some new glasses and new wheelchair just days before going on holiday. I wanted glasses just like my Mummy. Now we match.

I chose my first NHS wheelchair without any help. Some people can't tell much of a difference from my old chair, but for someone like me who literally lives in one, any small improvement or difference is a welcome change. The old chair was pink, smallish stripy wheels and flashing castors. The new one is dark purple, big flower wheels and soft castors. I like it. It's a bit easier to manoeuvre too. Although, don't tell anyone, as I'd rather be pushed around. It's difficult to propel yourself holding a handbag. I know. I've tried.

I had a nice holiday. Me Mummy and Daddy went on a big aeroplane to Disney World. Now I'm big, I was able to do lots of big girl rides that I wasn't able to do last time.

I went to the Bibiddi Bobiddi Boutique again. This time I was Sleeping 'Bootie'. Mainly because the dress is pink. Once fully dressed up with all my accessories, I did some serious posing. While still dressed as a princess, I then led the princess parade with the fairy godmothers through Downtown Disney to loads of clapping and onlookers. I did my special wave and absolutely had a whale of a time. I was born to do stuff like that.

I did lots of swimming while I was on 'oliday. I particular liked using my new 'rugger ring', cause then I could swim 'all by myself'.

As always, I saw lots of lovely characters, had loads of huggles and kisses and got lots of autographs too. All of which was super good fun.

Apart from some of my favourite rides: - flying like a butterfly (Soarin'), little TV's (Spaceship Earth) and zippadeedoodah (Splash Mountain) ... and apart from the princess parade perhaps, my absolutely most favourite bit of the holiday was possibly meeting the princesses and getting lots of kisses.

I'm home now. I was ready to come back. The flight home could have been better. Tea on the plane was yuck. Then no-one loosened my seat belt while I slept in my 'night time glasses', so I woke up after a whole 2 or 3 hours' sleep being sick everywhere. Not nice at the best of times, but somehow worser on a plane. Now I'm all confused. I want lunch at tea time; I want tea hours after I have gone to bed, even though I'm not tired. I don't understand. Is it morning yet? And when can I see Minnie Mouse again?

Bye, bye.  Like you to pieces,

Jess x

# September 2009

It's that time of year again, which means it is finally time to go back to school. I was almost ready to go back this time and had nearly started to miss my friends. It was just about worth going back. Now I'm in year 2, I was treated to a complete new school uniform, as I had almost grown out of the original uniform I had when I started in reception class. I'm still in the smallest size school cardigan they make though (aged 3-4... it's small considering I'm 6¾). It's an occupational hazard of being on the small side of tiny.

I went back to Rainbows as well. I like Rainbows. You do good stuff there.

I thought I was supposed to restart swimming too. We tried anyway. We turned up at the pool after a summer of the pool people renovating the roof, to find a pool with workmen and a cement mixture on the bottom. I hasten to add – no water in it. So, we went home again. You can't swim in a pool with no water.

Instead of a summer fete at school we had a School 'party in the park' on the first weekend back. I went with Nanny, Grandad and Daddy and it was really very good fun indeed. I went on lots of rides and slides with lots of friends. On the waltzer ride I got so incredibly excited, my friends had to put their hands over their ears!! I even made Daddy go on an inflatable slide which was funny as he nearly did himself a mischief. I think it's because his bottom was too big!

The tooth fairy has been suffering from the recent recession, almost entirely thanks to me. I lost one tooth last month and then I lost another 2 teeth in just 2 weeks this month. Weirdly the last 2 teeth I lost were both when I was asleep and we (finally) found the missing teeth in the bed the next morning. In fact, the 2nd time, the aforementioned bed was in a tent! Thanks to the mild-ish weather I managed to persuade Daddy that it would be a good idea to go camping in the back garden.

The only problem is, I think Daddy was pulling a fast one

when I woke up chilly as an ice burger early in the morning. I knew that the hot water bottle near me wasn't mine. This one was cold!

Over the summer holidays, Granny made me make loads of make-do things for the 'Flower Show'. I entered a very lot of classes with the philosophy of quantity rather than quality and it seemed to have paid off. I won loads of prizes and got several pounds in prize money as well. Out of nearly 90 children who entered I got the 2nd highest number of points again. And then I spent all my winnings on even more 'make-do' stuff.

I have started card making lessons. I am the teacher, as I'm now officially a prize-winning card maker. So far, I have made both Mummy and Daddy come to my lessons. They're not bad for beginners, although there was quite a bit of fuss (mostly from Mummy) as I insisted that my 'pupils' wore pink hair bands to my classes. Well, I need to have some degree of discipline and smartness in my lessons.

I had a go at hand bells for the first time this month. I'm quite good. So is Granny. Mummy definitely needs more practice.

We have had a bit of a team effort at home and decided to paint the outside of the house a lighter shade of pale. Well, we all got involved in the first coat anyway. Then me and Mummy got bored.

I have discovered that my new wheelchair is a lot easier to manoeuvre than the old one. Bigger wheels or something. I wasn't keen initially on actually bothering to do any of the wheeling myself, but then I discovered what it was like to be on the receiving end of some serious bribery. After a considerable amount of wheeling my wheelchair around the local supermarkets... Co-op, Tesco's, Sainsbury's, I have found I get suitably rewarded for my efforts. We accidentally discovered that supermarkets are strangely a really good place to practice – flat surfaces and wide aisles. And conveniently full of excellent 'good girl' prizes. In fact, the wheeling is going so well, Mummy and Daddy think I'm ready for real wheelchair lessons. So, we are all going down to

Brighton in half term, to go on a 2-day manual wheelchair course. I'm hoping, as its run by a kid's charity, that they'll be mostly children like me. Obviously not as pretty as me and I bet their wheelchairs won't be as jazzy as mine. But you know what I mean.

I've been doing a lot of sorting out and tidying up. I like neat and tidy. Just like Mummy. DVD's are one of my favourite things to sort out – that and stickers. A girl can never ever have too many stickers. And I have found they come in especially handy for my card making classes. Being artistic I also branched out and did a bit of painting on pottery. Mummy thinks she's good, but I am better. I did what I think was a rather impressive bauble for the Christmas tree. I think I may have to go back and do more stuff. It would be rude not to.

I like typing on the laptop. Doing 'work'. But I have to share the laptop with Mummy and Daddy. I try hard to share but it's driving me nuts. Pop Pop likes nuts.

Bye, bye. Like you to pieces,

Jess x

# October 2009

I went back to Brainwave after nearly a year since my last visit. I showed them how I can balance on the wobbly board. Then they put it on my list of exercises. I don't know why, I can do it already. I'm not going to do it again. And then there is the wheelbarrow exercise. I don't like that one at all. Daddy should do it instead. They also want me to learn to crawl. Well, I am definitely, absolutely not going to do that. Crawling is for babies. I am not a baby. So, all in all, another successful day of therapy... as always.

It was that time of year again for the school Harvest Festival in church. I practised my lines at home, but Mummy was not at all impressed with what apparently is an excessive and (unbelievably) unnecessary use of the word 'bum'. I personally find it hysterical. Especially when used several times in a sentence about field mice.

I went to the school disco just before half term. My friends all wore hoolie-skirts, shorts and tights, or jeans. I felt a bit more effort for the occasion was required. I quite literally made an entrance to the disco dressed as 'Sleeping Bootie'. My outfit was the complete ensemble of: big pink dress, white princess gloves, a ring, pink necklace, sparkly handbag, sequined shoes, hair ribbons and of course... a crown. I think I looked like a real princess. Daddy thought I looked like a real wally. The only problem was, the combination of energetic dancing (in a new harness that I've got) and the aforementioned outfit, meant I got really, really hot. This meant having to leave the disco early and in not quite the same dignified fashion in which I arrived. Next time perhaps I will manage without the gloves. I'm sure that'll make all the difference.

I explored the local woods in my off-roader. We hadn't been able to go there before in my normal chair, so this was a bit like an adventure. I collected lots of leaves for an autumn picture for my homework. It was almost fun.

At the very end of October, it was half term. I had the

busiest half term in the history of half term-ed-ness. Me, Mummy and Daddy travelled for ages. Well, for 7 episodes of 'Charlie and Lola' and half of 'Ratatouille' to be precise, before we arrived at our hotel. It seemed like a very long way. There was a restaurant right next door which was really handy. They did nice teas and even nicerer breakfasts. I liked that hotel.

Our first full day on 'oliday and we went to the zoo. The real highlights were: going down the slides in the play area, having my face painted like a pretty butterfly, going on a train ride on the real Thomas the Tank engine, and pretending I was a flamingo by standing on just 1 leg for over a minute. My favourite animal was a black and white monkey. Although it might have been a lemur or something. I got a bit confused and excited at first, as I thought they were pandas! To sort of remember this all, I managed to persuade Mummy to buy me a pink monkey. I can wear it round my neck like a sort of snugly scarf with legs.

The whole purpose of our trip away in half term, was to go on a 2-day manual wheelchair course for children. It was a bit weird though because the first thing they did was say that my lovely purple NHS wheelchair was too heavy and sensible to tip up backwards. They talked technical to Daddy and I think he understands. But the outcome was, I was transferred out of my new purple wheelchair (with the pretty hub caps) into a battered chair that was supposedly high performance. I was initially not impressed. Within minutes though I tried to run my stupid purple chair over and I asked if I could take the big old red chair home with me. Unfortunately, I'm not allowed. They need those chairs for training. We are now on a mission... again – but this time for a lightweight 'sports' wheelchair. I learnt how to do wheelies, which apparently is handy if you want to go up and down kerbs. It's a bit scary though coming down from the wheelie – especially when you fall out of your wheelchair and land on your nose. Which is exactly what I did. It took a bit of persuasion, some bribery and a make shift seat belt to get me back in the wheelchair, but I did it. My teacher also showed us how to get out of a chair if it capsizes backwards. I did the drill 3 times all in all, and think I was very brave. He lowered the chair so the handles touched the floor and you had to get safely out of the chair and then back in it again.

The other thing we did was wheelchair games. I learnt how to play British Bulldog and wheelchair basketball. It was okay, but being the only girl and the youngest one there meant the games were a bit rougher and louder than I am used to. Did I mention it wasn't just children in wheelchairs? All the parents and brothers and physios who came to watch had to play too. Daddy was so silly he fell out of his chair as well. Mind you, by the end of the course, most of us had!! I liked Mummy and Daddy having their own wheelchairs. I kind of miss it. Although I'm starting to get a bit bored of them whinging about their bruised knuckles. Welcome to MY world!

The other big thing we did in half term was go and see Disney Princesses on Ice up in London. It was in a big white round tent, called the 'Oh too arena'. We had front row seats, which was good but extremely chilly. I got to see all the princesses and as an extra special treat, both Mickey and Minnie were there too. It was really good. There were bubbles and fireworks and everything. And I got a princess banner and a bucket load of popcorn as well. Quite a good day. Problem is, I'm now extremely tired and I've got to go back to school soon. I need a holiday.

Bye, bye. See you spoon,

Jess x

# November 2009

I have done a bit of wheeling again all by myself. It is hard work and quite slow, but I am getting there. The new proper wheelchair gloves help a bit. The problem is people walk too fast. I am definitely speeding up... albeit rather slowly!

We have started practising for the school nativity. It is everyone in the infants. And in my school, that is a very lot of children. 5 classes I think. Which makes it all the more surprising that not only do I have a real and proper part... but I have lines to learn too. Mummy was so shocked when she found out I had 29 whole words to learn for the play, she hyperventilated and nearly had to sit down in the playground. I have been aptly cast as the head angel. My words go along the lines that 'I bring good news'. At school, I recite my words off by heart, and really nicely. At home, however, I have found it is excellent fun to ad lib while practising. I currently have 2 alternative versions to the official script. The first is along the lines of 'Mary, I bring you good news, pat pat, bum bum, poo poo.' This is perhaps my favourite. However, the other version, which usually gets a good reaction is 'Mary, I bring you good news... and bad news.'

Me and Daddy have been camping this month. I lost the battle to do real camping outside, so instead we put the tent up in my bedroom. It was quite good fun, however it was a bit squishy as I had to share the tent with Daddy. He snores and tosses and turns quite a bit. Then I have to wriggle quite a lot to get comfy, and then he complains if my foot accidentally ends up in his ear. After 2 nights with neither of us getting much sleep, we converted my room back into being a pretty pink bedroom again, rather than a pretty pink campsite.

We went to the first ever Edwardian evening in the village. It was rather extremely busy and chaotic but pretty good. I liked going into school as we had our Christmas market the same evening. It was really exciting as I saw loads of friends and teachers that I hadn't seen for literally hours.

We played tombola's and auctions and ate hot dogs. I got a new lumpch bag too.

Right at the end of the month, me and Mummy did a bit of a major bedroom sort out. We moved furniture and my bed and everything. I didn't like sleeping in it the first night. I felt all the wrong way around and upside down. But now I've got used to it, I like it and it's the best.

Better go, I want to help stick all the ribbons and bows on the Christmas presents.

Bye, bye.  Like you to pieces,

Jess x

# December 2009

The School play went really well. By the end my wings were exhausted and a regular supply of pink medicine got me through the last performance. I remembered all my lines and didn't ad-lib once. I enjoyed being centre stage. I think it may be something I could be good at, although I am not actually planning on being an actress. There aren't too many plays in which I can do what I do naturally. Be an angel.

I was invited back to LaplandUK. It was a bit scary discovering I wasn't on the 'good list', but then Father Christmas found my name on the extra special good list – so it was all okay in the end. It was quite the adventure. I cuddled a couple of very large reindeer, saw some real ones, stroked a husky and ice skated with a real Sami (Laplander). I'm hoping to get invited back.

Christmas was crazy but brilliant. There were 13 of us in the end for Christmas lunch... and everyone stayed the night. I got a sack full of pressies from Santa. The best thing in my stocking was a pink desk tidy. Mummy and Daddy got me a real pink mini laptop. It is great and I have got my school play and some photos on it already.

I got loads of nice presents this year and not a single dodgy one. Lots of lovely toys, handbags, jewellery, lip gloss and 'Joules' clothing. I had more big-girl presents this year than ever before. But that is because I am officially a big girl, and will be 7 really soon.

The lead up to Christmas was almost as exciting as Christmas itself, due to the serious amount of snow that landed the week before. Being nearly big, the plastic box that I'm usually put in when it snows, was a bit of a squash and a squeeze, so I have progressed to a real and proper sledge. We stayed on flat ground – but that was exciting enough as I managed to still fall off it 3 times!

Bye, bye honey pie.

Jess x (aka Lola or Mary!)

# January 2010

The year started with yet more snow. And I do believe we had even more than we did last month! Last year, term finished with school being closed due to too much snow. And then I only was back this year for 2 (and a bit) days and had to spend the rest of the week at home, as school was closed again! It actually started to get quite boring. It's a right pain in the bum bum getting my wheelchair through the ice and snow and I don't like playing in it either, as I get really very cold. Everyone else seems to enjoy playing in snow, but I guess their running around keeps them warm enough to have fun. I was in about a hundred layers, blankets, hats and scarves... and I was still cold. I just don't get it. I'd rather look at the snow from the living room, than actually go outside. This has made Mummy very grumpy though, and eventually I had to let her go out and play for a while, while I supervised from the patio doors.

Playing indoors, I love dressing up and pretending to be at the Disney 'Bibbidi Bobbidi Boutique'. It involves me having my hair, make-up and nails done and then of course putting on the princess outfit, complete with gloves and crown. This traditionally has to then be finished off with a photo session, while I pose like a princess. I'm not exactly sure if am actually a real princess, but I do feel like one sometimes.

At the very beginning of the year I did something absolutely amazing and without any nagging or prompting whatsoever. Just before my 7th birthday, I started to crawl! Not fast or anything, but it is real and proper crawling, all by myself, without anybody helping. I have now managed to go all the way down the hallway, which is absolutely miles. I even got a purple purse for my troubles. It has gone quite well, apart from a small mishap involving my nose and the carpet. While I was on a bit of a roll, I tried a bit of cruising (the walking while holding onto something, not the boating variety). I used the (newly erected) bar up the hallway and I shuffled my feet along the floor, moving along with no help.

Daddy did mention about putting a second rail in, but I'm concerned that we would end up with parallel bars in the hallway and then if we're not careful we'll find Uncle Billy Bob's upside down hanging off them!

I had my 7th birthday with Mummy, Granny and Nanny at Build-a-bear. It was great fun and the giant rabbit called Paulette came out 'specially to see me and to give me hugs. We each came away with a bear, complete with outfits. Mine was the best, but allegedly Mummy's was the coolest. After Build-a-bear we had a lovely party lunch for mine and Pop Pop's birthday.

I also went back to swimming, after the pool being closed for months and months due to a new roof and changing rooms and stuff being done. I amazed everyone by being just as good as I was last year when lessons finished. I have been told by the head club coach that I have potential. I think the new pink fish-shaped swimming hat helped though!

Bye.

Lola x (aka Jess)

# February 2010

Swimming lessons have been on the freezing side of chilly, now I'm in the big pool. So much so, my swimming teacher has been suggesting that buying a wet suit may be a good idea. So, that's what we did. Me and Mummy now have matching wetsuits and both look quite cute. It's done the trick too, as I'm nowhere near as cold as I had been. That and the fact that I look super cool... or do I mean, jolly jazzy! I have been told I have to concentrate just on backstroke, as I am supposedly a natural. A natural what... we don't know! They keep trying to teach me the proper backstroke arms, but they are so weird and confusing and stupid and boring, so I keep making up my own much better arm actions, to the obvious annoyance and frustration of my teachers. Arm actions also seem to look and work better if I sing. The only problem is, I can't sing and do arm actions AND kick my legs all at the same time. It seems to be one too many things to do at once. So, I have decided, who needs to bother with kicking. Anyway, that bit is quite hard work.

For a change my feet grew half a size, so that meant I got a new pair of shoes, which was good. Two new pairs would have been better.

I've been to another foot appointment and the orthotics man decided to adjust my current splints rather than have new ones made. They were supposed to be ready before I went back to school after half term. Well, that's been and gone, and so has the rest of the month... and still no splints. On the up side, my school shoes are over 2 sizes too big without the splints, so I have had to go to school in pink shoes.

We went to see High School Musical 2 at the theatre. It was really good fun and (with a bit of help) I got up at the end and did some very energetic dancing.

We had a busy half term and spent a couple of nights away in a moon hotel (a Premier Inn). I did some real big girl shopping, which I found I was very good at. It was good fun having a little 'oliday, but it really was quite incredibly cold. We had a very lot of snow, which meant that when we went on the roller coasters, we had to wear woolly hats and gloves... which was a bit weird.

I am still enjoying Rainbows and did a rather excellent wheelchair dance routine recently at 'Rainbows Got Talent'. Well I thought I was excellent anyway.

Bye-bye you silly nah-nah wally bags.

Jess x

# March 2010

I have been feeling on the poorly side of sick. I have been really hot and yuck and I had a cough that made me sound like a doggie. I had to have brown medicine which was so disgusting that I decided to get better again very quickly. Even so, I still had to have a couple of days off school so the rest of the class didn't start barking too!

I have had to point out to Granny that she has diamond hair. Well, no one else had told her, so I thought I had better mention it. Granny seemed quite pleased at first, until I let her know it wasn't actually a compliment. However, the other day I woke up with the weirdest bed hair – and Daddy had the cheek to point out that I had diamond hair too. Humph!

We did something really exciting at school. We did lots of singing and recorded it on CD. All the infants sang 'Yellow submarine'... all the infants, except me. My submarine was pink.

We went away to stay in a moon hotel again. It's the third one I've been to and I really like going there. They are my favourite and my best. Nice lovely comfy beds and huge yummy breakfasts. This trip was so we could go to a Primary sports camp at Stoke Mandeville, so I could learn real and proper wheelchair sports. Bowling felt weird as you nearly had to touch the floor to throw the ball and I thought I was going to actually fall out of my chair. Because of that, it might well have been the scariest sport I did!! In Kurling (yes, this sort IS spelt like that!) you sit on the floor and push discs on wheels to a target. It was good fun and after a while I started getting the hang of it. Fencing was hot in the hat and Boccia (pronounced bot-cha) was good, but my arm was aching a bit by now! And then I had to do even more throwing... with discus and then javelin. I got my 'trying hard and taking part' certificate from our lovely team leader Ernie. I never knew he was the fastest milkman in the west... but I can believe it. You should see him go in his wheelchair!!

Kiss me, cuddle me, tickle me!! Jess x

# April 2010

I have a sports wheelchair now, so in theory I can practise wheelies and other really clever stuff.

It can be a bit very scary though doing these tricks. Especially as it transpires, this chair is on the large side of enormous. It is an adult chair, not a child's one. I'm still holding out for one that is actually the right size for me, but until that day comes, this one will have to do. The problem was, this chair was apparently a bargain, and Mummy can never resist a bargain. Even if it means driving all day to collect it from the other side of the country. I was invited to go on a day trip to Yorkshire, but frankly I have much better things to do with my time... like making chocolate Easter nests, playing shops, drawing...

There have been Easter Eggs everywhere. I have been on a number of Easter eggie hunts, although I should point out, I eventually discovered it was actually the same bag of eggs that kept on hiding in different places! There isn't actually a never-ending supply of chocolate eggs. Which is a shame.

As the weather was unseasonably good, I convinced Mummy and Daddy into having a picnic outside. However, some of my comments created a bit of a stir. I usually really like celery. But I had some and it tasted purple. It was horrid. This apparently was a strange thing to say and I was asked to explain what purple tastes like. Well, it's obvious, isn't it? It tastes a bit like pink! I then had what I can only describe as 'hospital ham'. Mummy apologised. I don't know why, I really like 'hospital ham'.

I had a busy Easter holiday doing lots of different stuff. One memorable bit, was a trip to the cinema to see Nanny McPhee. The end was really incredibly sad, when the daddy came home from the war; I had to cry quite a bit. And I kept crying all the way back to the car... and then all the way back to Granny's house. It really was that very sad.

I have been repeatedly asked for years if I'd like a pet. Suggestions of pussy cats, hamsters and rabbits are the norm.

But I really can't be doing with these fluffy critters. They move a bit fast for my liking and all seem to have sharp claws or teeth or something. I then had quite a brain wave and decided what I really, really wanted was a pet fish. So, off we went on a bit of a mission, and with a bit of research by Daddy, I am now the rather proud owner of a very pink fish tank and 2 very little fish. I decided to call them 'Charlie' and 'Lola' the day I got them. The next day I changed their names to 'you' and 'me'. After that I am planning to call them 'Charlie boy' and 'Charlie girl'; and then 'snowy' and 'rainy'; and then 'fishies'; and then 'Ruby' and 'Elliott Elliott'; and after that 'Pinkie' and 'Purpley' and, well, I will just have to see after that. I'm running out of names already though. It is quite tricky having a pet. The first day I fed them, I sprinkled their food on the carpet next to their tank. Well, I didn't want their food to get wet. Mummy convinced me they would prefer to have their food in their water, rather than look at it through the glass walls. Each to their own I guess. Glad I'm not a fish. Their food tastes (oopps... I mean smells) absolutely disgusting!

I have done more bike rides and tri-cycled more miles in this month than I have ever done previously in my whole life put together. I'm getting quite good at the pedalling and okayish at the steering. Cycling along the pavements is fun as it goes down for each driveway. On these 'down hills' I scream with excitement and pedal really fast, but I do sometimes need a bit of a push to get up the other side. The 'up hills' can sometimes be almost a foot high, and my pedalling isn't quite that good yet! I like wearing my cycle helmet, so I look like a real and proper bicycle rider.

It's been a funny old month. The supermarket near school decided to do some fundraising for a local project. Well it was suggested they could get me a real child-sized sports wheelchair. One where I could do some proper practising of the wheelies I learnt, at that wheelchair course I did down in Brighton. A wheelchair that I could actually use right now (rather than an enormous one that will be suitable in about 5 years' time!) The 2nd hand adult one will be good one day, but it really is too big to manage right now.

So, there has been this massive fundraising event including a sponsored silence, bag packing and a huge raffle. We needed about £1,500 for a proper child-size chair. They are hideously expensive, as I guess they don't make that many. Well, the fundraising went brilliantly and I am even more famous than I was previously. There was a huge picture of me in the store being a 'princess on wheels'. I have been in the local paper twice, and I helped with the raffle by picking the lucky winners. As I was in charge of that bit, those with pink tickets definitely were at a distinct advantage... well it is my favourite colour. In the end, I was banned from picking anymore pink tickets. Well, the upshot is, they managed to raise enough money for me to have a new wheelchair... a real and proper child-size sports chair that tips up and spins and does all the things I learnt to do. I just need to order one now. Apparently, this is easier said than done. This hasn't been helped by Mummy, who in desperation to find suppliers who stock kid's chair, accidentally tried to make an appointment for me with a company based in America. When she finally found a dealer that was actually in this country, the trick was to then find someone within 200 miles of home that actually sold children size chairs.

What a palaver. Well, it seems you can't just buy these things off the peg. Not that they hang wheelchairs up on pegs. You have to go to a stockist in person, Monday to Friday, between 9-5pm to have a real and proper assessment. Well this is a pain in the bottom. I'm having to miss school. And Mummy and Daddy seem nearly as bothered at missing work. I have two assessments booked so far and I hope I will find something just right. The chairs do look exceptionally cool. I will have to be renamed the 'princess on flashy turbo charged wheels'.

Kiss me, cuddle me, catch me.

Jess x

# May 2010

I have had two sports wheelchair trials this month with different suppliers. Both only could see me during the day, and neither was open at weekends, so I had to have time off school for each one. To me this was a plan with no flaws. Especially as the first assessment was so far away, we ended up staying in a moon hotel for one night. I love staying away with Mummy and Daddy. It is like a very adventure. And breakfast there is my favourite and my best. Especially the mini muffins. I always have to have one (or two... or three!) of those.

I knew the first assessment was several hours drive away... as I was able to watch a whole DVD on the journey and I still had time to get bored. When I got there though, I'd never seen so many wheelchairs in one place. The people there were absolutely lovely. They were in wheelchairs as well and seemed to know everything there was to know about wheelchairs. I tried out a kids' chair called the Kuschall Junior. It was really cool and I went so fast at one point Mummy had to jog to keep up. Now that was worth seeing! I got all measured up and provisionally chose a red one. Problem was, I couldn't order it there and then, even though we all loved it, as I had a second assessment booked for a couple of weeks later.

The other wheelchair assessment was at home. This was never going to be as good, as for a start there was no overnight stay in a moon hotel and no mini muffins.

This wheelchair looked pretty flash, but it was not as exciting as the first one I tried out. I kept trying to run over Mummy, while Daddy talked to the wheelchair man. He was quite nice and actually admitted that this chair was not right for me at all. In fact, he went as far to say that I should really be looking at something more like a... Kuschall Junior.

Hang one. That sounds familiar.

So, within minutes of the end of my second assessment, I had a bright red and lovely Kuschall Junior wheelchair on order. And apparently, I will only have to wait a few weeks while it is being made to measure in the factory, to my actual and exact specifications. How completely cool is that?

Ironically, while in my current NHS chair, I actually got a speeding ticket at school! I was not very sure if this was a good or bad thing... but either way, I am especially proud of it, as doing anything at speed is not exactly my speciality.

While on the subject of receiving 'awards' at school, I also got a Special Achievement certificate for doing good listening, and remembering everything the firemen said when they came in to do a talk. I now know not to walk into a burning building. Well, I wouldn't, would I!! I can't walk! It wasn't clear though whether I should wheel myself into a burning building! I also learnt that you have to dial 999 as well. That's assuming you can find the phone in the first place. In my house, it's like a game of hide and seek... and the phone is exceptionally good at hiding!

I have been doing some indoor camping again. I have a new and very pink tent. I like a few home luxuries as I camp. Including a duvet, my DS and of course a snow globe. I even had Megan bear in the tent, complete with her luggage and toy wheelchair. It can get a bit squashy sometimes.

I've been to another disco at school. I really like discos. This time though I spent most of the time bottom shuffling around. It was the only way to stop Mummy constantly peering over my shoulder, which she does when I'm in my harness. This new-found freedom meant I was able to cuddle considerably more people than usual, which was definitely a bonus. Being on the floor, I also found lots of exciting stuff, including a 50 pence piece and a smartie. Mummy wouldn't let me keep either though, which was a shame. I wanted to eat the smartie. It really wasn't that fluffy.

I guess one of the main events of this month was another trip up to GOSH. I have to go up there every year just to see my consultant and talk about how I'm doing. As my appointment was later in the day than usual I decided that it would be nice to go to Hamley's before we went to hospital. So, this is what we did. They have a good build-a-bear department there and I find Mummy and Daddy usually let me have a little something if I have to go to hospital. So where better a place to go. This time I got a lovely 'Hello Kitty' which I have named 'Hello, Kitty-Mae'. We then went off to the hospital for a drink and cake before my appointment. I couldn't eat or drink anything though, as I was really nervous that the doctor might have an overwhelming urge to stick a plaster on my hand. They do that sometimes... well, they have done that every time I've had anaesthetic or a blood test.

Unfortunately, my doctor was so incredibly busy, all the outpatient appointments were running late... really, really late. 2 hours late in fact. I finally got seen just before 6pm! When we finally got to see my consultant, she was lovely and did lots of nice and easy tests. She wanted to look at my bendy wrists and ankles and banged my knees and elbows with a stick thing. Stuff like that. She asked lots of questions and took lots of notes. The good news was, that they did loads of genetics tests a few months ago, and they all came back negative. Bad news is, that means the next thing they want to do is a muscle biopsy. This means I've got to come back to GOSH in a few months, have another anaesthetic and... well, actually I don't know what else. Mummy was getting the low down from the doctor and Daddy kept distracting me from listening. I don't know whether it was intentional, or if he just wanted to talk to someone more on his wavelength. These doctors do get a bit technical sometimes and Mummy does a good job in pretending to follow what they are talking about. By the time they had got onto the subject of mitochondria, me and Daddy were having a much more interesting conversation. I guess we'll have to wait and see. I'm not too fussed as long as it doesn't involve plasters.

I had better get on. I really am a very busy and important person. I need to feed my fish, practise my spellings, do my homework, tidy my bedroom, write notes and pose for the camera.

Tickle me, kiss me, cuddle me, catch me. Jess x

# June 2010

I have got my new sports chair already... only 3 weeks after ordering it!! Compared to the old one it is much faster and twizerlier. The wheels are sporty and go out at the bottom a little bit. And it can do wheelies too. Daddy bought a 2nd hand one that was his size, so we could play wheelchairs together. We've been doing wheelies indoors and out. And although Daddy claims to be better at them than me, I haven't actually fallen out of my wheelchair yet... unlike him!!

I had to have some new hub caps for my new wheelchair... as my other ones clashed quite horribly with my sparkly metallic red frame. I have got a rainbow of colours which I think look pretty jazzy.

Talking of jazzy, I have been dressing up my many build-a-bears in numerous different outfits. Mostly pink ones, but then I do have mostly girl bears. I do however have one boy bear (cat), called Charlie. He comes in particularly handy when playing weddings. And he looks especially special in his red 'tie bow'.

I have been having a bit of trouble sleeping recently, which means we are all grumpy at the moment! For some reason, my pillow hates me. I don't know why, but I have had to borrow Daddy's pillow for weeks. It's a bit weird.

I've had a really busy month.

I was in the 'Wakey Shakey' group at the school Talent show doing a sing and dance routine to the Black Eyed Peas. I did a dress rehearsal in front of the school and a real and proper evening performance too. I absolutely loved it and I got 3 team points!

I've been cycling again, which was fun, but it can be very tiring.

I've been brave and adventurous and done real and proper camping somewhere other than my own back garden.

I did some good standing up (for a second or two) which earnt me some fantastic stickers.

I've had friends round for 'tea and toys', which was great fun, but they always mess up my room, which is 'nnoying.

A mobile zoo came to Rainbows, and I stroked a meerkat, a rat and a rabbit. I absolutely refused point blank to touch any of the creepy crawlies though. Eugh.

AND, I was in the local carnival as a fairy. Mummy and Auntie Piglet were big fairies. It was excellent, but so hot. And all that waving of my wand made my arm hurt. It's quite hard work being a fairy.

Tickle me, kiss me, cuddle me.

Jess x

# July 2010

We had Sports day on what was the hottest day of the year, which was just typical. The heat isn't great for athletes like me. I was in 2 races. The first was a sack race – I sat in my wheelchair, wearing the sack properly around my legs. And then a friend pushed my chair while I was in charge of the jumping action on my foot plate. I think we came 3rd. I then got another 3rd in the bottom shuffle race. This time I tried a bit harder than last year and I managed not to come last... mostly thanks to some very, very nice friends going even slower than I did.

I've had an icky yucky sicky bug. I thought it lasted days, but allegedly I fell asleep in the middle of the day after being very sick all morning. When I woke up I thought it was the next day and I wanted breakfast, but it was apparently nearly tea time. I was so confused and poorly sick and yuck. I obviously couldn't go to school being that poorly. Strangely though, there were 10 of us from my class, all off sick, all on the same day, and all with the very same thing! How completely weird and contagious is that!

As the weather has been so hot, we have been having some lovely outdoor picnics under the gazebo, complete with cushions, napkins and straws. It is my most favourite sort of meal ever.

I had a Physio session again. Only my 2nd one in 9 months... not a particularly good record, considering I'm supposed to see a physio now monthly. However, a combination of the long time since I was last seen, and all the cycling and wheelchair wheeling I have done this year, meant that the physio was incredibly impressed with my progress. And so she should... I was positively brilliant!

We went to the Mobility roadshow for the first time ever. It was absolutely heaving with people in wheelchairs, although I was probably one of the smallest ones there. I did get to do quite a lot of really cool wheelchair related stuff, including meeting (and getting the autograph from) a really famous man off the telly, called Ade.

I got a chance to do some hand pedalling on a kind of exercise bike. I did over a mile in total, all by myself. Now I want one for home. But apparently, they are a very lot of money.

I also tried out some really cool electronic car seats. These seats come out of the car at the touch of a button and swivel round so I can transfer out of my wheelchair and into the car seat really easily. Problem is, these cost a fortune too. Oh pickles.

Seems that everything we looked at was hideously expensive. We're not talking hundreds of pounds for each thing... according to Daddy, who picked up all the brochures, we're talking thousands and thousands of pounds. Frankly, anything more than £20 seems excessive to me, unless of course we're in Build-a-bear, and then it is perfectly good value for money as far as I'm concerned.

One of the most incredible things I have ever done, was while we were at the Mobility roadshow. I went rock climbing!!! I surprised everyone by suggesting that I wanted to actually have a real and proper go. I had to hold this handle thing, and each time I pushed the handle down, with my especially strong muscles, I went up into the air. It felt a bit like I was going to fall and it was a bit wobbly and scary, and very, very high up, but I did it. I felt very proud of myself and was quite amazed at just how brave I was. I also feel, I completely deserved the huge applause I got when I reached the top, which came from the then sizable crowd that had now congregated at the bottom of the tower to watch me.

I also had a wheelchair lesson while I was at the roadshow. It was by the same people I went to see in Brighton. I impressed them with my wheelies and I have some new stuff that I need to now practise at home. I also had a go at a slalom relay race, but this time I was loads faster than I was last time. This is due to a combination of my flashy twizly wheelchair and lots of wheeling practice. It means I am definitely getting better.

After my impressive sporting exploits at the Mobility

roadshow, I now have my name down for another wheelchair course at the end of the summer holidays. This one looks good, as it teaches you 'fishing'. I did think that I would need a net and a bucket for this, but apparently 'fishing' is when you pick stuff up from the floor in your wheelchair, and then wheel yourself while balancing it on your lap. Sounds tricky.

A few things are coming to an end. I have finished infants and have to go up to Junior's in September. We've had a couple of trial runs in our new class with our new teacher. Problem is I can't pronounce my new teacher's name. She's called Miss Skeggs. Honestly, when you have a speech problem, that's a bit tricky. I call her Mrs Eggs! It sounds pretty similar, and so far, I don't think she's noticed!

I've also finished Rainbows. I'll be a big girl Brownie when it all restarts after the holidays. I've got my nice new uniform already!

We had a bit of a fish incident that involved the biggest of my goldfish actually ending up flip flopping around on my bedroom carpet. After a bit of screaming (mostly from Mummy), we managed to get the fish back in the tank, which is where it was supposed to have been all along.

Am I famous? Everyone seems to know me wherever I go, and they always stop to say hello. Is it too early to start giving out signed photos? I have some!

Tickle me, kiss me, cuddle me... know me?

Jess x

# August 2010

The School holidays have been every bit as hectic as a month during term time. And the weather hasn't exactly been very summery either. However, I had a fun time and did some new stuff.

I went backwards and forwards between Granny and Nanny's for the first few weeks and stayed with each of them for a few nights too – well I did for first week anyway. Then I decided I'd rather spend every night at home with my fish. That and the fact I wanted to keep an eye on the house. Every time I stayed away, I'd come back to increasingly more chaos in the hallway at home. Mummy and Daddy were allegedly decorating the hall. However, to the untrained eye it looked more like demolition than decoration. I did help with a bit of paint stripping and painting with different test pots. The good news is, by the end of the summer holidays, the hallway was put back to a slightly better state than it started.

I did loads of good stuff with Nanny and Grandad, and with Granny and Pop Pops. I did lots of swimming and make do things, loads of baking and I went to the cinema to see 'Toy Story 3' as well. I also stayed away one night in Nanny's van, which was particularly good fun too.

I've had yet more new glasses. I have completely lost count how many pairs I've had now. I think though this is only my 2nd pair of purple ones. They really are very cool.

We went away on holiday to Jersey on a big boat. We had some really wet days while we were there, but spent those days swimming in the lovely hotel pool and lazing around on the indoor 'sun' loungers. I did some rather excellent swimming with my new Toy Story rubber ring, which earnt me a well-deserved pink butterfly hat as a reward. I did a bit of tidying up while I was on the beach, which caused a bit of a stir. It was on one of the warmer and dryer days, and I decided to collect up all of the sea weed from the beach and bring it back to where Mummy and Daddy sat... much to Daddy's disgust!

We discovered the sand was absolutely perfect for building sandcastles. And to help, I had a new pink heart-shaped bucket. Every day we were on the beach, our sand castle creations became ever more impressive, to the extent that by the last day I considered it to be more of a sand city than just a sand castle.

We went to a kind of zoo. Technically I think it was a conservation park, but it's kind of the same thing. It was really excellent fun and we saw some great animals. My favourite was the 'meerkat-dot-com'... simples, eeek! Mummy tried to tell me that they are just called meerkats, and not 'meerkat-dot-com'. I don't believe any of that nonsense!

After Jersey, we went away for a few days to do some wheelchair training, and we stayed in moon hotel, again. I learnt to pick stuff up from the floor and balance it on my lap while wheeling. It is trickier than it sounds. I did a wheelchair obstacle course too! I was pretty good.

At the end of the month we had a much deserved du-day (duvet) day.

Tickle me, kiss me, cuddle me.

Jess x

# September 2010

Back to school... unfortunately. I like being at home and playing toys and going on holiday and things. I did a lot of growing over the summer, which was handy as I am a junior now. This means I am really a big girl.

I have started Brownies. I don't like the uniform. It's brown and yellow. It is the sort of colour Pop Pop would wear! It should be called Pop Pop-pies and not Brownies. I'm in the gnome 'six'. But I'd rather be a princess. I'm not sure I want to be a gnome.

Me and Mummy changed my room around again, so my bed was in a different place. I wasn't good at sleeping upside down and back to front and the wrong way around. After over a week of not sleeping, me and Mummy decided to put my bed back to where it was, and finally I got a good night sleep!

I have decided that I don't want my hair cut long anymore, like the last twice I had a haircut. I'm fed up of tangles and knots and bobbles. I want to grow it short, like my 1 to 1. So, that is what I did.

Back to school means homework, and reading and spellings and hard stuff like that. I had some good and messy homework that involved papier-mâché. However, it did result in an unprecedented 3 unscheduled baths for just one piece of homework. I also have had to learn some harder spellings and there are more of them than last term. I didn't quite catch when the spelling test was though. I think it is April. That's handy. Loads of time. Uh oh... the test was Thursday, not April. That came around a lot quicker than I was expecting. It clearly is going to be a bit tougher being a junior than I was expecting.

I had a teddy bear tea party. All teddies were well dressed and most brought handbags. Me and Mummy were their carers. Just like I have a carer to help me. They still managed to have a little spill when they had their drinks though. 'Long ears' got soaked having her drink. I think it is because she doesn't actually have a mouth.

We went on a bit of a family outing to a wildlife zoo, kind of thing. It was a bit like the one we went to on holiday. It took ages to get there and the weather was yuck and grim. But when we got there we saw some really good animals, including my favourite (still)... meerkats.com.

I have started making a list of all the things I'd like for Christmas. So, exactly how many days IS it till Christmas?

Tickle me, kiss me, bath me, cuddle me.

Jess x

# October 2010

We went to the Primary Sports camp at Stoke Mandeville again. This time I was in the green team and had to wear a green t-shirt all day. I tried hard in all the morning sessions and was quite good at the two most unlikely (for me) Paralympic sports, Wheelchair shot put, and the club. I played Polybat too. It is a bit like table tennis, but with sides on the table. It's really hard to play in a chair. I was rubbish.

In the afternoon, everyone was supposed to play wheelchair basketball. I watched while some kids who could walk really well, 'play' in the wheelchairs. This really annoyed both Mummy and Daddy, so we all left early in a bit of a hump.

At least I got to stay in a moon hotel, I suppose.

We went to Brainwave again this month. I haven't been for absolutely ages. I showed them my crawling and everything, and after a whole day of trying quite hard, I got a list of exercises. The only problem is, my exercises this time are almost identical to the last list of exercises I had, and the same as the list I got from the NHS physio. Come to think of it, it is the same as the list before that, and the one before that too. I'm not going back. I've had enough.

We were supposed to go back to the really big hospital in London, GOSH. We had packed, I chose sweets, a magazine and everything and then a few days before we were due to go, they postponed it. I'm now not going till next month. However, I don't want to go any more. I now know that when I do go, I will have to go to sleep in the day, and that makes me really sick... I'm sad and scared about going now.

It has been a funny old month.

I did at least go to the Junior disco just before half term. It's a bit like junior scrabble... but different. I did some good dancing in my wheelchair all by myself. Now I am a junior, I did dancing like a big girl.

Auntie Piglet did a surprise visit to the playground after school one day. It was really very exciting and I had to give her a million hugs and cuddles and kisses.

Mummy's love for Harry Potter is starting to rub off on me. We had a Harry Potter Halloween party at Granny and Pop Pop's. Everyone had to dress up and they looked pretty good. I was 'behind me' (Hermione), and although I thought I was the best, Daddy was voted 'best dressed' as Hagrid and Uncle Lamby 'most handsome' as Sirius Black.

Expecto Patronum!

Jess x

# November 2010

I had a Roman day at school and had to wear a special, albeit chilly outfit that was actually hand made by Mummy. I had a really excellent time and did some fun things, including making clay pots, pendants and perfume. Thankfully we didn't have to build any long straight roads.

We had a special educational plan (or something) meeting at school and this time I was actually invited. It was not anywhere near as mysterious or as exciting as I was expecting. We just talked about what I was going to work on next, and then managed to digress onto talking about more interesting things like Minnie Mouse pens and Harry Potter. Easy peasy.

I spent a weekend at Granny and Pop Pops as Daddy had man flu and Mummy was on the exhausted side of tired. We had a really busy time doing cooking and make-do stuff as part of my Brownie Hostess badge. I also went to church where I was in charge of the collection and everything. It is all part of me practising to 'lend a hand' and trying to be a real and proper Brownie. I've been trying to learn the Brownie promise too, but it is a bit tricky to get completely right.

I saw the real and actual Queen. She was coming to the jam factory. I go there sometimes too. I like the shop. I was a bit disappointed that the Queen arrived in a big shiny car. I thought she'd arrive in a golden carriage. If I was a princess or a Queen, I think I would like to travel in a gold carriage.

I did my enrolment and I am now a real and proper actual Brownie. I remembered most of my words, although some last-minute stage fright, due to the audience being present, meant it didn't go quite as well as I had practised. However, I must have done enough, as not only did I get my metal promise badge, my gnome badge and my unit badge, I also got a well earnt hostess badge too.

I like to play 'sink and float' in the bath every time I'm in there. It's my favourite game. We get a right collection of things and guess whether it sinks or floats. I then drop each one in the bath in turn to see what happens. It is harder than you would expect. Mummy's new watch sank to the bottom straight away. Thankfully it is 'wet-able'. I checked.

I am getting more and more independent at school now I am a big girl. I am trying harder and harder to do my transfers with less and less help. A 'transfer' is not something you rub onto a piece of paper, well it is, but that's not what I've been practising. I've been working on 'transferring' from my wheelchair to my wombat chair to the toilet. I've also been wheeling myself into class in the morning and out into the playground at the end of the day. It is exhausting now I'm big. Mummy and Daddy agree!

Obviously, the biggest event of the month was my trip up to GOSH. It was the first time we have ever stayed in the GOSH hotel, 'Weston House'. It was really nice. It was more like a little house than a hotel room. It had a huge bathroom that was big enough for me in my wheelchair, a kitchen area, living room, dining table and two bedrooms. It was amazing. We went up to London the night before my appointment as they wanted us on the ward by 7:30am. We'd managed to do that from home before now, but you have to get up in the middle of the night, which is really grim when you have a long and stressful day ahead of you. So, this was fab. I didn't have to fast until 2am the next morning, so we got to the room/flat/suite and ate matchmakers until we all felt sick! We then went to bed and had a good night sleep, once Daddy had stopped snoring that is. In the morning, we woke up to Daddy's mobile phone alarm. I thought it 'looked' like Tinkerbell. Mummy thinks I'm nuts sometimes.

The hotel was only a 1 minute walk from the hospital, which was handy as it was pouring with rain. I was okay until we got onto the ward, and then I got all nervous and shaky. They did the usual 'obs' as they call them. That means, checking my oxygen (by putting a thing on my finger), my blood pressure, pulse and my weight. Boring really. Then we just had to wait until it was my turn to go to sleep. I was nervous. Really, really nervous. And sad. I kept asking really nicely if we could go home. But no. Apparently not. The promise of gluing, glittering and make-do stuff made me a bit happier and it made the time pass faster. It also made the wait not quite so scary and bad. I made some amazing Christmas baubles and decorations with a lovely lady who was the ward play assistant.

Because I had got so upset and nervous earlier in the day, it was decided I would have to have a pre-med this time. I don't think I've ever had one of those before. It was weird. I felt very funny. A bit like when Mummy has had one too many gins. All weird and giggly and chatty. I did some singing too. And when they put me on a trolley to take me to theatre, not only did I not mind, but actually it was quite good fun. The next bit I remember was not so good. I woke up in the recovery room with a really lovely nurse with the longest black plaits you have ever seen. I liked her a lot. Everything hurt, I was really cold and there was a lot of activity. Apparently, my pulse went through the roof, which is not good as I think it's a 6-storey building! Mummy and Daddy weren't allowed in and the nurse had to get help. I didn't know what they did, but I did eventually start to feel a little better, just really sore.

Once back on the ward it was just my mission to get home as fast as I could. That meant I had to eat, drink and wee, before they would discharge me. I had some extra meds while I was asleep this time, so I wasn't sick when I woke up.

That meant the eating and drinking bit was easier than usual. And on the 3rd attempt, I managed a wee. So, despite everything hurting like mad, I managed to get discharged and home in time for tea.

I've just got to get better now. I understand I have stitches in my leg under the huge plaster. I hope the surgeon sews better than me and Mummy.

Owwww! Be careful... please.

Jess x

# November 2010 Part II

Well, I thought, so wrongly, that was that.

The day after coming out of hospital I felt really sore and had absolutely loads of medicine, some nice, some not, but it was relatively uneventful. I hardly ate a thing, but that was not surprising in the circumstances. I did a little bit of colouring in, stickers and looking at magazines. When the pain killers wore off, I felt really rough and had to ask that anyone who touched me or lifted me was really very careful and gentle. I thought that was bad enough. But I had no idea what was to come.

The next day I had my early morning Calpol and soon after I was really sick. So, as everything was hurting lots, I was given the other nasty medicine. I threw that up too. Everything still hurt. And I felt hot, and shaky and wobbly (more than usual) and tired. All I could do was lie on the sofa and watch CBeebies.

Mummy kept trying to feed me, but I felt too sick. She tried to get me to play, but I felt too sore and she wanted me to talk, but I was just too tired. I just wanted to be left alone, so I could lie really still.

The next lot of medicine I threw up too. It was horrible and it made me cry. There was a brief time when I felt well enough to sit, rather than lay, and I even did 2 whole minutes of colouring in. It was a picture of Dora 'splora (Dora the Explorer). But that was enough for me. After one more load of up-chucking I asked to go to bed, a whole hour before bedtime. I'd had enough. At least I thought, it can't get any worse.

Next morning, I woke up for my first dose of Calpol. Soon after that, I was really sick. Again. Too de-ja-vous for my liking. I don't have the strength for much more of this.

The morning carried on with me being hot, wobbly and sick. By late morning I did my most spectacular up-chucking so far. Not only did it go everywhere, but it was brown. Totally and utterly disgusting. This threw Mummy into a complete wobbly, as all I'd had that day was water and Calpol. The next thing I know, I'm in the walk-in Centre seeing a lovely doctor. She was kind and nice and checked me over. She worked out why my sick was brown, and the answer was so utterly disgusting that I will be sick again if I think about it. It's enough to say, that because I had been so incredibly sick, and because my stomach was so empty, 'it' came out the wrong end. The lovely doctor said I needed some anti-sickness medicine. The same stuff they give after chemo. The only problem was, not one local pharmacist stocked it, and we tried loads. In the end, one pharmacy said they'd order the medicine in specially and we'd get it the next day. Better than nothing I guess. So, that's what we did. I think Daddy called it the law of 'sod', but I wasn't sick anymore after that. Although by then I'd lost over half a stone! And I didn't have half a stone to lose.

Bizarrely there were three upsides to this horrible series of events.

Firstly, Auntie Pigerlert did an unscheduled feel-better-visit, with a huge and lovely Minnie Mouse for me.

Secondly, I ended up having over a week off school.

And lastly, my hideously disgusting up-chucking, hot face-ness, and floppiness has frightened both Mummy and Daddy so much, that they have said that this is it. No more tests. Nothing. Not ever again. Amen to that.

# December 2010

I finally recovered from my horrible ordeal after GOSH, and my upchucking marathon. I was back at school one day before it started snowing. I managed 1 more day at school, despite battling through several inches of snow in my wheelchair (it isn't easy), before they closed the school for the rest of the week. Boy, did we have a lot of snow. A serious amount. And it snowed the next day too, so we made a snowman... and then it snowed some more, and it actually covered the snowman we had made the day before!

We got a new Christmas tree this year, which made a nice change. When we collected the new tree from the local garden centre, I also got to meet Santa... which was lucky, because I was invited to go to Lapland UK again this year, but after almost 5 hours in the car, we never got there... due to the aforementioned snow. I'm glad Santa is better getting around in the snow than we are!

I had a really good Christmas. Busy and with lots of presents. Which is just how I like it. One of my most favourite presents was an ironing board. So, me and Mummy can now iron together.

I did a school carol service in the church. Thankfully I didn't have a big part. I was just a carol singer. It would have been a disaster if I had a speaking part, as I was only in school for a couple of days during the three weeks leading up to the show, due to extreme poorliness and all that snow.

As it was Christmas time I went to two pantomimes: Aladdin and Peter Pan. I really enjoyed both pantos and luckily the 'goodies' won both times.

I have had my hair cut long again, so I look like a real princess.

I am so brave I can actually look at my stitches on my leg now, after my muscle biopsy. And out of the 13 stitches that I originally had, I think I just have 1 left hanging in there now. Pheweeee.

We thought we were going to have a bit of a timing

dilemma which could have meant the tooth fairy and Father Christmas would be arriving the same night. Thankfully the tooth held on for an extra couple of days. In honour of the tooth wobbliness, I insisted on a whole week of the Peppa Pig Tooth Fairy story at bed time. Except, to make it more exciting, I prefer to change the names. Auntie Pigerlert is Peppa, Uncle Lamby is Daddy Pig and Uncle Billy Bobs is Mummy pig (they have the same eyelashes you see!)

Night, night... don't let the beds bite!

Jess x

# January 2011

Christmas is over, and that means it is time again to go back to school. Oh bum. School is okay, but if I had the choice I would always prefer to stay at home and play toys, or Mummy's iPad. Either is fine with me. I love the iPad. I want one. Me, Mummy and Daddy have been trying to share really nicely, but it is hard sometimes. I do really cool stuff on it. I feed the fish (much better than feeding my real fish), I do jigsaws (better than real jigsaws), play the piano (better than my actual piano), do handwriting (better than getting my pen and paper out), talk to this cat called 'Tom', watch 'Simon's cat' on You Tube and make (and pretend to sell) clay pots. I'm really very good at the making and decorating pot thing. Probably due to all those times Mummy took me to painting on pottery. We can safely say I'm getting the hang of technology... and I like it.

Being that time of year again, it was back to Brownies and swimming lessons. I thought Christmas was busy, but my normal term time week is considerably more hectic!

Swimming went okay. Glad I have a helper to teach me instead of Mummy now. Mummy worked me too hard. The helper lets me bob along merrily, which suits me down to the ground.

Brownies has been good and we had a very late Christmas party, as the original one, quite festively, was snowed off! I had lots of new Brownie things for Christmas, as I sent Father Christmas a picture of me being a very proud and smart Brownie. So, I've been showing off my new 'boggy' warmer uniform, Brownies dolly and bear.

Can you believe this? A few days before my birthday, a man in the supermarket called me 'a little girl'. ME, little! I had to set the record straight right away. I said, 'I am not little, I am big... I am NEARLY 8'!

I have had a good month at school, despite being a bit snuffly, and coldy and sounding a little bit like a doggy. I got 5 out of 5 two weeks running in spellings and I was awarded a certificate for good numeracy as well. I think I'm on a bit of a roll at the moment!

January has been a month of birthdays – and lots of them. Even people who had birthdays last year managed to get in on the act and celebrate several more times during the month! My birthday was again a trip to Build-a-Bear. It is my most favourite and best place to go. I love it. I had a huge new bear wardrobe, so now I have plenty of room to store all the outfits. Great!

I think as I've had my 8th birthday, it means I must be nearly 9?! On that note, a week after my birthday, I had a present left for me left on the doorstep. A nice present, but I thought 'that's strange, it's rather early'... until Mummy pointed out it was actually for my 8th and not my 9th birthday. Oh. That's weird.

I like playing teachers and nurses at the moment. I've been looking after Mummy. She seems to need a bit of looking after recently, as she bent the car very badly and it is still at the menders. I even did good sharing and let her borrow my teddy for a whole night – I had a few spares, so I didn't exactly go without for very long. I did however ensure I got it back first thing in the morning.

There has been a bit of fuss and bother about me emptying all the toiletries out of the wicker basket in the bathroom and lining them up along the floor. I tried to do it neatly, but some silly nah nah wally keeps putting Mickey Mouse shampoos in Dora the Explorer's bed!!

I'd better go. Although... can I just make one more pot (on the iPad) before bed? And I need to feed the pretend fish, and say night, night to 'Tom' cat as well!

Night, night... don't forget to charge the iPad before morning!!

Jess x


Sorry, mummy is interfering again... at least she's promised to be quick this time!

# Ahhhh. Pity.

It is amazing how much pity comes your way, when you are a child in a wheelchair. People are forever "ahh-ing" and "shame" and "poor thing". And you would not believe the looks I get, if I dare to tell her off when she misbehaves! But in my opinion, being in a wheelchair is no excuse to not behave properly. However, I get treated like some evil witch, berating this poor, innocent child. Whereas, I'm just trying to treat her as normal as possible.

She is forever being stopped by people we have never met in our lives before, and asked her name and how old she is. I know they mean well. But it is behaviour that they would never show towards an ambulant, 'normal' child. It's a bit like being famous. You can't go shopping or out and about without being constantly stopped or stared at. We all do our best to remain polite and upbeat, but when you have been stopped numerous times in a really short space of time, especially when you are in a rush, it can be really wearing. And Jess soon tires of being civil, and frankly I don't blame her. Just let us be. Please.

# February 2011

We've had a half term this month. That meant over a week off school. Yipeee! My holiday was spread between Mummy and the grandparents.

I did lots of baking, cooking and making sweets, which meant I then had to eat lots of homemade cakes, buns and treats. Nice!

I went to the cinema twice and saw two 3D films. I also managed to get a bag of 'cinema sweeties' each time.

All that eating then might explain why I think I grew quite a bit one night. I thought I was now really quite big. That was until Mummy showed me a picture of me being held 'standing up' at Brownies. I was nearly 2 foot shorter than the Brownie next to me. Oh dear.

As it was half term I was allowed to have 3 tattoos... just the temporary ones you understand. But even they are rather tricky to get off when it is time to go back to school. Not as tricky as removing my scar I got from my 13 stitches though. I've been washing it every time I have had a bath with my strawberry soap, but it is not coming off at all. I think it is really annoying. I don't want a scar there.

I've been to the School disco again this month. I go to the Junior disco now. This means we do fantastic dancing, and stay up late! I like being a big girl. Sometimes.

I have been doing a bit of cycling on my brand new grown up tricycle. It has a back rest, seat belt, foot straps, and the most important added feature of all... streamers off the handle bars. As it is a bit 'woggily' to ride and as I haven't quite sussed that your legs should only go forwards, I haven't actually dared venture out of the house yet. I'm waiting for good weather, and a tail wind!

Know what? My bottom hates me. I've been having a few nappy problems at the moment and what I can only describe as nappy explosions. The other day I went through 3 pairs of trousers in one afternoon, due to an unexpected overflow situation. Luckily for me (but not lucky for Mummy) it happened when I was at home. I might have been a bit mortified if it had happened at school, as the nappy situation is a secret there. Shhhhhh. Don't. Tell. Anyone. I have even had to miss swimming as my bottom couldn't be trusted. Not even my 'sticky knickers' (my incontinence bikini) was up to the job. It isn't actually my fault that my bottom doesn't work. It seems my insides are just as wobbly as my outsides!

I've been playing hospitals, doctors and nurses a lot. Know what? I'm a great doctor. I do blood tests, use a stethoscope, have a clip board, and have 'killers for pain' and everything. Just about every single teddy in my room, and there are a lot of them, had to have either a bandage or some banana medicine. I think we had something akin to a bedroom epidemic.

Nurse! I need more bandages down here!

Nurse Jess x

# March 2011

I went to church with the Brownies. It was part singing, part Sunday school. I wasn't sure about going, I told them "I go to school already; I don't need to go to another one".  It was quite good fun, I suppose, as I did some sticking and pasting and make-do things. I wouldn't even mind if I had to go back.

I've not been at all well. I've had a week off school.

I missed: -

- a school outing to some lakes (and I had new 'Charlie and Lola' wellies especially),
- the speech therapist,
- open afternoon at school,
- a spelling test (phew, lucky escape!) and
- Brownies.

I have been ever so hot, been coughing like a doggie (again!), can't eat, and feel really tired and groggy. It's best if I just lie nice and still on the sofa, and then perhaps do a little bit of gluing and sticking when I'm feeling a bit better.

The constant coughing all night long, night in, night out, is starting to drive me bonkers. Mummy and Daddy aren't looking so good on no sleep either.

I have been swimming in a new local pool. The hot (steam) room is horrible, and the hot tub is a bit too hot. However, the swimming pool is really nice and warm and it has a lovely view. Some of my friends go there too, which is weird but quite nice, I guess.

I decided to have my hair cut short(ish) again after getting really fed up with the knots and tangles and bobbles and all the trouble and trauma associated with long hair. I like my new hair, and was polite enough to mention this to my hairdresser. I also let her know how nice and comfortable my new hair was too.

Yahooo! No more stupid hospital tests. It is official. Mummy and Daddy had a meeting with GOSH and there is good news and good news. The good news is, they don't want to do any more tests. Weirdly, we had decided that already, so thankfully we were all in agreement. The good news (the other one), was that the test results from the biopsy were negative. So, that is quite literally, that! They have run out of things to test me on. We have no clue what is wrong, and I guess we'll never know. But if it means no more blood tests, or MRIs or operations or biopsies, then I'm okay with that.

I have been doing a spot of gardening. It is mucky business! I have planted tomatoes and radishes, although they don't look like they'll be ready quite in time for tea.

We have a new car! The one that accidentally got a bit bent, eventually 'died' and was squished into a square. Cars often come and go and I'm really not that fussed usually, but this one is like an orange bus with slidey doors and I love it. I even open the window and wave at all the people we pass, letting them know that I've got a new car. Mummy isn't so positive, she just yells, "get your hand back in the car". Spoil sport.

I could not actually believe it, but this month I was 'Star of the week' at school. I got a certificate, a precious pencil and my picture up on the wall. I thought I would never ever be Star of the week. And I was SO excited.

The 'Star of the week', is...

Jess x

# April 2011

I had a bit of a bad splinter in my wrist. And there were a number of possible options of how to best sort out said injury. Plan (a) was to do the 1 hour round trip and get Granny to sort it out. Granny is an expert when it comes to splinters and it seemed the logical plan. Plan (b) involved a sterilised needle and tweezers... this made me very nervous. Plan (c) started like a good plan, and involved Daddy dashing to Boots, before it shut, to get some Magnesium Sulphate and then put it on and cover with a plaster... the plaster part was where it all fell down. Plan (d) was to saw my arm off... I'm hoping Daddy was joking with that one! In the end, we went for the easiest option (for me), which was handy. Plan (c), but we substituted the evil plaster scenario for a bandage, and it actually did work. No tears or anything. I even suggested keeping the bandage on for longer for sympathy. But apparently not!

I wanted to buy an "I love you Daddy" card the other day. The shop was full of 'Mother's Day' cards, but not one single "I love you Daddy" card. Quite annoying really. In the end, I had to buy him a blank card with a cake on the front and do the writing, 'all by myself'.

I made some chocolate covered strawberries. It was good messy fun, and I hardly ate any chocolate while I was cooking. Honest. But strangely we didn't seem to have quite enough chocolate to finish all the strawberries. I just can't think why.

We had a non-uniform day at school and rather than take in money we had to bring in an Easter egg for the Easter Tombola stall. I insisted on carrying my Malteser Easter egg all the way into school. I did really well too... I only dropped it once.

On sorting out my bedroom, to make it all neat and tidy, I found some real money. So, when Daddy dragged me off to B&Q one weekend, I was on a mission to find something actually worth buying there, amongst all the boring stuff... and I found a Disney princess kite! It was lovely, AND I had enough money. So, on Mother's Day, as a special treat, I said, I know, good idea, let's go fly a kite! "Let's go fly a kite, up to the tippity top, let's go fly a kite and send it soaring!" I love that song.

At the school Easter fair, I managed to win on the Treasure Map stall and was given a 5 'p' (pound!) note as a prize. I went straight to the 'Cheap Shop' with it and brought absolutely loads of stuff. Some of it was apparently tut. But if that's the case, then I like tut.

I've been wheelchair training on the decking at home quite a lot this month. I've done races, wheeling down small steps, negotiating through patio doors, swerving in and out of cones and some parking. I have tried practising with Mummy and Daddy, but Mummy is so rubbish that I had to give up with her and specifically request Daddy's presence for training. I did rather well, as you would expect. Daddy, despite being considerably better than Mummy, still managed to fall out of his chair... several times. The pair of them are really quite hopeless sometimes.

The Easter holidays involved a rather unusual game of pass the parcel, where I was the parcel, going backwards and forwards between Granny's and Nanny's house. Having said that, I had a really lovely time. I played toys absolutely loads, went out and about for picnics, the cinema, the beach, and even stayed over for 2 nights as well. Although it was apparently just spring, it felt much more like summer.

Because of the good weather, me and Mummy had a bit of a sort out of my shorts and leggings and stuff, only to find I had actually done some good and proper growing since last summer. So, I have had to have some new hoolie shorts (skirts with shorts underneath) ready for my holiday next month. I'm SO excited, I'm SO excited!!

I decided that I would change my name to Charlotte. Mummy freaked out at this, but it later transpired that was because she didn't fancy re-sewing name labels into all my school uniform. I offered a compromise that meant I would be called Jessica at school, to avoid the uniform re-naming issue, but I will only answer to Charlotte when at home. The fact it has 9 letters and that I couldn't even spell it, was not about to deter me from what I considered an absolutely genius plan. So, that is sorted. Oh, and before you get any ideas, it is NOT to be shortened in anyway whatsoever. My new name is Char-lotte.

"Let's go ride a bike!" I have been out on my new bike. It is a bit wobbily and I'm struggling to resist the urge to pedal backwards. However, I am sort of getting the hang of it and I think the streamers on the handles make me look very cool.

It was Easter this month. I always find it a bit strange though. Mummy is constantly on a mission that I eat properly. But around Easter I am practically force fed chocolate for every dessert for about a month. Despite the constant offers of help from Daddy in eating my Easter eggies, I feel it is only right and proper that I single handedly eat every egg myself. However long it takes.

There was a big wedding this month. I waved to them on the balcony (their balcony, not mine – you don't get many balcony's in a bungalow), before I got bored and wanted to play in my wheelchair.

How many days till we go to Disney again?

Jess (also known as Charlotte) x

# May 2011

I went to a party at the beginning of the month that was enhanced by a particularly good and quite unexpected party bag. So, understandably, I thought this was a good sign for the month ahead. However, next morning, when the school had one of their teacher training days and I was all set to have a day of toys and playing and picnics, I managed to kind of accidentally fall off the sofa and land on my face. Having the slowest reactions in history, meant my arms were still by my side when I landed, and my chin and lip took most of the impact. Good grief that hurt. I mean really, really ouched an awful lot. Daddy was just about to go to work and everything, and he thought a cold flannel and a dose of Calpol would soon sort this out, but what he didn't know was I had knocked myself into next week (mostly so my holiday would come quicker) and I was actually and properly concussed. To prove the point beautifully, and also because Mummy had specifically said I'd be okay as long as I wasn't sick, I promptly threw up everywhere. All over the place. Bleugh. A quick call to NHS Direct and I was put in the car ready for the off to A&E with Nanny and Grandad. They had cunningly just turned up ready for a nice day out. I just don't think they had envisioned their day out would be spent at hospital. No sooner had they got me in the car though, I was sick again. This time I managed to get it in the car, on my car seat, my outfit and Nanny's trousers. Spectacular effort. So, a high-speed change and spring clean and we were off. The nurse at the hospital was nice. A lot of waiting and a bit more throwing up and I eventually got to see a doctor. He didn't like the look of me at all, which is unusual, as most people think I'm quite pretty. Anyhow, I was kept in for observation, and after spending pretty much all of my day off in hospital, I was finally allowed to go home, with a fat cut lip and a grazed chin. I looked like I'd been in a fight... and lost. It's exhausting being ill sometimes. I managed to get in and out of hospital though without them planting a single plaster on me, which was a result. And I didn't even get any dreadful medicine, like I had before. So apart from my whole head hurting and feeling horrid and super tired, at least I was home. As a treat, and as I couldn't eat much with a poorly lip, I had a lovely bowl of strawberries for tea. Mummy offered me a second bowl, but I reminded her that I would be sick if I ate any more, and that I had had quite enough of being sick today, thank you very much.

My nickname is now apparently, Jessie Tumbleweed! Thankfully I have had no adverse side effects (apart from a bruised face), as a result of this incident. In fact, weirdly, the opposite is true. I've always struggled with numeracy. I find addition hard and subtraction downright impossible. However, the day after I hit my head, I got 10 out of 10 in subtraction at school... for the first time ever! I got 5 stickers at school in one day which is definitely a world record and I was told I'd been exceptionally whizzy in PE. The day after that I was complimented by my teacher in swimming lessons for doing so well. I am most clearly on a roll at the moment. Let's just hope that when this spurt of genius finally ends, I don't get dropped on my head on purpose, to initiate yet more clever goings on. I wouldn't put it past some doctors.

At school, we had to write our own 10 commandments. Mine ranged from, no. 1 - you must be nice; to no. 10 – you must not be a wally. So, I understand we now just need a couple of tablets of stone before we technically make this the official version.

One of my most favourite past times is dressing up my Build a Bears. I have, approximately, a million different Build a bears / rabbits / owls / cats / dogs / Hello Kitty's, all with quite an extensive wardrobe of clothes and accessories. Pinky is currently sporting a hand knitted jumper (by 'Weasley Wear', thanks to Granny). I can proudly confirm that I too have a matching jumper and that it is my favourite and my bestest one.

I guess though the most exciting thing that has happened all year was me going back to Disney World again, in Florida! It required a bit of a countdown before the holiday due to the incredible excitement. By the time I left for the airport, everyone in school, the supermarket and actually most of village knew I was going. I was also so worried that everyone at school would miss me, I convinced my 1 to 1 to take a photo of me and leave it on my desk. That way if anyone wanted to see my smiley face, they could look at the picture and wouldn't miss me too much. I thought it was a really good idea.

While I was on holiday (with Mummy, Daddy, Auntie Pigerlert and Uncle Lamby) I managed to do absolutely loads of swimming, rides, shows and characters.

The best bits of my holiday were: -

- Mickey and Pluto pushing me in my wheelchair, which I found really very funny. I also had some lovely stand up cuddles with most of the characters too.
- I got a badge and certificate from a cast member for helping behind the counter in the hotel shop.
- I also loved, going on Test Track 6 times (it is a big girl ride and it's ever so fast) and going on the 3D Toy Story Mania ride (and seeing Buttercup every time).
- Sitting next to Auntie Pigerlert at every conceivable opportunity.
- Seeing the princesses, and for the first time ever, getting to see Mary Poppins. She was beautiful and had a lovely hat. We had quite a chat and she was really nice, so I just had to go back and see her again on my last day and give her a big good bye kiss.

The not so good bits were: -

- Trying Butterbeer at Harry Potter World. Although I was in the minority on that one, as everyone else seemed to love the stuff. It is probably because I'm too young for the 'beer' bit.
- It was so hot you could have cooked bacon on the arm rests of my wheelchair. I even had to have socks on my arm rests to stop getting burnt some days. Apparently, it went above 100 on one day, and it never went below 90. Phewie.
- I was sick on the plane... again. This time though I was

sick in a sweetie bag. Mummy guessed what was going to happen this time, just before it did, and threw the sweets all over the place to get me a bag in time. Problem was, we then had to take the now lose sweets home in a spare sick bag! Yuck.

I had a very lovely holiday, and in the end, I just couldn't say 'Good bye' to the hotel when we left. It was too sad. Instead we decided to say 'See you soon' instead.

See you spoon Disney World.

Jess x

# June 2011

I kind of hurted my ankle a little bit. I thought it was actually probably very broken but no-one else seemed to take my injury quite so seriously. I convinced Daddy that I needed a real bandage to make it better. He strangely asked me how long I was going to need the bandage on for. Well, that's easy, about a metre I reckon. 20 minutes later it was all mended. Lucky I had a bandage, it made all the difference.

I am a little bit nervous and worried, as I am going on Brownie Pack Holiday next month, for 1 night and 2 days. I already have been allocated a lovely yellow Brownie sleeping bag, just for the holiday. And it is all arranged that I am going to be taking Granny with me as my 1 to 1. It is going to be quite weird, sleeping in a village hall with lots of other Brownies. I might get a bit homesick. I might fall out of bed. I might not like it. I am looking forward to the midnight party though.

I have finally been discharged from the hospital where I see the eye people. I have seen eye consultants and orthoptics people there and had 8 long years of glasses, operations and eye drops. No more. They have decided no more eye operations and the threat of eye-patching me up like a pirate has now passed. As I am officially a big girl, I am finally allowed to go to a normal and real optician. So, that's what I did. I went with Mummy and Daddy to an optician opposite school and I did just fine. Me and Mummy even got new glasses. Mine are purple. Purple is my new favourite colour. I think it might even be better than pink.

I had a bit of an accident at school. I was playing catch with a ball in the playground in my wheelchair and I rather energetically threw my arms and body backwards to catch it. Somehow the whole wheelchair went over backwards with me in it. I'm still not quite sure how it was even possible, as I have a rear tipper that is supposed to stop that happening. But anyway, over it went and I hit my head on the playground. It hurt a bit and shook me up enough that I needed quite a cuddle to recover. And then as a special treat I got to play being teacher in the afternoon. The children had to call me Miss Green and I did the register and Star of the week and everything.

I did some real and proper camping somewhere other than at home. In the end 5 of us slept in Granny and Pop Pops garden. Well, when I say 'slept', there wasn't much sleeping, what with constant nappy changes (I was having a bit of tummy trouble... not good in a tent) and the midnight snacks. Uncle Lamby definitely did do sleeping though. As he snored for England and then he did sleep weeing (it is a bit like sleep walking, but where the sole purpose is to go to the loo). He's weird.

Me and Daddy went on a school trip to Kentwell Hall. We both looked particularly cute, and we had quite a good time. Problem was, it was very wet, and rainy and muddy and wet. I was really worried that I had ruined my apron that made me look like a waitress. Thankfully Mummy did some magic on it, and made it as good as new, so I can play dressing up as a Tudor again. Shame Daddy can't – his outfit had to go back to the shop.

Jess x (aka Miss Green, circa 1533)

# July 2011

I went to the Mobility Roadshow again. It involved a two-night stay in a moon hotel, which is always fun. It's always amazing to see so many people in wheelchairs, especially other children like me. Except they're not like me. It seems most can walk... some just a few steps, but they can actually do it. I've only actually met a couple of people ever, who are in a wheelchair and like me can't walk at all. It's really quite odd.

I got to meet Ade Adepitan again. He is so nice and friendly. We had quite a long chat and I showed him I had a sticker of him on the side of my wheelchair. I even have a big poster of him in my bedroom now too.

I guess the highs and lows, literally, would be rock climbing, just like I did last year. The lows were mostly around my first attempt! It made me all nervous and I only got a bit higher than Daddy's head off the ground when I asked to come down. The high of the day was them letting me have a second go a few hours later, and this time I was really brave and got all the way to the top. I had to go fast as Daddy nearly beat me. He had to press the buzzer at the top for me though, as I couldn't quite reach.

For the first time ever for me, I got two certificates in assembly just before the end of term. One was for 'Personal achievement' and the other related to Sports day. I was so excited to get two certificates. I think it must be some kind of world record.

My 'Personal achievement' one related to going to the bathroom at school. I have had the odd success on my loo in the disabled bathroom, but it's all a bit hit and miss. I'm taken to the loo at set times in the day, between lessons and stuff. Because I don't know when I should be going. Anyway, we had a couple of days in a row where I managed to come out of school in the same nappy I arrived in. Not because anyone forgot to change me, but because I was so clever, I managed to save all my wees for the toilet visits. It was tricky, but I did it. Then, a day or two later I said to my 1 to 1, "can I ask you a question? Can I go to the bathroom?" I had never ever asked to go to the loo before. And not only did I go, but I managed a bit of a wee when I got there too. So, as you can see, a first like that truly deserved a certificate (and a sparkly purse and a Tinkerbell balloon). Usually I don't have the same toileting success at home, because at home I'm all relaxed and just don't want to try so hard. But I managed one whole weekend in pants. Just a couple of incidents, due to forgetting I had said pants on, but on the whole, not a bad effort on my part. The next weekend didn't go quite so well, as I no longer had beginners luck on my side, but the main thing is I tried. I'm also going to the bathroom at home all by myself. Sometimes it goes well. Other times Mummy insists that I need an impromptu shower and a general disinfecting of most of the bathroom. I'd like to say I'll get there. I don't know if I will. But I'm giving it a real and proper go this time, which is more than I've ever managed before. You never know, I may just do it.

I had great fun in Sports day this year. I was in 3 separate races. The first was the egg and spoon and my friend pushed me in my wheelchair. We were a winning combination last year, so we had a reputation to uphold. Thankfully, thanks to his good pushing and a suitable amount of blue tack, we managed to remain unbeaten for the second year running, in what is the high pressured and competitive world that is egg and spoon.

I was also in what they called the Wheelchair heel/toe race. About 4 of my friends lined up with me. They had to walk as if pacing out a distance, by putting one foot immediately in front of the other, heel onto toe. Meanwhile, I had to wheel myself in my wheelchair and try to beat them to the line. Grass is not exactly the best surface for competitive wheelchair racing, however despite this, in practise I had done really well. The excitement though of actual sports day and possibly some pre-race nerves, meant that I was taken over with the bizarre urge to do the walking part on my footplate as well as the wheeling bit. This slowed my progress down, but I still somehow was able to get a 3rd.

The last race for me was the Obstacle relay. I was the last leg of the relay race and I had to wheel myself to the end with a ring on my head. It must have either been the bumpy grass or my very round head, but the ring was forever falling off. This I found hysterical. Despite the ring spending more time on the floor than my head, I did manage to win this race as well. It was lucky I did win, as next year they may have suggested sticking the ring to my head with blue tack!

I loved Sports day. I haven't laughed so much in ages. I like being involved, with the parents cheering and winning races. So, then I was super pleased to be awarded a certificate in assembly for "setting an outstanding example to others, by being an inspiration". I was dead chuffed.

End of term was a whirlwind and almost as soon as the holidays started, I was off to Brownie pack holiday. It was great fun. I took Granny with me as my 1 to 1. But as there were rumours that Granny snores, we agreed to just stay the 1 night. Well, I think we both did great. Granny didn't get drummed out the Brownies, after having a quiet night in the leaders' room, and I had a busy and exciting time. Brown Owl even woke me up in the middle of the night so I could take part in the midnight feast. How cool is that!? And I got a certificate for being 'The Politest Brownie'. Why, thank you! And, don't say 'what' say 'pardon'! So... pardon were you saying?

I went for an annual review at GOSH, and despite expecting that they would discharge me this time, they want to see me again next year, with the continued promise of no more tests. So, that's ok. Especially as a trip to GOSH always means a trip to Hamley's too!!

Jess x (and Buttercup and Pooh Bear and Hello Kitty and Minnie Mouse too)

Here we go again. Mummy putting her two-penny worth in again (as that is all they are actually worth!)

# A life of extremes

Is it really my imagination, or is living with a special needs child, a life of extremes? It seems like our 'highs' are just so much higher than what is the norm, but our 'lows' are literally the pits. One way or another there seems to be a lot of crying involved, whether it is in joy or in utter despair.

I am always amazed at the lengths some people go to ensure my child is included. I am aware it is my prerogative to get her involved. It just surprises me when other people are just as intent on letting her have the same experiences as everyone else. Sports day at school to me is a good example. The easy option would be to exclude her altogether. I mean she just can't do what the others are doing. But that does not seem to be an option for school. Instead, they made up races specifically for Jess. Ones that she could do, and where she could race as an equal. The inventiveness of the races and the utter dedication of the staff to ensure total inclusion makes me want to cry every time I go to a Sports day. I was proudly watching Jess in her egg and spoon race. She was in her wheelchair and a friend was pushing her. As her balance is quite dodgy to say the least, school blue tacked her egg to her spoon. If they didn't we'd still be there today! But despite Jessie's complete and utter concentration on the task in hand, it remained reasonably obvious to the crowd that Jess's egg was defying gravity. One by one her friends had to stop to pick up their fallen and un-blue tacked eggs. Slowly Jess found herself in the lead. It was then, although I was pleased for Jess to find herself out in front, that it occurred to me that the other parents may find the whole blue tacking situation, as well... cheating! Because it was actually putting their children at a disadvantage. While all these conflicting emotions are running amok around my head, I decided I should at least cheer her on, even though the position she found herself in, out in front, was technically through no ability of her own. It was then a huge cheer erupted behind me. It was the other parents realising that Jess was now in front, and they were cheering her on. Actually, calling her name and encouraging her to win. Jess was having the time of her life. She was so incredibly excited, having so much fun and enjoying the crowds, the attention, and the winning. But it made me cry! Happy that everyone was really behind her all the way. Happy that Jess had a chance to do well in something and to be able to do it so publicly too. It was a really special moment.

Then we have times when things are less good. And thankfully this is usually a less public event. Knowing Jess's cerebellum is shrinking. That apparently (still a bit of denial here!) she has this progressive degenerative brain disorder, is something that never leaves you. No day goes past without it nagging somewhere in the back of your head. Whether it is concern for the future, or just plain resentment that no-one else really seems to understand exactly what it is we're going through. The other day Jess kept falling over more than usual. She couldn't manage to crawl, kept forgetting stuff and had a general vagueness about her. All I could think of was, the day has come. The day the consultants warned us about. She has actually started to regress. It is going to be all downhill from here. The utter and all-encompassing low that puts you in is indescribable. You think you will never be happy again. If I didn't know better, I'd have said there were a few dozen dementors about. Then the next day she was back to 'normal'. Well, normal for Jess and you realise she was just having an off day. It wasn't the end of my world at all. Days like this, although you go through the despair, also drive you relentlessly to ensure you do everything you possibly can, and do it as soon as you can. Don't waste time waiting to live. Do it now. You may not get a second chance. So, we do what we can as soon as we can. If the regression does come, then we've done the best we can. If it doesn't, then she would have hopefully had a very full and privileged childhood.

# August 2011

I have had such a busy summer holiday. I've been backwards and forwards, and forwards and backwards, between Granny and Pop Pop's and Nanny and Grandad's. So much so that I was worn to a frazzle on several occasions and had to spend a couple of days just snoozing. It is absolutely exhausting keeping the grandparents busy. I have done everything from camping to crabbing, kite flying to sailing, drawing and cinema, played hotels and plane journeys, had picnics both indoors (due to rubbish weather) and out (on the occasion when it actually wasn't raining), shopping... and swimming. Phew. No wonder I've been on the exhausted side of tired.

I did have a short holiday at the end of the month with Mummy and Daddy. It was only for a few nights, as allegedly we had already been to Florida this year. But that was ages and ages ago. In fact, I'm sure it must have been last year, it was such a very long time ago.

We did get to stay in a holiday house cottage place, and it was nice. They had an indoor pool too which was lovely and warm, and we managed to swim in there every day. We went to one place and I did some real and proper drawing, and then painting on actual canvas. It was probably my best piece of work to date and is now proudly up in my room.

I went to a great Model village which had buttons to press that made funny noises. It was a huge village, in a small miniature way, if you know what I mean. I liked the churches and the trains best. The trains were funny because there was a meerkat on one and a penguin on another. Weird.

I got to go to a Sea life centre. This was cool, as my favourite section in a zoo is the fish. So, it was like the best zoo I'd ever been to. So much so, we ended up going around it twice. Once slowly, answering the quiz, searching for treasure and looking at the fishes. And the second time I was 'photographer lady'. And I was pretty good too. I know. I also bought a baby turtle in the gift shop. Not a real one though. I wasn't allowed.

I went to a real and proper(ish) Theme park, where I got completely and utterly soaking wet going down a water slide. It was a bit like zipperdeedoodah (also known as Splash Mountain). I saw a sea lion show where he balanced a ball on his nose. I can't do that. He did trip over his keeper though... now I CAN do that. Apparently, I'm forever getting under people's feet. An occupational hazard of being on the floor most of the time.

On our last night away, there were fireworks. Which were really cool. Well freezing actually. We didn't know they were going to happen until they had actually started, so out I went in just a Dora the Explorer nightie and a blanket. I was as cold as an ice 'burger'.

Mummy and Daddy had to have some blood tests this month. When they were in the waiting room I rightly said "Welcome to my world!"

Ha!

Jess x

# September 2011

September meant it was time to go back to school...
again. I went last year. And the year before for that matter. I
had to go back though, otherwise they'd all have missed me.

It also meant back to Brownies too, after a couple of
months off. Low Owl presented me with all the badges I had
earnt on pack holiday and Mummy then almost earnt a
sewing badge by putting them all on my Brownie sash. I have
a very lot of badges now and look quite smart in my uniform.

I like looking smart. We went to Pizza Hut and I insisted on
looking lovely in a straw hat, scarf and handbag.
Unfortunately, Mummy and Daddy are usually a bit scruffy,
but I have decided that it's no reason for me to let the side
down as well.

I sort of broke my toe on the carpet at home, because
Mummy hadn't hovered for years (give or take a few weeks)
and I stubbed my toe on the bumps. It needed a bandage and
ointment and it hurt for ages.

A big event of the month was a trip to a moon hotel
(again) and another wheelchair course. It was with a charity
called Go-Kids-Go. I saw them for the first time nearly 2 years
ago, and it was during that course when I realised my NHS
wheelchair was a bit rubbish.

Since then I have been on two 1 hour courses with them
at the mobility road-shows, but I hadn't been back for a full
and proper course again, until this month. I tried really hard
and did well, despite my stinking cold. I've been having
trouble doing a wheelie on the move without stopping, but I
think I sussed it on this course. You need to do this natty trick
(apparently) to be able to get up a kerb. I can do the tipping; I
just need to perfect the timing. So, I'm still crashing into kerbs
(most of the time), but am getting closer to actually getting it
right. It's really hard to do.

I also did a controlled 'capsize'. Megan Bear and Daddy
both had a go at a controlled wheelchair capsize too. Megan
Bear did well. They are really quite incredibly scary to do. I

hope I don't have to do an uncontrolled one. Daddy did... and cut his thumb. I thought we might need an am-blue-ance or perhaps even a hell-a-copter.

After the wheelchair course we went to an Anglo-Saxon village. It reminded me of Kentwell Hall. All olden days and people dressed up and stuff. It was quite cool and I was the camera lady again.

I know, good idea, let's play wheelchairs. But don't forget the crash-mat.

Jess x

# October 2011

Well at the very end of last month I thought I sort of broke my toe. Two days later and at the very beginning of this month, my little tiny toe, wasn't so little and tiny any more. It was all swollen and bruised and yuck and looking at it made me want to gag. Usually I'm told not to make a fuss, but for a change Mummy actually agreed with me and said that my toe did actually look disgusting. In fact, she said she didn't like the look of it one bit. It was bruised up to my ankle on top of my foot and the underneath of my toe was black. And there was this horrid red line on my fat little toe that made it look like it was bleeding. So, off to casualty for me, on what I think was apparently the hottest day ever. This made the 'no shoes' situation not quite so weird. I would have worn shoes, but we were struggling to find any that would fit over my increasingly swollen foot. In desperation, I did take my slippers... just in cases. Anyhow, we had to wait for long enough, and then I was seen by a really nice nurse who thought I may have dislocated my poorly toe. But to make sure, they would x-ray it. Mummy had to wear a funny apron that looked like she was going to do some painting, when she was with me in the x-ray room. Daddy missed the picture taking bit as he was dashing back to the car while this was all going on to get some more nappy supplies. My bottom had been a bit poorly anyway, but the thought of hospitals and x-rays meant that I was most definitely in need of a new nappy. The x-ray camera was absolutely huge. Even bigger than Granny's. Anyway, the picture of my toe showed that it wasn't dislocated at all, but actually a little bit broken. So, I had to have it strapped up, but with no plaster touching my skin, as per my very strict instructions.

I wouldn't normal talk about furniture, but I am going to have to make an exception with our new table. I love it. I've washed it twice and was even caught kissing it!!! Which in itself would usually be a tad weird, until you realise it is a giant statue of Mickey Mouse holding a tray and it's the tray that is the table part, if you get my drift. Anyway, it is just fab.

An exciting adventure was a two-day trip to LEGOLAND. We stayed in a hotel at an airport, which was cool but a little odd and we met Auntie Pigerlert and Uncle Lamby there. Then we all went to LEGOLAND together. I did some scary and very screamy roller coasters, which were great fun.

I love doing rides. I had my face painted as well while I was there, which I always really enjoy getting done. It feels so nice and it tickles too. But then after a couple of hours, it gets all itchy and just plain annoying and I have to rub it all off.

The airport hotel was really huge and nice and quite posh looking as moon hotels go. When we were in the hotel restaurant, I was big enough and brave enough to order my own tea, all by myself. And I even asked for a straw nicely too when I ordered my drink. I need a straw sometimes as my drink can get all spilly. I am still a bit of a messy Jessie.

In the LEGOLAND shop there was a huge Lego statue of Hagrid. Lamby posed next to it and you couldn't really tell who was who, as they are both really tall and exceptionally hairy. I like Harry Potter. But that is mostly Mummy's fault. Although I now want a real and proper wand for Christmas, instead of a pretend one. Mummy says I'm a half blood princess. Daddy is a muggle you see. I also now have a habit of dreaming about Dobby, ever since I found out that Dobby died. Dobby is in heaven. With my fish. And Michael Jackson. Don't worry, be Dobby.

I got a puppy on a lead when I was away. Not a real dog you understand. I hate dogs.

I do not believe it. I was 'Star of the week' and then a few days later I had to go up in assembly twice for two separate 'Certificates of Achievement'. One for reading and writing, and the other for maths. This must be a record for me on the certificate front. I struggle with maths. It makes no sense to me at all. I mean, if you had 5 smarties and then got another 5 smarties, well you would then have quite a lot of smarties. Does it really matter exactly how many? Well, according to my homework, apparently, it does matter. I just don't know why. School is hard sometimes. Is it half term yet? I'm tired.

Half term was busy considering I started on the exhausted side of tired. We went and stayed with Uncle Billy Bob's and Del. In my aim to bath in every house I have ever been to, while I was there I had a really lovely bubbly bath with one of Del's bath fizzers, and got bubbles absolutely everywhere.

Also, while we were with them, we went to a place with an iron bridge... but I can't remember what it was called! And there I did drawing in a nice coffee shop while everyone was having hot drinks. Tea, I think.

On the way back from Billy's, as a real last-minute decision, we decided to meet up with Auntie Pigerlert and Uncle Lamby, and together we all went to a big girl spicy chicken restaurant. And then we went on to a car museum which had a speedy ride where we slid all over the seat. I thought I might cry. But I don't believe it, I really liked it. It was a good ride.

The low of half term was doing my homework. It's always hard work and I don't like hard work.

To make up for it I did lots of shopping with Mummy and Daddy.

We went to an indoor shopping centre, which was huge and busy. I went to both the Build-a-Bear and the Disney shop, so it was almost a perfect day for me. We also went out for lunch and did some shopping at a garden centre near home too. It has lots of lovely Christmas bits and bobs there. Although, apparently, it isn't Christmas yet. The funniest shopping we did though, was looking for beds. It was in a shop on the first floor, so we took the lift up. All was fine until we went to leave. We got back in the lift, and... got stuck! The door wouldn't open. We had the staff there trying to get the door open. It was like being in prison, I think. All was okay in the end, and unfortunately, we didn't need the firemen after all.

Love Jess and doggy x

# November 2011

'Trick or treating' is something I'd never done before or had ever planned to do – so I thought it was safe to round off last month's journal a whole day early. As is always the case when I do this, something noteworthy then happens. We had a few trick or treaters that came to my house on Halloween. It was tea time for us, and I ended up eating my tea in at least 3 sittings, as I was up and down the hallway giving out sweets. I like to be in charge of sweeties in my house and due to Halloween, we had a cauldron full of them. One of our trick and treaters was a friend from my school. It was then I thought... hang on, I know, good idea, let's go trick and treating ourselves. Mummy felt that an announcement like this, at 6:30pm on Halloween itself, was a little late to make such a decision, considering I had no costume, or trick or treat bucket. However, by 7pm, thanks to a planned Harry Potter party in a couple of weeks, I was able to look like Harry, complete with uniform, scar, broom, wand and a bucket from the seaside (for my sweeties). So, the bucket didn't look too sad, I part filled it with sweets from our own cauldron. In effect, I trick or treated myself. Daddy put on a Hagrid beard and wig and Mummy put on a Gryffindor cloak and off we went. We visited 2 of our neighbours, who were really generous, lovely and nice and then we came back home. We were back by 7:05pm. It all seemed over a tad quick for me. Then I decided, I know, good idea, let's visit my 1 to 1. So, with that and one additional unplanned stop at another friend's house, we managed to be out for almost an hour and we doubled the number of houses we trick or treated, bringing the grand total to... four. Now that WAS enough excitement for one night. I really enjoyed trick or treating, it was great fun and I really want to go again.

It is a bit of a pain sometimes living near 2 schools, especially when I don't go to either of them. But we are always rewarded every year with a great firework display in one of the playing fields, and we are able to watch the fireworks lying on the living room floor through the sliding doors. This year was no exception. And in fact, it was a better display, and a good deal warmer, than the real and actual one we went to see the following day. Some of the bangs we heard were even loader than Daddy's bum bum. It's hard to imagine, I know, but it's true.

I've been doing some cycling on my new and improved bike that I had for my birthday earlier this year. I can now pedal and steer all by myself. And I go so fast that Mummy and Daddy now have to run to keep up. I am now a real and proper cyclist.

Our crazy family had a Harry Potter party. But this time I was Ginny Weasley and not Harry, like I was for my trick and treating. As Mummy wanted to be Harry! There were a load of us, and technically we all dressed up, although some were clearly more impressive than others. Auntie Pigerlert was Professor Umbridge and I kept forgetting she was supposed to be scary and kept accidentally giving her huggles. Doughnut (Auntie Pigerlert's friend – who has a weird name) was Professor Trelawney and was really very good. I liked Doughnut. Uncle Lamby was Filtch... 'oh, we are in trouble' and Daddy was Hagrid... 'oh, I shouldn't have said that'. Me and Mummy looked smart in our school uniforms. And when Gryffindor won the cup we both cheered. Expelliamus.

This month is also Pudsey bear month and I was told to go to school all spotty. I did consider chicken pox. But apparently, that was not what they meant when they said it was non-uniform day.

Bedtime is becoming a logistical nightmare. Before I can go to bed, I have to make sure that my teddies and dollies are all dressed in their pyjamas and are in bed. I don't do this with every single one of my teddies, as if I did it would literally take all day. Instead I have a select few that have to be looked after, some of which even go to 'school'. So, before I can get to bed, 3 Barbie's have to be collected from 'school' tucked up in their individual beds and wrapped up. Then there are 2 dollies and pooh bear that have to get their bed things on and into a sleeping bag. And then there's Dora the

Explorer, Boots and Penguin who all sleep in baskets in the bathroom. Oh, and both Barbie and Dora have teddy bears too. It is actually quite a feat to get us all in the right beds every night.

I know it is not normal for someone my age to be in nappies. I am pretty sure no-one else in my class is. So, I am learning to not publicly announce it every time I need a nappy change. But the subtle approach doesn't always work either. My favourite announcement to date, which seems to make Daddy chuckle a bit is 'I have a problem with my bottom'. The thing is, I really actually do have a problem with my bottom most of the time. I either can't go to the loo for literally weeks on end and my tummy gets so full and sore I can't eat, or alternatively I'm going all the time. And I mean ALL the time. When it's like that, I can't go swimming or anything. It's a bit of a pain really. And I now have 3 different tummy medicines to try and help and they all taste yuck. Why can't they make medicine taste nice?

I went to a surprise leaving party. It wasn't a surprise to me, but then again, I wasn't the one leaving. One of our neighbours was moving out, as just like us, she was starting to struggle with stairs. I think stairs are quite overrated. We seem to manage perfectly well without them anyway.

One evening I went out to the Edwardian evening nearby. It was good fun. I brought a flashing star wand and I even painted a Frisbee and decorated it with glitter. I don't know if that is exactly what they did in Edwardian times. I should ask Granny. She'd know. If it was like that then, I think it would have been quite cool to have lived in olden times.

Love Jess x

# December 2011

As it is now December and therefore very nearly Christmas, Nanny and Grandad took me to their Yacht Club children's Christmas party (it wasn't as posh as it sounds, believe me!) Santa parked his sleigh on the roof, which was really cool and a little bit dangerous, and he even brought me a present. We played games and everything. I love parties and had a really nice time.

At school, we learnt some Christmas songs complete with sign language ready for the carol service. My class song was 'we wish you a merry Christmas'. It had loads and loads of versus, and I knew most of the words. But my favourite bit was when 'we all want some piggy pudding... and we won't go and get some'. Or something like that.

I was lucky enough to get invited back to Lapland UK. I must have been very good again. It was a really excellent day and this time we helped the elves make teddy bears. These teddies were really lovely. I gave mine lots of love and hugs, so the lucky person who gets it at Christmas time will get a very special bear. I like Lapland. Nice place. I like meeting Father Christmas. He lives in a snowy wooden cabin in a snowy forest. He told me that both me and Auntie Pigerlert are on the extra special good list. Which was surprising.

I also got to go ice skating again, but this time I managed to push, all by myself. Daddy skated on his own. He didn't fall over once. He fell over at least 3 times, and I went faster than he did when he was actually on his feet!! It was excellent fun.

While at Lapland, after icing my gingerbread biscuit Christmas tree decoration, I was sitting on a log listening to Mother Christmas reading a story about Christmas trees, and I fell off... well it was as easy as falling off a log!

I hope I get invited back again. We all had such a lovely day there. What was nice, was a week or two later, just before Christmas, I was at home having tea and the real and proper (Rotary Club) Santa came right past my house on his sleigh and stopped for quite a long chat. It was nice to see him again. I love Father Christmas. He's very kind.

I went to what I thought was my last swimming lesson of the year, only to discover when I got on pool side, in my new purple wetsuit (the pool IS that cold!), that there were no lessons at all and the swimming club were having a real Swimming gala. 'Oh blow', I thought. I got dressed in my swim stuff specially. Then they pointed out, I was down to swim in three races and I was actually going to be competing. 'Oh blow'! The gala was a bit like Sports Day. Lots of waiting and clapping, and when it was my turn and I had to try very hard. I was in the very first race. '25m on your tummy with a woggle and a helper'. I swam really fast (for me) and tried hard and managed to get a 3rd! I was presented with a special green 'third' ribbon. I was also in the '25m on your back with a woggle and a helper'. However, between me, Daddy and the helper we decided I might just be able to swim 25m without a woggle! So, that's what I did. For a good swimmer that doesn't sound overly brave. But for me this was quite a big thing. My helper swam in front of me with my woggle in case it all went wrong and I tried my absolute bestest. It is a long way to do kicking and I got tired, especially as I was racing other kids who had quite rightly decided to wear their woggle. Anyway, I was exceptionally proud of myself by getting another 3rd (and another ribbon) and as I was especially brave and didn't use my woggle at all, they gave me a certificate for achievement too. I also was the last leg in a relay race, in which I think we came 2nd, but it was a bit manic and to be honest I was not completely sure what was going on. The upshot was I took part in my very first gala and came away with 2 thirds, and a certificate, knowing that I had done my very best, and I was pretty proud of myself for that. My ribbons and certificate were framed when we got home. Mummy and Daddy were rather proud of me too.

I went to two pantomimes just before Christmas. The one with school was pretty good, but I was really worried about my bottom. My 1 to 1 forgot my spare nappies, so when I went to the loo and had a change I came out in just pants.

That was even more scary than any baddies in the panto, as I then had to try really, really hard not to piddle on the coach on the way home. You could tell it was Christmas, as a miracle happened... I managed to get all the way home clean and dry. My bum is quite unpredictable sometimes and is often out of my control, so any mishap would not actually technically have been my fault.

I also got to go to the panto with Nanny and Grandad and it was a really good one. Lots of 'it's behind you' and dancing and stuff. A really excellent show. And at the end of the show the prince came off the stage and came and talked to just me. It was so very cool. The prince told me how beautiful I am (he probably thought I was a princess) and he asked if I liked the show and I was able to tell him, 'yes I did, and... well done, you were really good'.

It is Christmas, and I am SO EXCITED!! As always, Christmas time was mad at home as everyone came to my house AND I was door-girl as people arrived. That meant I got to see everyone and was able to give them all huggles, and kisses and everything.

I got loads of good presents and nearly got everything I asked for. And I got lots of things I didn't. I had some lovely dollies and clothes and make-do stuff this year as well as some big girl grown up things including a rug and a real and actual iPod. I like my iPod. I haven't had to play with Mummy's iPad once, as I now have all my own photos and games and music in one place without Mummy's tut getting in the way. And it is a camera as well. Excellent. By Boxing Day, I had taken over 400 photos and nearly 40 videos. Most of them of me! Well I am the most photogenic one in the household.

As always, the New Year started by being frightened witless in the middle of the night by nearby fireworks. Never a great start to a year I think. But I made up for it by having a pyjama day, which is the best kind of day.

Happy very New Year.

Love Jess x

# January 2012

It's been a bit blowy out. The wind has been whistling around the bungalow so loud and fast that I did wonder if we would wake up in Kansas or the Emerald City or somewhere. It has meant I have not been sleeping too well. I'm not good at sleeping if it is too windy, or for that matter, if it's too rainy, or fireworky, or too hot, or too cold, or too dark, or when my pillow hates me. I guess I'm just not overly good at sleeping in general. And I don't like being awake all on my own, so I usually request back-up of some sort. That probably explains why Mummy and Daddy are sometimes on the grumpy side of grouchy.

I had a dolly for Christmas and got another one with my Christmas money. Now I like to spend time feeding, changing, cuddling and putting my dollies to bed. I'm a good Mummy to all my babies. I like dollies now. As long as they don't make a noise or do anything. Dollies like that are just too scary for me.

I was 9 this month. Good bye 8 and hello 9. What a big girl I am now. And I've done some growing, so I may finally be too big for at least some of my smaller age 5-6 clothes.

Birthday time also meant lots of nice new toys, clothes, make do things and games. It had been a few weeks since Christmas, so I was ready for more presents. I've just got to find room for them all now!  Birthday time also, now traditionally, meant a trip to Build-a-bear. It is one of my favourite places in the world. This time I got a nice new Olympic teddy bear with Olympic type clothes. It is really quite cool. Apparently, I am going to the real and actual Olympics in a few months' time, so now I have a special teddy ready for it. I am almost excited. But not as excited as I am about going back to Build-a-bear. I might have, roughly, a million build-a-bear teddies, give or take a few, but they have all been acquired entirely due to just 2 different scenarios. 1st, I have been to quite a few Build-a-bear birthday parties. Three of my own, and even more for other people's birthday's. I'm not so keen on other people's parties as they usually are a tad noisy and busy for me. I like MY birthday parties best. They are quieter, mostly due to a lot less children. Children can be really noisy and quite annoying sometimes. They are noisy at school and at Brownies. I prefer the quiet life. The other, 2nd scenario as to why I go to Build-a-Bear, is as a treat to make up for going to hospital. Unsurprisingly, I have loads of Build-a-Bears because of this too.

So, it was a surprise to be offered a trip to Build-a-bear on an occasion not related to Birthdays or hospitals and to go twice in one month. Pop Pop had promised me a treat, if I could stand up all by myself for a count of 30. Well, at 9 years and 5 whole days old, I did it. 37 counts. (It was really about 10 whole seconds, but it felt like years)! Mummy did the counting, which is handy as she is good with numbers and managed to count very fast. And doubly luckily, I did my standing in Granny and Pop Pop's kitchen with them both as my witness, so I was then eligible for the treat. It was decided that a trip to Build-a-bear would be a good idea, and who was I to disagree to that.

I had an excellent month. At school the head teacher gave me a 'Praise postcard' and 10 team points for excellent standing and hard work. And the same day I was told at Brownies that I was the new Sixer for the Gnome six. I don't believe it. Me a sixer. I haven't even been a seconder yet! I've even got a sixer badge!

Love Jess (the new Gnome sixer) x

# February 2012

Well, we had snow for quite a lot of the month. It was good fun to start with, and then just became a pain in the bum bum after it was still around and causing problems a whole week later. I was going to do snow angels, but the back garden was so deep there was concern I would disappear entirely. Despite many attempts to build snowmen, we found we had the 'wrong type of snow'. It didn't roll at all. Rubbish. It was however, good for igloos. Me and Mummy built one that resembled a 'well' for the first few days, and then it looked more like Stone Henge a week later! The snow was also rather good for sledging. And I had a new purple sledge to try out too. Except I managed to fall off it 3 times on the flat. So, it was decided that sledge wasn't really up to us all going for a long walk/drag/slide. So, we dusted off my old wooden sledge again which has sides and I was wedged into that. Luckily, it was quite a tight fit as we ended up going, for the first time ever, real and proper sledging down an actual hill. It was very fast and quite excellent fun. After about half a dozen goes though it was decided to call it a day, as allegedly I'm a tad heavy to drag up a snowy hill on a wooden sledge. We need a ski lift nearby it seems. Getting to school in the snow and ice was really bumpy and hard going. Wheelchairs are just not designed for weather like that. And even when we did manage to get through, my chair was like a snow magnet and would collect loads of snow en-route that would then drop and melt all over the place whenever we got anywhere vaguely warm. Mummy spent the first 10 minutes of Brownies running behind me with paper towels mopping up the floor. Bit embarrassing really... wish I'd left her at home.

I went to the garden centre twice during half term. Once for lunch, and another time for breakfast. Both times though involved quite a lot of bacon and beans. I love it there. It has a good restaurant and a lovely shop. It is very hard not to spend an awful lot of money. I also went to the cinema in half term and saw the 'The Puppets'. Although most people call them 'The Muppets' for some reason. It was funny-ish.

Daddy is going to get a LandRover Defender. Bored with it already and he hasn't even got it yet. Me and Mummy keep coming up with better things (mostly from the aforementioned garden centre) that we should buy instead.

I finally got to go swimming again in the new local pool, once my bottom had stopped misbehaving. It's a lovely pool, as it is really warm and has a nice view. Due to my silly bum bum, I have ended up missing 3 consecutive swimming lessons. Not even my new purpley pink sticky knickers (incontinence tankini) could be trusted with what I would potentially be throwing at it. It did make up for it though at the end of the month, because as part of a fun session at swimming lessons, I got to 'coo in a narna' (canoe in a yellow kayak). I was really nervous about falling out and getting wet underwater, but I quite enjoyed it in the end.

Love Jess x

# March 2012

Mummy and Daddy took me on another wheelchair course at Stoke Mandeville. I was excited about staying in a moon hotel and getting a 'free' t-shirt, but other than that I wasn't overly bothered about going on the course.

We went pretty much straight from school to the moon hotel. I had been wiggling a tooth of mine for most of the journey there, so it was good and wobbly by the time we arrived. Problem was, I was then worried about going to sleep with it so wonky, in case I swallowed it in my sleep. So, we got in our jarmas and had a few matchmakers as a pre-bedtime treat. Next thing I know, my tooth is missing. We can't find it anywhere. We soon come to the only possible conclusion that I must have swallowed it. We were just having quite a debate about whether the tooth fairy would still come if you can't actually put the tooth under your pillow, when thankfully Mummy found it. We were then just left with the question, "Does the tooth fairy visit moon hotels?" Well, none of us were really sure, so just in case, we popped the now found tooth under the pillow. Well, amazingly the tooth fairy did actually come and I had a lovely coin under my pillow the next morning. Such fun!

There were loads of different sports to try on the course. But we started with my least favourite. Wheelchair basketball. It always frightens me and it literally ended in tears. Mostly mine. And then it kind of went downhill after that. The course this time was really good. I just didn't really want to play. Being one of the older ones, I was put with others more my age. But they seem to cope with it all better than me. It just seemed so difficult, and noisy and busy.

The sports that suited me best were the quiet and slow ones, like bowls and boccia. It's kind of more my pace. I'm really not into things like contact sports, or team games. It's all a bit too much for me.

One thing I did discover I liked (other than the bowls and boccia), was taking photos. And I did become the only child who was also a 'Registered Photographer'. I even got a sticker on my t-shirt to prove it.

We never did make it to the end of the day. I became increasingly less interested in what was going on, and more and more unhappy about being there. Eventually it was decided that we were fighting a battle that was probably lost before we had even left home. So, despite having a second night of bed and breakfast booked (and paid for!), we came home. I'm not cut out to be an athlete.

At school, I did rather excitingly get the 'Most team points in my class' for the spring term and my team, the 'Hedgehogs', won over all. I'm so clever.

I have done some great standing at school. Over 2 minutes apparently although I haven't been able to repeat it at home. I think my 1 to 1 must blue tack my shoes to the floor. That or have a very fast watch!

I have noticed recently how many weird sayings there are. If I ask a question, Mummy often says, "we'll see." See what though? Or does she mean 'a sailor went to sea, sea, sea' type of 'see'? It's very confusing. Then I was told 'not to blow all my pocket money at once'. But I didn't want to blow on it. I just wanted to spend it. And another thing. People are forever 'pointing things out' to me, but they don't actually point. I think it is all a bit peculiar.

Love Jess x

# April 2012

I really like taking photos. I have kind of traded up and now use Mummy and Daddy's camera most of the time. My favourite things to snap are my dollies and toys, films on the TV, my feet and any houses that I see out of the car windows. I am actually a very good photo lady.

We have sort of got 2 pet ducks. I say 'pet' in the loosest sense as they are entirely wild, but they like to visit a very lot and we like to feed them special duck food. I have even named them. Donald and Daisy, after 2 ducks I know in Disney World. I'm really hoping they have baby ducks as that would be quite cute.

I've not been at all well. I've been upchucking, had a bit of a temperature and a sniffly cold. I even had to miss Brownies and 3 days of school. I was back at school less than a week and then the whole upchucking started again. This time however, it was right in the middle of the supermarket car park. Which was a combination of a bit disgusting, embarrassing and downright horrible. But I am feeling a bit better now, which is a relief.

As soon as I was feeling up to it, I decided what I needed was a bit of girly shopping with Mummy. I got some great new Hello Kitty pants, and a Hello Kitty nightie which are lovely and will be good for my holiday later this year. We also went into the Lush shop as we both absolutely love their bath bombs. After choosing a very many smelly, glittery and colourful bath fizzers, they asked if we'd like to sign the door of the shop, like some of the other customers had done. Well, we couldn't resist that. So, me and Mummy are now a little bit famous, as we both signed their door with their special pen and we also drew a flower each, which was nice.

I had a bad day at school. It didn't go too well. I got 0 out of 0 in my numeracy test. Or it was something like that anyway. I struggle with numbers. They are just weird and make absolutely no sense to me.

Mummy heard about a centre for the riding for the

disabled and asked if I would like to go. Well, I gave it quite a lot of thought and was naturally worried about many things; top of my list was obviously the falling off. But eventually I decided to have my name put down on the waiting list and see what happens. It was only then I voiced my only remaining concern. Would I be riding a real and actual horse? Well, apparently, it seems that I would. Oh dear. I might have changed my mind already.

I went to see the tummy lady again. I really didn't learn anything new. But to be honest, we rarely do. The funny thing was, my tummy was checked and I was given the all clear that it was soft, no problems, and no blockages. And then that night I literally did a months' worth of pooping in one go. It was so impressive I got Daddy in from the garden to admire it and then I took a photo of my award winning giant poop. I may frame it. The photo, not the poop.

I have done a really clever first at swimming lessons. I went underwater on purpose and held my breath properly and everything. I didn't even die. I'm actually quite proud of myself.

Love, Jess-the-mermaid xxx

# May 2012

We had a fire drill during my swimming lesson. They are a bit weird and not like the fire drills you do at school. For a start, you don't have to line up in the playground. Which is handy. I was all wet and in my swimsuit and goggles. They got me out the pool and one of the big strong teachers carried me to the fire exit where everyone was waiting. We had quite a nice cuddle and a chat. It was good fun in the end, despite it scaring me half to death at first.

I like baths and bath fizzers. After my baths, I like a bit of talc to dry me off and make me smell even nicer than I do already. Being quite a big girl, I decided I would be clever and do the talc-ing bit all by myself. However, Mummy had a complete hissy-fit when she checked on me a few minutes later. For some unknown reason, she thought I had been neither big nor clever, using the entire pot of talcum powder in one go. I did smell gorgeous though.

I did my Agility badge at Brownies. It's a badge for doing exercises and stuff. The list of things that the Brownies had to do was stuff that was beyond me. Skipping, standing on one leg, star jumps etc. However, the Brownie leader came up with a Jess friendly version. I did a wheelchair obstacle course, wheelchair limbo and some bat and ball control. The other part of the badge involved dancing. Well, I had learnt how to do wheelchair dancing on my last wheelchair course. So, me and Mummy used that music and added our own cool moves to come up with a dance duet. We even got to perform our wheelchair dance in front of all the brownies and leaders, and despite being a bit nervous half way through, we got a big clap when we finished. I think they were quite impressed with how speedy and whizzy and clever we were.

Auntie Piglet came down for a few days and we talked Disney a very lot. Well, I think it's less than 6 months before we go back again, so we are doing some serious planning and listing. We also got some spare pin badges ready to do pin trading on holiday and me and Piglet pin traded for hours between ourselves. It's good fun doing pin swapsies.

I surprised Mummy the other day by knowing what a Pterodactyl was. Well I'm quite good on the names of Dine-zee-cores, mostly helped by liking a program when I was littler than I am now, called 'Harry and his bucket full of Dine-zee-cores (Dinosaurs)'.

An exciting highlight of the month was a school trip to an activity centre. Daddy came along as he was jealous he'd miss out on all the fun. We did rock climbing and boating. Both were really good fun. In the rock climbing I took it in turns to be both the anchor (which I was naturally very good at) and the climber (which was more tricky, as they didn't have a hoist like they do at the mobility road show). Having said that, I think I did really well. I also went boating, although Daddy insists it should be sailing. I don't know why. We were in a boat, not in a sail. He is a silly nah nah wally bags sometimes.

Love, Jess xxx

# June 2012

In what was probably the driest day over the half term, I did some good cycling down near the sea. I also went crabbing in the boating lake. However, as Daddy had greedily caught all the crabs himself, mostly with the help of my pretty pink net, there weren't any left for me. But the dry weather didn't last long and soon me and Grandad were sheltering under a picnic blanket together. We then did a mad dash back to Nanny's motorhome. Some of us got a good deal wetter than others.

We also had the Queen's Diamond Jubilee this month. I did lots of patriotic things, including making a very glittery hat and wearing it to a street party that we had one lunchtime at school. To add to the red, white and blue décor, my wheelchair also sported 2 Union flags. I really did look quite the part. We went looking for some jubilee celebrations too, as there wasn't much going on near us. And we found some good fetes, live bands, make-do arty crafty tents and everything.

I lost a tooth this month. Now I don't mean, it fell out and I put it under my pillow. No. I actually lost it. Never to be seen again. Weird. It had been a bit wobbly at school. And I woke up that night and it was missing. It was traumatic. How would the tooth fairy know to come? I came up with a good idea that involved Mummy writing a note to the tooth fairy (in the middle of the night) to explain what had happened and that although my tooth was out, it was missing, presumed lost, for ever and ever. Well, I was lucky as not only was the tooth fairy in the area, but she saw my note and left me a coin. She also left a special fairy note for me that said she knew my tooth had come out as I was smiling in my sleep. She could see the new gap. It was a lovely little note. I hope she leaves one every time.

We had sports day at the end of the month and I did 3 races: - Egg and spoon (again), skipping!! and a walking race. As usual, the egg was well glued onto the spoon and I think I came 2nd. Skipping was very exciting and I had to twizzle the skipping rope while being pushed by my boyfriend. We were brilliant. I think we were 3rd. And last, but best, was my walking race. Everyone else did heel to toe walking while my carer (also known as my 'handler') helped me walk super speedy fast, like a proper athlete. Everyone was cheering me on. I was a real and actual winner. I came 4th, I think. I was ever so excited. Granny and Mummy were at the end ready for cuddles and kisses. It was a really special and smiley day.

The next day, in front of the whole school, for the 2nd year running, I was awarded a very special certificate for being an outstanding example and an inspiration to others. That's what I've done today to make me feel proud.

Love, Jess xxx

# July 2012

We found an injured little bird in the garden and we actually took it to a real animal hospital. I was in charge of carrying the shoe box that we had put the poorly bird in. I carried it really carefully all the way to the vets. It was like a special delivery, and I didn't drop the box once. Even so, the poorly bird had apparently broken its hip and despite lots of trying, the vet doctor person had to put it into a special sleep so it could go to heaven. I don't know how you get into heaven. I hope it's a lift. I am going to really struggle if it is a stairway!

I literally did the biggest poo in the world this month, and it made me very poorly. I hadn't had a proper poop in about a fortnight. Although that is an incredibly long time, it hadn't beaten my previous poop-free record. So, we didn't originally put my poorliness down to me being super-duper constipated. I was running a temperature, was even floppier than normal, really confused, and then I was horribly sick on the carpet. Twice. Eventually, after a whole day of this, I practically gave birth to a poo the size of my head (almost). As soon as it was out, my temperature went, and I felt almost instantly better. Better out than in, I say.

I've decided I am going to have a real little girl and I'll call her Sophie. This however came as a bit of a surprise to Mummy. I'm not going to have a baby right now though. I think I'll get married first, when I'm bigger, and then I'll have Sophie. It was mentioned that I may have a boy baby instead. Well that is nuts. I don't like boys. It will have to be a girl. And I am definitely only going to have just one baby, not two. I'm not completely crazy. And I've also decided (after learning about babies at home and school), that I will have her through the sunroof option and have a big smiley face on my tummy, rather than do it the huge poo way. Well after the other day, I don't think I can go through that again.

The Olympic torch came through our county this month. School were nice and said that we could have the morning off if we wanted to see the Olympic torch relay. We came up with a cunning plan, which was a bit like a real adventure as it involved getting up in the middle of the night. Or that is what it felt like. We left home just after 6am to make sure we could be parked and get close enough to see the Olympic torch go through our nearest big town. It was special as it was the first town it came to in the county, and there was music, and soldiers and police and everything. It was really exciting. AND we saw the torches kissing. How rude! It was wet. The weather, not the kissing. Very wet. It did a lot of raining. In the end, I wore a tracksuit, Daddy's jumper, Mummy's waterproof and a blanket. And I had two umbrellas. I was still cold. But it was worth it. It was cool seeing it for real. I mean cold.

Piglet came down to stay for the weekend. I think the highlights were having lunch at the jam factory and Piglet buying me some pink glue. It may not sound like an exciting weekend to some, but I had a really lovely time.

I hurt my eye this month. I think I got an eyebrow in it. Mummy unkindly thought that was very funny. And it really hurted. It sorted itself out in the end though.

One of my favourite things at home is my baby dollies. My most favourite dolly is called Brooke. I love her to bits and she is not even broken. I give her cuddles, get her dressed, put her in her pushchair and wheel her around the house. When the weather is all rainy, I push her to the sliding doors so we can sit and look at the garden together. I'm a good Mummy. It is all good practice for when I have Sophie.

I went on Brownie pack holiday this month. I was so excited about going. But it nearly didn't happen at all, as I felt quite poorly the day before. But a good dose of Calpol and three different sorts of tummy medicine made me almost better just in time. So, me and Granny were dropped off at the hall ready for a 4 day, 3-night adventure. Well, apparently, I am the princess scupperer of best laid plans. I was only on pack holiday for a couple of hours and the Calpol started wearing off and then I felt all hot and sniffly, and poorly and yuck. So, Mummy was called. And even though another dose of Calpol brought me a couple more hours with the Brownies, I bailed out just after tea. I wrongly assumed that as I had left pack holiday, that all the other Brownies would leave too. Well it would hardly be worth carrying on without me. But apparently, they did. After lots of lying on the sofa, some fresh air and medicine, and two nights at home, I started feeling better. Better enough in fact to go back to Brownie pack holiday to join in for the last 2 days. That way I would get to do an overnight as well. And not just any night stay… but the night with the midnight feast! The very best night. I had a great time. We did real campfire songs around a proper and actual campfire. I love Brownie pack holiday and have asked to go back again next year, although technically I might be a tad old. I know Granny was there as my handler / carer / helper person, but sometimes I just wanted to show everyone I'm quite a big girl now. I had to tell Granny to 'go away, I want to do the mushrooms all by myself, I don't need you'. And I was right. On the last day, I was awarded 'best chopper-upper of mushrooms' and I still had all my fingers intact too. Which was a bit of a surprise.

The Olympics started this month. I know this as I was allowed to stay up really late and eat popcorn and matchmakers and watch the Opening Ceremony, with the sole purpose of trying and see if I could see Mummy on the telly. See was there! I didn't see her though. But I did see people from GOSH and Voldemort, which was a weird combination. I finally gave up and went to bed when all the athletes came out. When you are 9 years old, that bit is exceedingly boring.

I've discovered that being big, not whinging too much, taking all my medicine without too much fuss, trying to use the loo rather than my nappy, and blowing my nose rather than sniffing, as well as everything else I'm trying to do, can be so much like hard work. That sometimes I don't want to be big any more. I want to be little again.

Cuddle me.

Love, Jess  xxx

# August 2012

Being the summer holidays it has been a busy, exciting but unfortunately quite a wet month.

I went to the zoo, just me and Mummy. The best bits were buying a huge balloon, having my face painted like a monkey and going to the shop. The animals were okay, but by no means the main reason why I like to go to the zoo anymore.

Me and Daddy went real and proper camping in a tent with Lucy the LandRover. We also had Nanny and Grandad come with us, as the back-up and catering team. They stayed next to us in their motor home. It all started really well, but soon went horribly wrong when we had a huge thunderstorm. I don't like lightening. Or thunder. Or rain. And especially not when you are in a tent. Thankfully the storm didn't last too long and despite getting close to an abandon camp situation, we stuck it out the one night, like the true and hardy campers we are. We took the Hippocampe (the off-road wheelchair) camping, so we were able to go to the beach. I also wheelchaired all by myself across the country park the next day, just so I could have a BBQ. I am such an adventurer.

I have been watching the Olympics on TV. Some sports are better than others though. My least favourite sports are hitting (Boxing) and kicking (Taekwondo). I really can't stand either of them. I was lucky enough to actually go to the real 2012 London Olympics. Me, Mummy and Daddy all went up to see the synchronised swimming team finals. Mummy liked the boosts, Daddy liked the swimsuits and I liked the music. So, there really was something for everyone. We all went to support Team GB and were suitably dressed with flags, wearing Olympic t-shirts, and Team GB tattoos. It was amazing. I was particularly excited when Team GB did their synchronised swimming routine, as they did it to the Disney music called 'Flying'. So, for me that made it especially good. While we were there we had a look around, and did loads of stuff. I insisted we went to the BMW stand, as it looked like you were underwater. And we were glad we went, as we saw a short film that was good, and we got free wristbands and top trump cards too. We went to the huge Olympic shop which was fun and there was a giant Wenlock in it. We had a picnic tea on the grass and then explored some more of the Olympic Park. By the time we had to head back to the train station, I had decided that I wanted to be in the Paralympics one day and that I wanted a gold medal. So, in preparation for that, I was insistent that I wheel my wheelchair, all by myself, really fast, most of the way back to the train station. It must have been at least a mile, and by the time I stopped I was doubled over in pain. I think at the very least I had pulled a muscle in my tummy. Although it hurt so much, I did wonder if I had actually pulled a bone. We had a week in Devon and stayed in a lodge. It was very nice. It even had its own private hot tub, which I went in several times. In it we practiced some of the synchronised swimming moves we'd seen a few days before. And staying on the Olympic theme, while we were in Devon we got the chance to have our photo taken with a real Olympic torch. So, that was quite exciting. It was much heavier and colder to hold than you would think. The torch bearers made it look so easy.

I tried glass blowing (and sucking!) … I ran out of puff part way through and accidentally breathed in and it made my glass thing-a-me-jig go all wrong.

I went to the beach twice and got very sandy and incredibly wet both times, but that is because I had bottomed shuffled for miles across the sand and partly because it rained. I had a new bucket and spade and we made castles complete with walls. One time I got so mucky and wet that Mummy had to buy me an emergency dress, as I was apparently too soggy and sandy to get in the car.

I did some posh make-do stuff which was fun, including painting a lovely pottery plate, as well as doing glass painting too. I have already used both creations when having my tea.

I discovered CBBC when I was in Devon, and although I haven't properly converted from CBeebies, as I miss my most favourite programs, I now at least have a few big-girl TV shows that I like to watch.

I have been on a short bike ride near home. I really enjoy going downhill. I'm good at that and I am quite fast too. I really do not like going uphill though at all. I pedalled a lot but was too tired to keep going. It is definitely too much like hard work. Makes my legs ache. And my arms.

I have been to the cinema with Mummy and we watched Brave. It was a good film. Afterwards we had lunch and did shopping. We brought some bath fizzers and the lovely lady in the shop very kindly gave me a couple of free bath fizzers and some little soap testers too. I always knew I was famous. People everywhere seem to know me, or at least know that I am a princess.

I think I may have had chicken pox again (this would be about the 5th time!), so it seems unlikely. However, it looks exactly like the poxy chicken. The good news is I just had 5 spots this time, so not a real problem. Weird though.

My two goldfish (one of the original pair, plus a new and identical replacement) have been getting bigger, and bigger and the pink tank they were in was getting more and more cosy for them. I thought the best plan would be getting a bigger tank, but I was over-ruled as allegedly I am not the one who feeds and cleans them. Anyhow, the decision was made to re-home them in a lovely pond. And I helped. It took a while, but they soon got the hang of it and made lots of new fishy friends. I might miss them. What's for tea? What... fish? I don't have any fish!

Cuddle me.

Love, Jess xxx

# September 2012

I had the chance to see Athletics at the Paralympics, which was exciting as I got to go into the main stadium. Because I needed a wheelchair ticket, I could only have one person sit with me. So, I chose Mummy. Daddy then had to sit somewhere different and look after Granny.

I wore several Olympic Lanyards when I went to the Paralympics, kindly supplied by Uncle Billy Bobs and Del. They were both, very impressively, officials at the actual Olympics, so they managed to get some real and proper Olympic bits and bobs for me. Which was really rather cool.

I was actually quite famous while I was at the Paralympics. Even more than I was before. One of the big TV guys with his huge TV camera wanted to film just me with my GB flags. So, I got to be on the big screen in the athletics stadium. I might have even been on telly too, but I don't know for sure. Shame, as it would have been my TV debut.

For me one of the highlights was doing a Mexican wave in the main stadium. As the wave came towards us, Mummy grabbed me round the middle, stood up from her flip up seat, and helped me to my feet. We did the arms in the air and cheering bit and then Mummy helped to sit me back down again. Except, her chair was now up. So, as she lowered me back into my wheelchair, on her way back down to her own seat, she missed... and ended up sitting on the floor. It was hilarious.

After watching the Paralympic opening ceremony and being very jealous of Team GB's wheelchair hub caps, we have managed to get me my very own set of GB wheels, and I have had a load of great compliments already. Mind you, I usually do get a lot of compliments, so it may not all be down to the new hub caps.

September also meant back to school and Brownies. Which is good and bad. I like playing at home, but I was just about ready to go back this time. I had missed everyone. And I'm sure the feeling must have been mutual.

I really have had quite an eventful month. I think I was in my first ever car/motorhome breakdown. We had a tyre blow out in Nanny's van when we were on our way to the beach and had to be rescued. It was a weird combination of a bit exciting, annoying, scary and then quite boring. But I kept myself occupied nicely until we got underway again.

I have been really poorly this month too. I was supposed to be watching the closing ceremony of the Paralympics on the TV while Mummy and Daddy were actually there, in Stratford. However, I felt really sick. Nanny put me to bed, but then I was really sick everywhere, so my duvet ended up in the bath. Which is a weird place for it to be. I then went to sleep for a while, but when Mummy and Daddy came in, in the middle of the night, I was ready to be a lot more sick. And my poor bottom really hated me too.

Between midnight and breakfast time I had gone through about 10 nappies, 4 sick bowls, 2 more pairs of pyjamas, another set of bed clothes and a blanket. And my favourite doll, Rapunzel, was on the radiator drying, after having sick on her dress and in her hair. She wasn't the only one with crunchy sick-hair by morning. It was a disaster. Neither me or Mummy had slept at all and we were completely exhausted. By the time everyone else was getting up for the day, I was empty, both top and bottom. Nothing more to come out of either end. Thank goodness. I just needed a rest and a few days off school to get over it all. And Mummy reckons we're going to need a new washing machine too, as I don't think the old one will ever completely recover after what we threw at it. My poor duvet was so yuck after the up-chucking incident, that I ended up having to have a new duvet too.

Auntie Piglet and Uncle Lamby came down twice in the month, which is unheard of, and both times I had a wobbly tooth. And it was the same tooth each time. It wibbled and wobbled for weeks, and eventually fell out in bed. Now, that is the third tooth in a row I've had that fell out in bed. That is just plain weird, I think.

I did an all time, very proud of myself, first. I went to school in pants (no nappy), not once, but twice, on two consecutive days. And no mishaps or anything on either day. Problem was, to do this I had to have no tummy medicine for days to make sure I didn't poop. I then well and truly suffered for it afterwards though, as I had a really bad tummy ache, and temperature again as I got another poo stuck. I even felt so grotty, that I had to go to bed and to sleep in the middle of the day. The only problem was, when I woke up at tea time, I didn't know if it was yesterday or tomorrow. It is very confusing being ill sometimes. And I am starting to get quite fed up of being ill, as it seems to be happening more and more often. Eventually, a whole week later, I finally did an enormous poop, and it was as big as my head. Almost. They really make my poor bum-bum ouch a bit.

I did an absolutely amazing thing. I stood up, all by myself, without holding on to anything, for a staggering and world record breaking eight minutes and 15 seconds. I couldn't believe my eyes and neither could my carer or my teacher. 8 whole minutes. I even got a certificate for it in assembly and everything. When I got home, as a special prize, Mummy and Daddy gave me the Flynn Ryder doll (from the Tangled film). He is Rapunzel's boyfriend. I've wanted that dolly for ever.

We did World book day at school and I dressed up as Hermione Granger. I refused to answer to Jess all day. Everybody had to call me Hermione. I really like being in Gryffindor. But it is not as good as being in Hedgehogs.

I had a really good idea this month. I said, 'I know, good idea, let's paint my play house purple'. It used to be pink but it was getting really old, and tatty and yuck. Well, we eventually had a dry day that meant me, Mummy and Daddy were able to go out in the garden and paint my house purple. Allegedly it is one of the only colours of glossy paint they don't make, so in the end Mummy had to do some clever paint mixing. It was quite hard work painting it, but it looked fab once we'd finished. I really like purple. It's as nice as pink.

One thing, other than standing up, that I have got a lot better at recently is reading. I've loved writing for ages; I just couldn't read that well. Well, not well at all. However, my reading is really starting to get loads better.

I've been quite proud of myself recently. And rightly so I think too.

Cuddle me, please. Love, Jess xxx

# October 2012

A couple of really big and special things happened this month, to the extent I don't know which was best or where to start. As I've literally just landed, I think I'll start with my holiday to Disney World in Florida, again. I was looking forward to it for ages, but as I'd been a couple of times before, I did wonder if we should go somewhere else for a change. Well, when it was time to come home I remember saying that I didn't want to ever leave Disney, that I loved it more than home and could we come back again sometime soon. Loads happened as always. Me, Mummy and Daddy stayed in an airport hotel the night before our holiday, which was weird but handy. That meant, rather than getting up in the middle of the night so we could get to the airport in time, we were able to start the day with a big and lazy breakfast. I think this is an incredibly good plan, considering I really don't like plane food at all. The flight was long and boring, but at least I got to watch 'Brave' on the plane, so that was good. When we got to the Disney hotel, Auntie Pigerlert and Uncle Lamby were already there... in fact, they had been there for days. Considering we had been to Disney before, we did some completely new things:- We had some 'magic' photos taken (like Tinkerbell sitting on my hand!); I had breakfast at the Hawaiian restaurant with Lilo and Stitch, which was very cool as we got flower garlands to wear; I met Russell and Dug from 'Up' and I saw Merida from 'Brave'; I did some big girl simulator rides that I had been too small and scared to do previously, one in space and the other with dine-zee-caws (dinosaurs); I did trick or treating in Magic Kingdom for the not-so-scary Halloween party, and apart from the spooky music it really wasn't too scary; And for Halloween I dressed up as a mermaid pirate, and the other four were actual pirates. Mummy kept freaking me out though, as she had a beard... in the end that had to go, and then she looked like Mummy again. Daddy really got into the spirit, but unfortunately kept the pirate act up for the following week and even came back through customs on the way home still in character. Boys!

While in Disney I bought a Jessie the cow-girl hat, with a badge saying 'Jessie' on the front, which was so appropriate I just had to have it. What was cool though, was wherever I went in that hat, people seemed to know my name and shout 'hello Jessie'. I knew I was famous at home. But now I'm famous abroad too.

We saw a real wild alligator at the hotel. It spent the days near one of the lakes, not far from the pool. That was a bit scary. The hotel people did put a trap out for it, but the alligator just sat next to it. I think it liked the hotel and wasn't quite ready to check out.

Anyway, it was a good holiday. It started hot, but then some big sandy storm passed nearby and it got all cold and really very windy. Now that was a first, as I had never been cold in Florida before. But for a few days I was in trousers and jumpers and I was using a swimming towel for a blanket. Once that weather had passed through though, we were back in shorts again for the last few days, which was nice. The journey home would have been boring, had it not been for me seeing a girl from my school on the plane, and me being sick on landing yet again. I'm not good with flying home. I blame the plane food. It is disgusting. Anyway, I'm back now and it is absolutely freezing here.

The other really exciting thing that happened, is I got some little and very cute tripod walking sticks. Mummy found them on the Internet. They are red and yellow with 3 feet on the bottom of each stick, which make them slightly less wobbly than regular walking sticks. Mind you, they are still a tad wobbly when I'm in control. Anyway, I had a go with them, and a week and a half before I went on holiday I managed a few steps with my sticks, and I didn't have anyone helping. I actually WALKED!!! However, I do need someone on standby to catch me, just in cases. I did a bit of practising at home, without telling a soul (other than Mummy and Daddy obviously). It was all top-secret. Then, I visited Granny in hospital just after she had her bionic knee fitted. As a really special treat, and without any prior warning or anything, I just walked into her hospital room, all on my own (with my sticks obviously). I did another demonstration when Pop Pop arrived too. We needed a lot of tissues that day. For a prize, I am going to have a walking party next month, to properly celebrate.

I showed my teachers my excellent walking at school, and in total I was awarded a massive 40 team points. Wow.

I celebrated my new-found walking when I was at Disney World in a rather special way. While we were there, we went out for one particularly posh dinner. Auntie Piglet told the people at Disney that we were celebrating me taking my very first steps. So, Disney gave me two helium balloons, a 'celebrate' badge each, and they decorated the table with Mickey glitter. Then part way through the meal the waiter told us it was time to go outside and watch the 'Wishes' fireworks, while he promised to keep our dinner all warm. It was amazing. And as part of the fireworks, you have a chance to make a wish, so all your dreams come true. Well, Auntie Piglet said that last year when she saw it, she wished for me to be able to walk, and there we were celebrating it really happening. So, wishes really do come true. It actually is magic in Disney.

Cuddle me, catch me. Love, Jess xxx

# November 2012

I went on my first proper 'poppy day' parade with the Brownies this year. And half of the village seemed to have come out to either march or watch. It was so cold though. I was as freezing as an ice-burger. And that was despite me wearing my new and very fluffy brown boots, a vest and a Brownie 'boggy' warmer. The highlight of the parade for me, was that I was chosen to lay the poppy wreath on behalf of all of the Brownies and Guides. Low Owl pushed me in my wheelchair to do the actually wreath laying bit, but being in my chair I couldn't quite reach, so a nice and actual soldier man helped me. It was really special and I did very well.

There has been a lot of talk of something called 'Movember'. It is a bit like November but everyone has moustaches. Well in my weird family, all the boys, apart from Uncle Billy Bobs that is, have got moustaches already. So, both Daddy and Uncle Lamby went one step further and grew beards to match their moustaches. I like beards. They are all hairy and tickly. I couldn't quite manage a beard myself, but in the spirit of 'Movember' I was twice seen sporting a moustache of sorts. One was a chocolate milk one, and the other a chocolate ice-cream one. Both of which were very tasty.

My hair drove me completely nuts on holiday. I hate knots and tangles and it was worse than ever. So, I decided to have my hair cut into a bob again, and if I say so myself, I look a bit like a princess now, I think.

I took my walking sticks to Brownies to show Low Owl. I have never known the Brownies to ever be quiet. But when I got out of my wheelchair and stood up they went completely silent. Then I took a couple of slightly wobbly steps and someone said 'look, Jess is walking'. Then they all started clapping. I was very proud.

I had my very well deserved walking party at Granny and Pop Pops. I had given Pop Pop quite an extensive list of what makes a good walking party, and I do believe he remembered everything. From carrots, dip and party rings to eat; posh party hats; a 'Well Done Walking' badge; presents; pink balloons and party poppers; and pass the parcel. I even had a well done 'Brave' cake, complete with candles. And after a bit of persuasion, I got everyone to sing 'Happy Walking day to you'. To show all my guests that I had properly earned my lovely presents, I did some very good walking demonstrations and I even tried dancing with my sticks too. It was a really wonderful party. Just for me.

Love, Jess and Hubert the bear xxx

# December 2012

I was lucky enough to be invited back to LaplandUK again this year. Unfortunately, though, the day started with much swearing (not from me, I must add!) as we woke up to the first snow of the winter. Amazingly, we did manage to get there without too much of a hitch. However, I was able to watch 1 and a half films, which means it was quite a long journey. When I found out I was going to see Father Christmas again, I was adamant that this time I was going to get him a present. So, I brought him a lovely chocolate Father Christmas (in the shape of himself), as well as a Christmas card, lollypop and a postcard of me walking with my sticks. He seemed very surprised and pleased with his pile of treats. Oh yes, he gave me a present too.

I had an excellent time again in LaplandUK. I made this lovely teddy bear with a red Lapland jumper in the toy workshop, which helped out Santa and the elves get ready for Christmas. I iced and nicely decorated a gingerbread man biscuit with Mother Christmas and I went ice skating too. Even Mummy skated this time, although she had to use this penguin thing to help her stand up. Daddy thought he was too big and clever to need a penguin, and that is why he fell over. Twice. We had such a lovely time that we want to go back again, and again and again,

I have been in another gala at my swimming club. I even had a proper club swimming hat this time, so I really looked the part. I came 5th out of 5 in both of my races. I tried really hard, so I am very proud of myself. I even got a certificate.

Christmas was good as always, and I got loads of excellent presents. This year though I was more excited than ever before and I was able to break my all-time record for an early start on Christmas morning. I know the exact time, as Mummy said it over and over again. "2:18am. it is only 2:18am!!!! It isn't morning yet, it is barely night. 2:18am. I can't believe it. 2:18am." Well, you get the gist anyhow. After much persuasion, I had to get a few more hours sleep before

I was allowed to have any presents. Which I don't think was very fair. It is Christmas, after all.

The house was a squash and a squeeze as always, but it was really nice to see everyone. One of my most favourite presents this year was a 'Brave' bow and arrow. I was rubbish to start with but after a lot of practice in the hallway, sometimes with a not-so-willing victim/assistant sporting an orange on their head (we didn't have an apple), I got better and better. By New Year I became quite the accomplished archery person.

Love, Jess xxx

# January 2013

I had a birthday this month and I am now 10 whole years old. Which is quite big and grown up really, considering I am still on the little side of tiny. For my birthday party treat, I went to the Harry Potter studio tour with Mummy, Daddy and Granny. I was SO excited about going. As I had beautifully decorated my wheelchair with bows and banners and stuff, the people there knew it was my birthday, so I got a badge and everything. As part of the tour you get an iPod to borrow, which was all about Harry Potter. I loved it. Unlike the Butterbeer that I tried, which was absolutely disgusting. While on the tour I saw a model of Hogwarts. Mummy had told me all about it, and I had pictured it to be a bit like my dolly house. So, when I saw it I nearly cried. It was huge. While we were there, I also got to fly a broom (it was a Nimbus 2000 I think) and I flew Mr. Weasley's car too. I was brilliant. You could tell I am a half-blood princess. I am a natural.

I came home from school very excited the other day. Know what? My teacher got married to a wife and had a baby. It was very cute. The baby that is, not the wife. I was hoping they'd name the baby after me. As I'm famous, you know. But they didn't.

I had a friend round after school for tea, shortly after my birthday. I don't usually have friends around. But I'd thought I'd give it another go and I had a really lovely time. We made soap (from a kit I had for my birthday), we played Scalextrics (and crashed a car into the bin), and we even had posh ice-cream. Cool... Well freezing actually. A bit like the weather!

We had a lot of snow, which has really confused me quite a lot, as I was convinced that if it is snowing, then it must be Christmas. But apparently, Christmas was only a few weeks ago. I don't understand at all. We built a little igloo and an enormous snowman, which Daddy gave a bottle of wine (empty, I hasten to add!). I also played snowballs, did sledging on the flat along the pavements and made a few snow angels.

I had to give up and come indoors in the end, due to getting snow in my eye. An occupational hazard of playing in the snow when it is still snowing quite hard.

I've been to Centre Parcs for Auntie Piglet's big birthday. I had a lovely time, and for the first time ever I had an actual proper bow and arrow lesson. I was nearly as good as Merida from 'Brave'. While at Centre Parcs I did lots of swimming too, but no slides this time, as they scare the skin out of me. I'm actually hoop-less (hopeless) on water slides. I manage to end up a different way up and round at the bottom compared to how it all starts off. Weird. Anyhow, the swimming bit was great fun and I tried out every possible pool I could.

Such Fun!! Love, Jess xxx

# February 2013

I had half term and spent it with both Mummy and Daddy, which makes a change, as I usually take the opportunity in the school holidays to wear out the grandparents.

We tried to take it a bit easy, as we all had just recovered from poorly colds and were on the exhausted side of tired, again! Having said that, there were a load of things we wanted to do and we managed to get it all done. We all needed an eye test. And as a result, me and Mummy had to have new glasses. They were both purple-ly, although mine were much nicer and much cheaper. We went out to lunch a couple of times. I had my favourite combination of prawn cocktail followed by ham, egg and chips. I like being a big girl... sometimes. We also had lunch at the garden centre again, which was good but chaotic, as they were having loads of building works going on. I did manage to try out their very nice and brand new disabled toilet and I also bought some lovely bath bombs while I was there.

We have had a seriously overdue major sort out of all my clothes in my chest of drawers and wardrobe, and they both now actually shut. Mostly because they are no longer full of clothes that don't fit me anymore. It was amazing how much had to go. But I think that may be due to me growing quite a lot the other night.

There has been much talk at home about 'big' schools, as I will have to leave primary school next year. The thing is, next year seems ages away. But apparently, we need to make a decision as to what school I want to go to, within the next couple of months. It is becoming quite a challenge and it has so far involved looking on the computer at loads of different special school websites and then driving half way round the county to check where they are and what they look like from the outside. Some look a bit scary. I want to go somewhere nice. Not too noisy. No football. Not too far away from home. And it would be nice not to be the only one who is in a wheelchair, like I am at school at the moment. But the biggest and most important factor for me though, is that I most definitely do not want to be staying the night at school. I do really worry that I'll be sent away to a boarding school, a bit like Hogwarts, and that I will have to sleep at school. And although I would quite like to learn magic, I absolutely do not want to sleep at school. Mummy and Daddy have promised they'd never ever send me away, but all this talk of big schools is starting to make me a bit nervous. I think I'll feel a lot happier once I have been able to visit a few schools for myself and I can see that there are definitely no beds.

I have had some wobbly teeth. Two at the same time which was a tad disconcerting. One is still hanging in there at the moment. The other one fell out in the middle of the night while I was having a nightmare about a kangaroo and a lion. It was all very weird.

The latest TV programs that I am into at the moment are 'Doc Mc.Stuffins' which is on Disney Junior (and I love the little sheep on it called 'Lambie') and 'Miranda' (which is, what I would call, absolutely hilarious).

Bear with. Bear with.

Such Fun!! Love, Jess and Lambie xxx


Mummy again…. Feel free to skip this bit, as usual. I won't tell.

# Mind the gap

This is a concept that we were warned about a long time ago, but we have done well to ignore it for this long. What I refer to, is what happens when you have a child with developmental delay, or what has happened in our case anyway. The gap between your child and their peers starts small. It begins with them sitting up a little later than usual. Or their talking is delayed a bit. The gap between where they are and where they 'should' be may not feel like a big issue to start with. But that gap widens. And it keeps on widening. Until, before you realise it, you are facing some insurmountable chasm. You suddenly realise that you have been watching CBeebies for over a decade, and you only have the one child. That Barbie's, and dollies, and most pre-school toys and puzzles are still being used and loved. It paradoxically gives you the bizarre combination of real worry and strangely, joy. You get to have and cherish that little child for much longer than you ordinarily would. But it also means that the things that currently interest your child, their peers left behind many, many years ago. It means making and keeping good and true friends is almost impossible, as other children continually develop, evolve and change their tastes so much faster than your own. And you find they have been left far behind.

So just be aware. Anyone with a child with complex difficulties, please mind the gap.

# March 2013

On the wobbly tooth front, something rather odd occurred. My second wobbly tooth fell out in the middle of the night while I was sleeping. That is twice that has happened in so many weeks. Odd.

For Comic Relief, we had a 'mad hair' day at school. I decided I wanted curls. This would have happened naturally for me when I was about 2 years old. But now, as I've got bigger, my hair got straighter and straighter. So, to relive my curlier days, Mummy washed my hair and then covered it in hair gel, so my hair went all stiff and peculiar. Then it was wound round some material which was then tied in knots. To keep it all in place I put a hat on top. And that is how I slept. In a woolly hat with curler things underneath. In the morning, Daddy took all the bits of material out. It worked! I started the day with loads of neat-ish ringlets… but finished the day with the craziest bushiest hair you have ever seen. My hair is 'totes' mad. I thought that I looked a bit like Hermione Granger, but on a particularly bad day.

Mummy and Daddy have now visited the first two possible big schools for me. One is a definite 'no' and the other is a probable 'yes' at this stage. They have even found me a new and potential boyfriend at the school they liked. He is a speed demon in an electric wheelchair, he is handsome, with blonde hair and green glasses. I think I like him already and can't wait to visit the school myself now. I have even drawn a picture of what I think he looks like.

I have had another yummy high tea at the jam factory. I love it when they bring out the big three-tiered plate arrangement, full of sandwiches, cream teas, and cakes. It is my most favourite treat. Ever.

I have had a complete nightmare with my splints (they are the things that go on your feet, under your shoes, to stop your feet going all weird). Back in November we asked for an appointment for new splints as they were already rubbing and getting tight. We eventually got an appointment through for... June! However, last month I had to give up wearing the now too small splints altogether, as they were making my feet really hurt. The problem is, without my splints my feet go really weird and wonky and any standing up makes them hurt. So in desperation, Mummy and Daddy brought, at great expense (apparently)... some real black Piedro boots (suitable for school) and pink fur-lined Piedro slipper boots (that actually are fine to wear outdoors). I used to wear Piedro's, years and years ago, before I had splints, so I knew they should be okay as a temporary solution. Then, a week after my hideously expensive footwear arrived, my splint appointment was moved to next month. How blooming typical is that.

What have you done today to make me feel proud? Well, I think this month, my most impressive achievement is learning to swim a whole length on my front, without woggles or floats or anything, for the first time ever. Swimming on my front is quite a wobbly option for me, but doing wide breast stroke arms and special mermaid legs has sort of solved the problem. I half swim, half walk, half drown. My numeracy is not much better either. Thanks for asking.

You could tell we were heading for an end of term. As I definitely had the traditional 'end of term tiredness syndrome'. I had been really exhausted. And what with my ongoing tummy problems, meant the last week of school before Easter became a real struggle. I even had to miss one Brownie night and a couple of swimming lessons due to my dodgy tummy. I hate my bottom. And it hates me. I also hate taking so many different and really disgusting medicines. If only they helped. But even with them all, my bottom still doesn't work properly. It is a serious and complete pain in the bum bum.

On a happier note. After years and years of waiting (I hadn't mentioned it previously – didn't want to jinx it), we finally got the all clear from the Council about having the garage converted into a wet room at home. It won't be happening in the next few months, as the builder is a busy bee. But it now has to happen sometime in the next year.

That is the rules. As a special treat, and as a bit of a celebration for the 'go ahead' we went out and looked at ideas for tiles and toilets and taps and sinks and soap dishes and grab rails and showers and toilet seats and lights and... Well, there was just so much we needed to look at. And it wasn't just a case of choosing a sink I liked. I had to find one that I actually could get my wheelchair under. That was easier said than done. Some were absolutely rubbish. And I want a toilet with a real handle and not one with a weird push button. Looking at wet room stuff was quite exciting. Considering.

It being Easter, I have been busy making and doing things. Which is my favourite pastime. I've drawn, glued and stuck some lovely cards, made lots of chocolate Easter nests, buns and cakes. I've been quite a busy little princess chef in the kitchen.

On Easter morning, the Easter Bunny left me an Easter egg hunt. Except it was bunnies I had to find, not eggs. So, it was really an Easter bunny hunt. He obviously thought I was very clever this year, as they were all very well hidden. In the end, me, Mummy and Daddy had to find the bunnies between us. Then at the end, we had to do a thorough stock check to ensure that Daddy hadn't eaten any. When it comes to chocolate, Daddy cannot be trusted at all.

Billy, Del and their dog Piddles (also known as Pebbles) came down for the Easter weekend. Because of this, I decided to spend all my pocket money that week on my very own dog (a toy one obviously... I don't like dogs). I named it Puddles (also known as Piddles, and Pebbles). It was really lovely to see everyone again, and I enjoyed all our lovely cuddles and kisses. Apparently, I am a bit of a sloppy bucket.

Love, Jess xxx

# April 2013

We are going on a holiday on a huge boat later this year. It is called a cruise apparently. And Mickey Mouse is going too. I am so incredibly excited now, since I watched a few clips of our actual boat on YouTube. I don't think I can actually wait until August. In the hope of making the holiday come a bit quicker, I decided to start packing already. Mummy thinks she is organized. But she's not as organized as me. She has never packed over 4 months before a holiday. I am so excited, I even brought a special pink cruise hat ready for our holiday. I can't wait. I can't wait!!

My bottom continues to hate not just me, but also Mummy, Daddy, Granny and Nanny. The school Easter holidays were not a good time at all for my bottom and I had to have numerous unscheduled baths and showers, and I was still called a stinky gizzard. Not very friendly considering I can't really help it. One of the impromptu showers happened at such a speed, I ended up in the shower still in my socks! It is quite literally a mad house here sometimes.

I finally had my appointment for new splints. It was brought forward as a result of moaning to my new physio about having to wait so long. This appointment was called a 'casting' and they put both feet in plaster cast. A bit like if you break a bone. And then once it is dry, they cut the cast off and then use that as a mold to make my splints. It is quite clever really. The design I have chosen is pink butterflies. Now, I did choose this design years and years ago, and it turned up as bunny rabbits. So, fingers crossed this time that they are actually butterflies.

Love, Jess xxx

# May 2013

Mummy got me a new and scary book about growing up, called 'What's Happening to me'. We have only got half way through it so far and already it has given me the heebie-jeebies, big time. I really do not want to get a tatty bottom when I get bigger. I like my neat little bottom, just the way it is. There was also a picture of something called reproductive organs. I don't understand it at all. It just looks like a monster with long arms to me and I'm not sure what that has got to do with anything. The whole thing has freaked me out so much I am having sleepless nights, nightmares, and everything in between. So, I have decided I am not going to grow up at all, but instead stay little for ever, so I can always have cuddles and kisses and stay at home with Mummy and Daddy.

I have not been at all well. All snuffly, and sneezy, and sleepy, and grumpy and dopey, and hot and yuck. It's been like Snow White and the seven dwarfs, but without Snow White. And as a result, I ended up not just having a pyjama day, but I had an actual pyjama weekend. And I even had to have a day off school too. I have to be really poorly to miss school. My head has to almost fall off before I'm allowed to stay at home. It's not fair.

I really hate spellings. I have a spelling test every week at school, and I'm rubbish. Mummy and Daddy tried to make me do my spellings outside for a change, to make it a bit more interesting. But no. It didn't work. Spellings make my head hurt wherever I am.

Apparently Mummy and Daddy have been looking at more special schools. I know this as Nanny and Grandad had to pick me up from school one day, as they weren't back in time after seeing these other schools. Neither of the schools they saw were any good for me. One doesn't want me, which is surprising. I assume it is because they haven't met me. The other school is supposed to be wonderful, but it is huge and miles away and not really right for me. So, it has now been decided which school I am going to next and we had to officially announce it at my year 5 meeting at school. It was a bit of a weird meeting. Everyone was happy with our elected choice of school, which was a good. However, we were asked if we had considered not waiting until year 7 to move schools, but instead me starting a special school sooner rather than later. Well, frankly we hadn't seriously given it a thought. I assumed I'd go to big school when everyone else went. I'd just go to a different one, that's all. So, we had to give it an awful lot of thought. And quickly! Eventually, we decided that despite the chaos it is going to create over the next couple of months, what with letters to the education people, transport sorted and wheelchair problems to overcome, that it may be best all round if I do start my new school this September. It should be possible, as the school I hope to go to is both a primary and secondary school combined. It was just never the plan that I go to the primary school bit. It is not definite yet, as we are still waiting for the 'all clear' from the people who make these decisions. Although we are hopeful, as we know the school we have chosen actually has a place available, just for me. It has a blue uniform and is only about 5 miles from home (and it just happens to be the closest special school to where I live – so our house move a few years ago, was more cunning and better planned than I could have ever imagined). That's all I know about it at the moment, although I am going to visit it next month and I am really quite excited already.

In half term at the end of the month, me, Mummy and Daddy went away to Norfolk. We stayed in a lovely bungalow cottage that had its own huge hot tub. And I miss it already. I don't miss the weather there though. Norfolk is a very cold, misty, windy and wet place. I don't know if it always is like that, but the bit I saw most definitely was. We still went out and about every day. A small issue like horrendous weather doesn't seem to deter my parents. However, I was as cold as an ice burger most of the time. Having said that, we still did have a lovely time away. I went to the beach and had a picnic, but even the kite fliers had to give up as it was too windy! I got Mummy to make me a couple of sandcastles while I went looking for shells and stones. I like the beach. The sand is really soft. But we couldn't stay too long as it was just freezing. I made some amazing bread, all by myself, at a windmill. That was excellent fun and when we got back to the cottage we had my bread with oil. It was absolutely delicious. I'm a good baker. In desperation to go somewhere warm, Daddy decided we should go to a museum all about the war. I was not convinced at first, but on learning it had a gift shop and it was mostly inside, I decided I would give it a try. It was actually pretty good. I took loads of photos and posed for many more. Some of the stuff they had was absolutely enormous. While we were there we also went on a truck ride that was good but bumpy fun, and I got a certificate for tapping out my name in Morse code. That was really tricky to do.

On the last day of our break we went to a wildlife reserve where I: collected stamps for a nature trail; picked up as many feathers as I could find; did pond dipping and caught a fish; and went on a rather cold LandRover safari where we saw wild deer. A good but rather chilly holiday.

Love from Jess and my new dolly, Bella Ballerina xxx

# June 2013

The night before I went to look around my new school, I finally found out I had definitely got a place there. So, the pressure was on to then actually like it. But we shouldn't have worried at all. I loved it. Also, I was expecting to start in the primary school bit. But I'm not. I'm a big girl now. I'm going straight into class 3, which has years 6, 7 and 8, and I'll be a year 6. It is known as the middle school. I spent the whole morning there, in my new class. I even had lessons about butterflies, which I think had something to do with fractions and symmetry, but I could be wrong. A big excitement for me there was that my new desk goes up and down, so it is just the right height for me. It is amazing. There are buttons on all the doors so I can open them 'all by myself'. And I had a tour of the school and playground by the lovely Headteacher. My Mummy, Daddy and my current 1 to 1 came along for a nose too. There was a beautiful sensory garden and the plants smelt all weird, as well as an outdoor classroom that was really cool. There was even a wheelchair accessible roundabout and slide. I have never even seen one of those before. So, as a result of my morning at my new school, I am really very excited about going now.

The timing of going to a new school couldn't have been better really. A naughty infant at my current school, she must have only been about 5 years old, was really rude to me the other lunchtime, taking the mickey out of how I talk. It isn't my fault my words come out all higgledy piggledy sometimes. But she upset me and made me cross. Also, I have been starting to struggle a lot at school. It is just too hard for me. It means it definitely feels right for me to now go to a special school. It makes sense. I always knew I was special.

I have adopted some new quotes, and they are specifically used where Daddy is involved. If he calls me smelly… which he does rather a lot, my new retort is "How dare you!" Which seems fair. Also, I have a new nick-name for Daddy, as he keeps annoying me. "Stoopid snore-a-boy". Which seems accurate I think.

I have had 2 days out this month. On the first, I went around some posh gardens of a big house, on Daddy's birthday. That was quite good and I liked the swing and hedge tunnel best. The other day out, was a country show on Mummy's birthday. I had a go at archery again. It was quite good, although it hurt-ed my finger a bit. The best bit for me that day though, was off-roading in a LandRover. It went on a massive see-saw and it felt like a flying car. I think it was Daddy's best bit too.

I went to the Mobility roadshow again. But this time it was a long, long way away. 2 films and a play on the iPad away to be exact. It took absolutely ages to get there. We left home to go up there as soon as Daddy had got home on Friday afternoon, but didn't get to the hotel until hours after my bedtime. We normally stay in a moon hotel. Not this time. We stayed in a hotel at a motorway service station. It was quite nice actually and I had a low bed, just like at home, which was great as I could get in and out of bed all by myself.

We did so many things at the roadshow I just don't know where to start! We met a magician man who made me this huge duck out of balloons. He was really funny and did card tricks, walked on stilts and everything.

I took part in a Wheelchair dancing demonstration, and Mummy had a go too. We were quite good.

I enjoyed having my make-up done. It was this funny powder on a brush that made me look very grown up and some nice sparkly lip gloss too.

I found the people that sell hand exercise bikes again, broke all their records and did over a mile in less than 5 minutes. I am an actual cycling champion I think.

I was very lucky and got loads of free stuff at the roadshow. I got two little teddy bears. One in a t-shirt and another in a headband that looked like he was playing tennis. Wimbledon was mentioned, but I am not exactly sure what Wombles have got to do with tennis. I was given a nice but enormous t-shirt, and absolutely loads of sweets too. Some were nice.

I had my face painted like a pink glittery butterfly. And I also had a princess tattoo done, but they put it on a bit like a plaster, and I nearly had to cry. I didn't like that one bit. It looked nice, but I won't do that again.

I did rock climbing there again too. Twice. One time I got to the top with Daddy. The second time I got about three quarters of the way up, but at least I did better than Mummy, who stopped about half way. What a sissy.

I met the Stig and had my photo taken with him, and later saw him whizzing around on a mobility scooter. It was hilarious.

We met this lovely man who we thought looked like Johnny Depp, and he was called Johnny too. He had bionic (exoskeleton) legs, because his own ones didn't work at all. It looked quite cool, but they didn't have any bionic legs small enough for me to try. Mummy and Daddy said I couldn't have them anyway, as allegedly £45,000 was a tad expensive for new legs. Cheapskates.

I am famous again. The official press at the roadshow kept popping up and photographing me all around the show. And naturally, I posed where I could. It would have been rude not too. The photographers were even radioed in by some of the organisers when I was wheelchair dancing, just so they could get a picture of me then as well. I was officially the most photographed person at the show. I just knew I was famous.

While we were away we got to see Billy and Del. Weirdly they live in the same town as the roadshow which was handy. We went out for a nice meal and I saw their dog called Peddles (also known as Pebbles). We even did some princess posing.

After all of that, I was quite literally falling down tired. I need to sleep for England.

Night, night. Love Jess xxx

# July 2013

Summer has finally arrived. And in celebration of the sunny weather, we went for a picnic on the beach. It was lovely, but busy. Despite planning to go for a swim, once I had put one whole foot in the sea, I decided that it was far too cold to do real swimming. So instead we just played in the sand and ate a cool bag full of food.

Being that time of year again meant it was sports day. I did pretty well. A couple of firsts, a second and a last. Helped by the fact that I technically cheated in every single race. In the sack race, I was in my chair, but with my feet in the sack and my tall friend pushed me very fast. We won that one by a mile. In the egg and spoon race my little friend pushed me slowly. We lost that one, just. But we would have lost by miles if my egg hadn't been blue-tacked to the spoon, again. In the obstacle race I had to hold onto the ring on my head as it kept falling off... think I was second in that one. And finally, the walking race. Which I did in my walker all by myself. Problem is, I have trouble steering it, so I sort of had to 'borrow' someone else's lane, because I struggled to stay in my own lane. I won that one too. It was an exciting but exhausting morning. But all my excellent efforts meant that my house, the Hedgehogs, won Sports Day. Well done me.

I was in a school play just for the year 5 and 6's. It was about bullies, and I had to pretend to be in a fight. I chose to be one of the nice school children though. For me there was no acting involved really, as I am already a nice child.

I have now finished Brownies for ever (don't call me Heather!). The last 2 Brownie evenings were a bit special. I did some pond dipping and also went swimming. While pond dipping, we caught a leech, which was really gross and also a ginormous water boatman. Going swimming with the Brownies was okay, but it was a bit too shallow and splashy for my liking and all the other Brownies wanted to do races and underwater games and stuff that I couldn't actually join in with. I let them play. I decided to stay with Mummy instead. It can be lonely being me sometimes.

Auntie Pig-er-lert and Uncle Lamby came down to see me one very hot and sticky weekend and as usual they brought me some lovely pressies. I then proved that I truly deserved them, when they came to watch me at a sponsored swim. I swam length after length after length. All by myself and without a woggle. In the end, I managed to swim 11 lengths. It meant that I easily got my 200m badge and certificate, which I am very proud of.

But that isn't my only proud moment this month. At the end of each school year there is an awards assembly for things like reading, numeracy, and literacy and then a few special awards at the end. Well, the head teacher had given out all the awards but one… and she had got to the largest and most special award of all. She said this was for a really special girl. One who smiles and is cheery all the time. One who brightens up the whole school, despite having to deal with a lot of problems getting around.  A good inspiration to everyone. At this point, the description seemed a tad familiar. Then the head said, "I can see you grinning Jess. Yes, I AM talking about you. But I haven't finished telling everyone how lovely you are yet!" I was lucky to hear her tell everyone how I was going to a new special school and how much they would all miss me. There was an awful lot of blubbing and sniffing happening all around me. But eventually, it was time to go and collect my award. It was the 'child achievement of the year' award. My 1 to 1 carer helped me up and walked me to the front, where I collected the largest and most breakable award of all. And when I was turned around to head back to my space, there was half my family sitting at the back of the hall. Mummy and Daddy, Granny and Pop Pop, and Grandad and Nanny. They were all there. In my very special assembly. All of them were smiling and sniffing and clapping. I was rather pleased with myself.

It has been weird, but I have now left my current school for ever. Ready to go to my new school in September. I took in loads of presents for all of my teachers and I gave out special bookmarks (with a picture of me in my new school uniform on the front) for my friends. I took in a special book so I could collect autographs from friends and teachers alike, and as I did, I cuddled my way around the school. I was very lucky too. My class had made me a huge photo book with a picture of each person in my class in it, and they had all written something nice next to their picture. I was given loads of super presents too. It was a bit like Christmas. But very hot and sunny... and at school. I'm going to really miss my old school. But not half as much as I think they are going to miss me.

I have really grown up recently and two specific purchases can prove it. The hot weather has meant that I have been a bit of a sweaty smelly bags. So, I have now got my very own deodorant. I chose a pink spray one first, but that made me cough, sneeze and moan about how chilly it was. So, the next day Mummy bought me a pink roll on. I like it. It's got a ball in it. And it makes me smell nice. I also got my first ever crop top vest. It looks just like a teeny-weeny booby holder, just right for my teeny-weeny boobies.

I have been on my last ever Brownie pack holiday. And this time I managed the whole 3 nights and 4 days, and so did Granny. Although we will both probably sleep for a month to recover.

Pack holiday was busy and great fun. We did loads of stuff. I made a hobble-y (hobby) horse, and a pink papier mâché pig, washed a car and my socks... but not using the same bucket, laid the table, played games and sang songs. The only thing that made me cross on pack holiday was that I was awarded a certificate for being the naughtiest Brownie. I think they were joking, as I am not really naughty. A little cheeky perhaps, but not naughty. I was so cross, I actually threw my certificate in the bin! It was all due to a biscuit related misunderstanding. I may have taken too many of the good biscuits... twice. That aside, it was a great pack holiday. I made lots of friends and had a lovely time. I have to leave Brownies now. I'll miss it.

Love Jess xxx

# August 2013

I love listening and singing and dancing along to music. My talent is that I can usually guess a song within the first few notes. Which amazes Daddy, as he is hopeless when it comes to music. Anyway, I sometimes come up with my own unique and alternative lyrics. I bet you can guess which song this is… "I kissed a goat, I didn't like it, tastes of hay and carrots'. I also like dancing along to "Gammon star" (Gangham style) too. I think my versions are loads better.

The school summer holiday is a bit like a marathon relay race, but where I am the relay baton. I'm passed from Granny and Pop Pop to Nanny and Grandad, and back. Back and forth, forth and back. I've done loads of different things though. Including going to the cinema, the library, shopping, playing, and picnics on the beach. Sometimes when Mummy collects me I look like I've bum bummed through a hedge forwards, sometimes I look just like a princess.

I went to this cool 'Kidfest' at the local farm with Mummy and Daddy. It was great fun. I saw the real Mister Maker from CBeebies and I made a cardboard melon! I danced along with Bob the Builder and the Zingzillas, and I went to an actual circus. Probably one of my favourite bits though, was getting my face painted. You can't really beat having that done when it comes to special treats.

The big excitement of the month was going on my first ever cruise. It was a Disney cruise that sailed from Barcelona, which is in Spain, I think. We stopped in France and Italy. In one of those countries (my Geography isn't too good); we got off the boat and went to see the leaning tower of Pizza! (Pisa). It is a really wonky tower, being famous because it hasn't fallen over… yet. I actually thought the buildings were a bit boring. The best bit for me was buying a pink bracelet and a pink t-shirt with the wonky tower and the Disney princesses on the front.

The cruise was really good. I saw loads of different characters on board, I watched three shows in the boat theatre (and in one of the shows, Tinkerbell made the boat fly), I went in a hot tub and in the pools, I watched lots of Disney films (on poolside, and also in the cinema on the boat), and I ate loads of pizza and ice cream.

I was also invited to be an honorary crew member for an hour or so, where I traded pin badges alongside the crew, including the captain. For that I was given 2 certificates and loads of free pin badges. It was excellent fun. Aye, aye Captain.

We had a pirate party on the top deck of the boat. There we saw Mickey Mouse actually fly on a zip wire between the two funnels of the ship. It was amazing. And afterwards there were real fireworks as well.

I had a great time, and by the end of the week I was well and truly famous.

I've also had my first real sail on a small boat with Daddy and Nanny. It was in Nanny and Grandad's boat. I helped with the turns... ready about "Lee ho". I think doing this as well as the cruise, means I am now an official sailor person. Just like Daddy.

I had a day out of sorts, looking at new wheelchairs, as my sports one is getting a bit snug. It has done well though, as it has lasted over 3 years. However, my recent growing means I could do with a new one. I have chosen one that is extremely very pink, and we managed to order it before the month was out. That means in a few weeks' time I'll be sporting some new wheels.

I'm off to start my new big school in a few days. I am excited and nervous and a bit scared. I also heard that I'm definitely going to be on the minibus to and from school too. And I am lucky, as I'll be the last one to be picked up in the morning and the first to be dropped off at the end of the day. So as far as I'm concerned, it is a perfect plan. I'll also be starting guides a week later.

It really will be a complete and new beginning for me, in so many ways. New wheelchair, new school, start Guides. Time to start growing up... a little anyway.

It's an end of an era.

So, this is Jess, signing off.
Out. xxx

Just remember...

Everything will be alright in the end.
If it's not alright, then it's not the end.

Well, the plan was to end it there, after 10 years exactly of journal entries. All, had been relatively static for a while. We'd got no diagnosis, but one was unlikely to ever be found. Tests had stopped. Which meant no-one was really looking at Jess that closely any more. The plan was to still keep in contact with GOSH, as her unusualness meant that a local GP was always flummoxed when they saw her.

Progression both at school and physically, continued to be very slow, but steady. But a new special school seemed the right way to address that. So, at least we were moving in the right direction. No regression. No signs that things were going to get worse. The doctors admitted that as they hadn't seen anyone quite like her before, that it was possible that other parts of her brain would compensate for the bits that were deteriorating. That the brain is so complex, who knows what her outcome would be.

However, we should have guessed she would always keep us on our toes, one way or another. We had a couple more months of relative normality, and then things once again, started to go awry.

So, we'll pick it back up, straight where we left off. But this time, now she's bigger, the updates have moved to be quarterly not monthly. Other than that, it is business as usual.

# Jess's Journey...

## continues

# Sept–Dec 2013

(age 10 years, 7 months)

This really is a new start for me.

Time to grow up. Be a big girl, like Mummy. Well, perhaps not quite that big!

So many new things seem to be happening at the moment.

I have just started my new 'big' school, even though I'm only now beginning year 6 (which usually is the last year in primary school). I'm here in a new place because my mainstream school was getting too much for me. Truth be told, it was getting a bit much years ago, but I liked it there, in my old school. I liked the people, and they seem to like me. So, I stayed. In hindsight, I probably stayed there longer than perhaps I should. Now I'm in my new school, things make a bit more sense. My lessons are more understandable, more my level. My new friends like the same sort of things as me. Most are in wheelchairs. We even talk the same. So, it is probably unsurprising then, that I found a very close friend very quickly. He is called Ron. He is sort of blonde-ish and handsome and 'drives' an orange manual wheelchair. We pretended to get married in the playground, and when we are bigger, we are going on a cruise for our Honeymoon. We even go to the toilet at the same time, and chat away happily in our adjacent cubicles. He is my new and very special friend.

I have had my first birthday party invitation in absolutely years. Although I had good friends in my old school, their parties were never exactly accessible, or suitable for me. For many, many years, I hadn't been invited to a single birthday party. It was quite a shock getting an invitation, especially as it was from a friend at my new school. The theme was 'Princes and Princesses'. I was naturally a princess, complete with tiara. There was face painting, although I opted to have my arm painted instead, picnic food, homemade buns, glow-in-the-dark bracelets, make-do things and music. My kind of party. And Ron went too, so it was even better fun.

I have started Guides as I got a bit too big for Brownies. Age wise, not height wise you understand. If it was done on height, I'd still be a Rainbow probably! It is a bit of a struggle though, as it finishes half an hour after bedtime! Mummy did threaten to take me to guides in my pyjamas. But thankfully it transpired she was only joking, and after just a couple of week's trial, I got my very own big Girl Guide uniform. It is good fun. We do lots of make-do stuff, which I love, including baking and printing our very own pillowcases. It's quite cool really.

'Obviously'. It has got to be one of my most favourite words at the moment. I love the way Professor Snape in Harry Potter says it to that Professor Umbridge woman. He makes it sound like the longest word in the world. When I say the word, I am often asked to repeat what I've said. Originally, I thought this was because people didn't quite understand me. I do have trouble saying all the right vowels and all the right consonants when I say a word, and when I do, they aren't always necessarily in the right order. But apparently, the way I say this word is something else. Ob...vi...ous...ly.

One weird thing about going to my new school is that I get picked up in a special mini-bus from home in the mornings, and then after school, I'm dropped back off back at home. I feel very big going off on a bus. The only problem was, as my sports wheelchair didn't fold, it was not allowed on the bus. A small issue like this doesn't deter us for long though. I test drove and chose a new wheelchair last month, but as it is custom built, I had to start my new school in my big NHS chair. But only 3 weeks into term, my new chair was delivered and adjusted and was all ready for the off. It is extremely pink, with light up castors and princess hub caps. VERY me.

Although I like my school, it doesn't stop it being tiring or a bit annoying sometimes. I always come home tired and hungry, but sometimes I come home a bit cross too.

I have started doing my own hair, as we are going to have to find a new hairdresser. Our usual hairdressing lady is actually going to have a litter of babies. THREE! All at once.

She must be bonkers. Anyway, I have been practicing, as I think it would be a good idea if I became our new hairdresser.

I have been to my first after school club, ever. It is where you stay at school after most people go home and do fun stuff. I enjoyed it but it was a bit boring and tiring as I get home so late. So, I'm not sure I will actually go again.

At the end of my first half term in my new school, we had a Halloween party. It really was excellent. I made a lantern with a battery, scooped out a pumpkin and decorated the hall. Once we had done all the preparations during the morning, we stopped for lunch and then partied all afternoon. I even got to dress up a bit like Hermione from Harry Potter. Complete with a broom that was fixed underneath my wheelchair. It didn't fly though. Which was a tad disappointing. My wand didn't work either. I definitely had some dodgy equipment.

At school, I did an audition for a part in our Christmas play. We are going to do 'Charlie and the Chocolate factory'. I must have done really well, as I was given the part of Charlie, and I am not even a boy. There are 2 downsides to this amazing news. The first has something to do with the 143 words that I will need to learn, the longest of which is a huge word... 'Scrumdiddilyumtious'. The second problem, is I am going to have to wear this yellow checked shirt and brown cardigan (I refused point blank to wear a jumper). I am the girliest girl ever, and these clothes are... well... let's just say, they are boys' clothes. Yuck!

I have lost 2 baby teeth that used to be at the very back. Well, when I say, 'lost', I know where they are. The tooth fairy has them and she has made them into 2 particularly large and shiny stars in the sky, as they were 2 particularly large and shiny teeth.

I went to a wheelchair course in Norwich and stayed, as always, in a moon hotel. It was a good course, although being at the very end of term, I was predictably on the tired side of exhausted. I did my best and I even volunteered to have a go on the evacuation chair, which can be pushed down stairs in an emergency. I was worried it would be scary, but it was quite good fun, and almost like a ride. My best achievement on the course was doing a back-wheel balance in my wheelchair, using the mat to lean on. I've never been able to do that before, so I was quite understandably rather proud of myself.

After many years of talking about it and meeting with loads of different people, we are finally having the garage at home converted into both a wet-room and dressing area for me to use, as the current bathroom at home isn't wheelchair friendly at all. Building works are now underway. It is all noisy and dusty and horrid. Already I can't wait for it to be finished. The weirdest thing so far, is being carried in my wheelchair, by the builders, across a big trench that they had dug across the drive, so I could get to the school minibus. Daddy would have usually done that sort of thing, but he is limping around on crutches at the moment. But that is quite another (boring) story!

Me and Mummy got into the Christmas spirit in November by making some Christmas crackers especially for Christmas day. We made loads and they were actually pretty good. I can hardly wait for Christmas now.

Also, before November was out, we had a Christmas Decoration Day at school. It was great fun. It involved covering the ceiling, doors, and computers in tinsel. I helped decorate a Christmas tree and we all decorated our wheelchairs too. We had a fantastic time.

In preparation for all things Christmassy, the learning of my lines for the Christmas play has been going quite well, considering how many words I have got to learn. My main practicing place has been in the bath and after much bobbing about in water, I have now pretty much sussed all my lines... as well as the lines of some of my friends too! I have even come up with a festive song, relating to me playing the part of Charlie Bucket. 'Tis the season to be Charlie, fa-la-la-la laaaaa la la la laaaa'.

For the last few years I have got an invite from Father Christmas to go to Lapland UK with Mummy and Daddy. I was getting quite nervous this year as there was no sign of an invitation. I started to wonder if I had actually been put on the naughty list. By accident, obviously. Then, out of the blue, with just a couple of days warning, I was asked if I would like to go to Lapland UK… with my school!! And even more excitingly, with my boyfriend Ron. Well, at least this explains it. My invitation must have gone to school instead this year. It was a very, very long way to Lapland on the school minibus though. Despite this, I had a great time. I made a puppet and a bear, saw an enormous and very cuddly husky, decorated a biscuit, saw Santa and went ice skating with my boyfriend. A really brilliant but tiring day out.

I went out on the school minibus again, but this time for a Christmas school party, and I came home with the biggest party bag in the world. It had a huge play dough set and a hat and pen and... well, it had absolutely loads of stuff. We had a nice lunch out, with crackers and posh hats, I did some dancing, I'm sure I met a real princess and I had my photo taken for a newspaper. So, all in all, a pretty cool school trip.

I was lucky to actually get to Lapland and the party as the next day I was not at all well. In the course of the day I went through 5 pairs of pyjamas, one pair of which was Daddy's! and I got sick in my hair. Not a good day at all. It meant that I had to have several days off school, which was sad. We had been quite excited, as I had been nominated to have a Christmas lunch with the town mayor, but due to my rather spectacular up-chucking, I never made it… which was a shame. I was also supposed to be taking part in a swimming gala, but I never got to do that either.

Thankfully, once recovered, I did manage to go along to the Christmas party that was held at my school. It was great, as I got to show Granny and Pop Pop around my school for the first time. They saw my classroom and desk and they met my teacher and boyfriend. I had a buffet tea, and I saw Father Christmas there too. He gave me a make-do perfume set which looks like excellent fun. I like Christmas. Not that long now!! I literally can't wait until Christmas day.

I also went on an outing to do some Christmas shopping with my school, and we had lunch out as well. I had my absolute favourite meal of hot dog and chips. I had a shopping list and some money and I had to buy a Christmas present for both Mummy and Daddy. But that is a big surprise, and top secret, so I really can't say anymore on that.

I was in the school Christmas show, Charlie and the Chocolate factory. And I was the hero of the story, Charlie. I did really well, and I even sang a little solo... all by myself. Lots of people came to see me perform. Granny and Pop Pop, Mummy and Daddy, and Nanny and Grandad all came along to watch me.

I went to the Christmas fair at my old school. And I spent most of the time cuddling my old friends and teachers and letting them know that I was getting on just fine in my new school. Highlights included: cuddling my old one to one; having my face painted; and Daddy winning the hamper of cakes at the auction. Yummy!

The next day I went to the pantomime to see Cinderella, and weirdly I bumped into loads of my old school friends that I had only just seen the day before. A good show and another late night. The run up to Christmas can really be exhausting.

As part of the crazy run up to Christmas one of our special school treats was to go on an outing to the cinema to watch Frozen and to have a McDonalds. My new school is great.

After 9 weeks (ish), all our building works have finished, at last. This means I've now got a lovely shiny new wet room, with some very pink accessories. I've managed to have several showers in it already, and I have been really enjoying the underfloor heating too. I feel like a very big girl with my own wet room. We've got a new drive too, that I can wheel across, all by myself. I've never been able to do that before, so it's very exciting.

I went to the farm again to see Father Christmas with Mummy and Daddy. Me and Santa had a lovely long chat, as I gave him a home-made cracker and a card. I also stuffed a flamingo, a toy one obviously, and then I dressed it in a hat and summer dress so she looked 'boot-a-full'. I made a tree decoration and I iced a biscuit. It was pretty good fun. I think I might go back again next year.

Christmas was busy as ever with absolutely loads of lovely presents, and I don't think I got a single dodgy one. So, that was excellent. I also got to see lots of family too. Which, I guess, was quite nice as well.

Happy New Year.

Big squishes and squashes,

Jess xxxx

# Jan-Mar 2014

The first exciting thing of the New Year was my Guide enrolment. This did mean though, that I had to learn the new guide promise, which proved to be quite a challenge, due to some tricky words in it, but I got there in the end. I was so pleased I did it, as I really wanted my very own guide scarf and woggle. I also had to light a candle, which was dangerous. I'm not good with fire! I am now a proper and official guide. And am rightly proud of it too.

2 days later I celebrated my 11th Birthday. As my birthday always seems to follow Christmas a little bit too quickly for my liking, I was given a lot of money this year for my birthday. Which I thoroughly enjoyed spending at the Disney Store. I also had the promise of some new bedroom furniture, for my lovely new bedroom. And I helped put some of that furniture together, as I am big now. I even helped with some of the hammering. Although my heart wasn't entirely in it, as I was continually distracted by my new pink DVD player.

Moving into my new bedroom unfortunately involved a huge amount of sorting out, which took weeks, as allegedly I have been a bit of a hoarder, and have managed to acquire an extraordinary amount of tut. It does mean that my new room is now relatively neat and tidy. At the moment, anyway. Or at least it is compared to my old room.

I have started horse riding at school. This is miraculous as I don't like any animals, not even kittens. So, the thought of getting on an enormous horse was a bit daunting, to say the least. However, once I realized some suitable bribery was ready and waiting if I just went for my first lesson, I gave it my best go. And I loved it! My horse is brown, is a boy and is called Tawny. I can tell him to "Walk on" and "Whoa" so far. But that is quite enough to be getting on with, thank you.

I had an absolutely disastrous half-term. It all started just after swimming one evening. We'd picked up a Chicken Mc.Nugget Happy Meal for me to eat in the car on the way home, as I was starving. But my right chip-holding hand was all pins and needles, so I persuaded Mummy to sit in the back of the car with me and help me with my tea. Then my shoulder felt weird. And soon after that I had a fizzy lip and couldn't eat my nuggets at all. They got all stuck in my mouth, as my tongue didn't seem to be working properly. Thankfully I was clever enough to tell Mummy I felt weird and she turned the light on in the car. Mummy thought I looked weird, but you should have seen her face. She looked like she'd seen a ghost. Apparently, I was having a stroke. Daddy skidded the car around and we headed to A&E really fast. On the way, I was struggling to speak properly and I think I started to talk a bit like Uncle Lamby (as he comes from up north. Well, the Midlands to be precise!). And I was getting really muddled. I couldn't remember Mummy's name and thought my name was 'Barbie'. It was really very confusing and scary. It was mostly a blur after that. I was told later that I thought the horse on my t-shirt was a pear, that my face went all droopy on one side, and that I wasn't able to move either my right arm or my right leg. I spent an hour or so in a room called 're-sus' and during that time I was put in a CT scanner, which was weird. After an hour or two though, I started to feel a bit more like my old self. I started to move my right hand and foot. I started to talk more normally, and eventually I even knew who I was. Quite a relief all round, I must say. But by this time the hospital doctors had spoken to GOSH, and between them they decided that they should keep an annoyingly close eye on me. So, they found me a bed on the children's ward, which was loads better and nicer and quieter than being in re-sus. But it proved to be a very, very long night. I got to the ward just after 9:30pm, so it was already way past my bedtime. But there was going to be no sleeping. Every hour, on the hour, I had to have a load of tests. Blood pressure, a crocodile clip on my finger, a light in my eyes and a strength test in my hands and legs. Shortly before midnight I was so washed out and in shock, that I threw up absolutely everywhere. Thankfully Daddy had just got back to the hospital with some pyjamas, which was uncannily good timing for him. I did apologize to the nurse for being so sick, but she was really nice about it. By the time my bed was changed and my pyjamas were on, it was time for my hourly 'obs' (it is short for 'observations') - you get to know the lingo when you are an in-mate! And so, it carried on all through the night. I didn't really sleep. So, me and Mummy spent half the night just chatting. At 3am I was hungry and ready for breakfast, as I never did get very far with my McDonalds the night before. It seemed like a very long night. It didn't stop me though, from being chatty and smiley with the nurses during the night for my hourly 'obs. And as soon as the TV was allowed on, we had that working too. Both Mummy and Daddy did threaten to put the Winter Olympics on, but in the circumstances, they let me watch CBeebies. It was a bit baby-ish, but it was the best thing I could find. Later that day I met the hospital radio DJ, put in a special request and even got to hear my name mentioned on the radio, twice. And they played my favourite song at the moment 'Because I'm Happy' from 'Despicable Me 2'. I'll just be happy now if they discharge me. But that doesn't look like it will happen anytime soon. Amazingly, we were allowed out that afternoon so we could sleep at home, but on the promise to come back very early the next day. And we were back so early, the ward was in darkness and everyone was still snoring!! Before the people on the ward had even woken up, I had some hideous blood tests and the first attempt to get a cannula in (that is a horrible needle that they put in your hand, and then leave this kind of tube thing behind). As I've had so many before, they tried my hand and my foot, but no luck. So, sore and bruised, they had to give up for a while. Then my Godfather turned up. He actually works in that hospital. And he held my hand while the nurse finally got the cannula in. It was still really horrible, but at least it was over quickly. And before I knew it, I was being wheeled through the chilliest parts of the hospital as they had decided to put me in a washing machine (an MRI). Which looks a bit like being in a plane. Then there was lots of waiting around, more blood pressure tests, and keeping a very watchful eye on me. Eventually, at bedtime, I was able to come home at last.

Properly discharged this time. Why is it, that I am forever in and out of hospitals? I have had enough! I guess, at least I am now in 'recoverment'. I am never going to eat chicken nuggets ever again. Next time I'll be having a burger.

I've been doing physio at school, and afterwards I got my shoes and socks back on all by myself. The other week I came off the minibus with a hat-trick of wardrobe malfunctions. My socks were on inside out (but they always are after physio), my shoes were on the wrong feet (that or my feet were on the wrong legs) and I was wearing someone else's school cardigan (as it was nicer than mine). This apparently, was good going, even for me.

Anyway, lots to do and see.

Love, Jess xxxx

# Apr-Jun 2014

I have had a load of hospital appointments over the last few months. Here we go again! Mostly harmless ones that involved just talking to the doctors about my 'fizzy lip' episode that I had the other month. I did have a real test though, an EEG. That is where they stick those electrode-y things to my head. The most annoying part about it was that I had to wash my hair 2 days in a row. You have to go with clean hair to do the test, but then they put this glue stuff in which means you then have to wash it all out. Really 'nnoying! I suppose one upside to it was that I was brave, so I got a pot of special 'cinema' sweeties, thanks to one of Daddy's friends insisting that I thoroughly deserved them.

Most of the family came along to watch me in my Easter show at school. I sang a solo of a couple of lines, as I'm in the choir at school now. "Easter bells ring; Easter bells ring". In the play, I was on the jury, although I wasn't entirely sure what was going on. I was quite worried that I'd have to wear a bandage in the play, as I'd bumped my arm the night before. But a bit of cream sorted that out. I had to have the special lotion on both my elbows though, as I couldn't remember which one hurt. But it worked. As I was all better by morning. Until that was, my tooth fell out. And there was 'bleed' everywhere. I get in a right pickle sometimes.

I won an award for the very best decorated Easter egg competition out of the middle school. I made my egg into a bubble bee. I hate bees. But I wanted to win. And I got a £10 book token for my prize. And I will even be able to keep the book that I buy. Not like when I go to the library. I have to give those books back.

My new bedroom furniture has finally arrived, has now all been put together and is up in my bedroom. I am now officially a real princess, as I sleep in a four-poster bed complete with pretty curtains. It is a real bed too. I used to sleep on a bed with no legs, one really low to the floor, so I could get in and out 'all by myself'. But Daddy built a step for this one, so I can get in and out my big girl bed without any help. It is very exciting. I also even have a wardrobe with slidey doors, my own mirror, and a bedtime table. It is really a very 'me' bedroom.

During the Easter holibobs (holidays), I went backwards and forwards, and then forwards and backwards between Nanny's and Granny's houses, staying the night here, there and everywhere. It meant lots of packing, un-packing, re-packing and unpacking again. You get the gist. Weirdly though, I love packing. You're weird. I won.

Me, Mummy and Daddy went to a place called Alton Water on one of the Bank Holidays. There was a lot of cycling to be done and I was exhausted by the end of it. Even though I technically didn't actually do any of the cycling myself. Mummy and Daddy took it in turns to have me as a passenger. When Daddy was cycling, he went so fast down the hill, he cycled off the path and across the grass. It frightened me so much I nearly piddled myself. And when I say nearly, I mean actually.

I was in a Panathlon competition. It was an inter-school thing, where I was chosen to represent my school, and I had to race against other schools. I did something called New Age Kurling, which was pushing this round disc on wheels down a ramp towards a target. We won one game and I think we came 4th. Out of 4. But I'm not very sure. Anyway, I did several races and I was super speedy wheeling my chair in and out of cones. I came home with 3 medals. And one of them looks like it might be a gold. They even look like real medals, just like you would get in the Olympics.

I have been having quite a growth spurt recently. Which is really odd for me, as I've been on the tiny side of small for absolutely years. However, I am seriously making up for lost time. The good news is, I keep getting lots of new clothes. The bad news, is that Granny says I am growing like a weed. I think I'd rather grow like a flower. They are pretty. Like me. I've grown so much, I have new boobies and even have my first ever booby-holders. I don't like them at all. Really uncomfy. So, I mostly opt not to bother. And at the moment that's okay. Although, Mummy did say that I may have to start wearing them sometime soon, whether I like it or not. Apparently, if they carrying on growing the way they have been these last few weeks, they'll be as big as my head by this time next year. Odd. I hope she was joking.

I've got a new horse at horse riding. I don't always ride the browny-coloured one called 'Tawny' anymore. My new one is white with spots. Not yucky spots, like measles or chicken pox. More freckly, mole-y kind of spots. I call him 'Oliver'. Although I'm not sure that is his name. He is nice and my riding lessons are still good. I like horses now.

I have been awarded 'swimmer of the week' at my swimming lessons for my brilliant breaststroke arms. And in the same lesson... I did my first ever sitting dive. And then, I did about 10 in a row. It was a really big thing for me and I was SO excited and proud of myself for finally being brave enough to dive in.

In the half term, we went away on holibobs (holiday) and stayed in an actual little lodge with its own sauna and hot tub. I really want a sauna at home now. It is magic. It made my cold go away and it is very relaxing. Although I don't have it anywhere near as hot as Daddy did. He likes it like an oven. Me and Mummy have it like we are on holibobs somewhere hot, like Disney World. It was rather cold and wet and yuck outdoors on holibobs, so we were very pleased with our posh lodge and we went in both the sauna and hot tub every single day. We did do other stuff. We went to a nature reserve. Some of it was good fun and some of it was really boring. We went to a museum too and I dressed up as a Victorian girl and tried on an old fireman's hat and I did some colouring in as well.

One hilarious thing we did in the lodge, was we added some body wash to the spa bath... and then turned the bubbles on. We had foam and bubbles everywhere. And I mean, everywhere!

Nanny had a big birthday in June. And when I say big, I mean huge. We had a surprise party for her on a boat. She likes boats. Daddy likes boats too. I was worried I would get all seasick like I did on the cruise. But as it turns out, a boat on a canal is much calmer and more relaxing. It was actually quite good fun.

I had a small disaster after horse riding with the school one day. I came back without my hairband. It was one of my pink ones with a bow. I have a few pink ones with bows, and it was one of those. Anyway, it got all lost. In desperation, I came up with a good idea. Missing hairband posters. I was going to make loads. Put them up around school and home. I perhaps could give a reward if it was found. Anyway, I was persuaded to check with school the next day before we spent a whole evening drawing posters. And luckily it was found all safe and well at school. Phew. What a relief.

I hurt my leg in swimming. At first I thought I had hurt a bone, and asked if I would have to have my leg in plaster. As it happened it was all better by tea time. I was a little disappointed though as I was already looking forward to having a go on crutches!

I like baking. And for 'Daddy's day' (also known as Fathers' day), me and Mummy did a load of baking. Mummy is not great in the kitchen, something the guides have now discovered after my patrol tried to make pizza from scratch and ended up with a complete mess. So, when I wanted to make something nice for Daddy, Pop Pop and Grandad we 'cooked' things that we could actually manage. So, we made chocolate crispy cakes, and chocolate covered marzipan vegetables. Apparently, marzipan fruit is more normal. But who wants to be normal. Oh, and I didn't lick the spoon. Honest. It wasn't me.

I have been to the local Country show again. I got to have another go at archery. It makes your fingers hurt a bit though. And it was next to the shooting, and that was really noisy, so it was a bit tricky to concentrate enough to do well. A highlight for me was having some chocolate covered strawberries. They were mega delicious. I ate most of them, but allegedly wore the rest. We then finished the day watching these dogs jumping around a course. It was sunny, I had my feet up on a bale of hay and I had a lolly. I could have happily watched them all day.

I have discovered though, that growing up not only makes you taller, it also makes you feel very cross and very angry sometimes. I don't like that bit much. I like being all big and grown up. But I don't like the other bits that go with it.

Anyway, I'm bored. I don't want to do this anymore. Go away and leave me alone.

Love, Jess xxxx

# Jul-Sept 2014

School has been going well. I just cannot believe I am at the end of my first year of my new school. A whole year! But then on the other hand, it seems like it was a lifetime ago that I was in my old school. Weird, isn't it. I'm glad I'm already at my new school, as if I wasn't, this would have been the end of my time at primary school and I'd be starting secondary school in September. This school is plenty big enough for me. There are about sixty or seventy of us, and we range from the 'ickle little tiny 4-year olds down in the primary end, right up to these enormous 19-year olds in Post 16, or College, or whatever they call that bit. I've heard what real big secondary schools are like. Each year group is bigger than my entire school. Scary. Don't think I'd like that at all. I don't like noise, or too many people, or pushing and shoving… and I don't like the sound of the tricky lessons they have either. I am most definitely better off right where I am. Although having said that, I may have got myself into a little bit of trouble at the end of term. I got a real and actual detention for talking to my boyfriend in class. I was in big trouble. I had to stay behind during break and the teacher wrote it in the 'school to home' book, even though I begged her not to. And to top it all, I have been told I am not allowed to sit next to my boyfriend in class starting from next term… as we keep secretly holding hands under the desk. I can't help it if he's handsome. Not my fault.

At the end of term, we had sports day. We were in groups that represented different countries. I quite rightly was competing for the England team and we had to wear red and white. I took part in quite a few different events. I did the throw the bean bag onto this big number chart thing, and I did exceptionally well at that, scoring maximum points on several of my throws. I had to throw a ball into a net, but no matter how much I tried to blow it, it still rolled off in the wrong direction. I did a wheeling my wheelchair race, which went well as I am pretty speedy, and then a walking race in my walking frame. In fact, it was rather novel to be in a sports day where they didn't have to adapt each race for me, as we were all already on a level playing field. Well, technically, level playground. Anyhow, the upshot was, me and my team did so well that England got the most number of points and as a prize I actually got a real medal. I am getting such a collection of medals, that I have had to have a cork board put up in my room to display them all.

At the end of term assembly, we sang a song about summer, and for some reason we were all wearing swimming goggles. Ron wore armbands too, but that is because he can't swim. I didn't wear armbands, I can swim all by myself. What was exciting was in that assembly, in front of all the parents, and grandparents, and everybody, I got 2 horse riding awards!! Grade 1 horse riding and Grade 1 horse care. Not bad going considering the first time I even got on a horse was just a few months ago.

I am not going to the Saturday evening swimming lessons at the moment. We made a unanimous family decision that we would have a term off. And as it happened, it all worked out just fine, as in my school holibobs we went on an actual holiday to Madeira. While I was there I did absolutely loads of swimming, and I practiced doing my sitting dives at every occasion. We were staying at this posh hotel, but I expect no less nowadays. Anyway, they had several pools. A huge cold outdoor one that was next to the restaurant, and then an indoor one that was part of a spa, but where you could swim through a door to the outdoors. That was my most favourite thing to do. And I literally spent a week going between the indoor and outdoor bits of the spa pool. And it paid off too. When I arrived in Madeira I swam like a dog. By the time I left, I was swimming like a fish.

The weather there was lovely. Not Disney-hot, but not Norfolk-cold. Somewhere nice and comfy in the middle. Perfect for sitting around in your swimsuit, reading books and magazines and stuff. Which was handy as we had the most enormous balcony attached to our room and we spent many an evening all sitting out there on our sunbeds reading.

We did go out for a day trip adventure in a coach into the mountains. And boy, aren't mountains a long way up. And when you are up there, isn't the sea a long way down. It was fun (when I ate a scrummy ice cream), then scary (when we met another coach on a bend up the mountain), then it was boring (when we went and tasted Madeira wine, as they didn't let me have any). I did get to try Madeira cake, but that was just wrong and yuck.

This school holiday was a bit of a revolutionary turning point for me. I was finally ready to have a good and proper go at switching from pull-ups to knickers in the daytime. The thought of going through the night in knickers gives me the hebbie jebbies still, but I was ready to give it a good and proper go in the day. I did really well on holiday and wore a real swimsuit, rather than my sticky knickers (my incontinence swimwear). And I just had to resort to pull-ups for the day trip up the mountain, and the plane journey there and back. And all the nights too, obviously.

The rest of the summer was good. As is traditional, I suitably wore out all the grandparents by keeping them constantly on their toes. With never ending make-do stuff, cooking and baking, shopping and cinema, days out and days in.

I wore out Daddy one weekend by challenging him to a water fight. It was a proper one involving the hose pipe and the watering can. He was losing, so in the end he cheated by standing up and running away.

Before I knew it was time to go back to school. I was missing school quite a bit and I was really excited to go back and tell them that I had made the best achievement possible over the summer, by coming back to school in knickers.

School was just how I'd left it and remembered it. I still have a boyfriend, except now the other boys want to love me too. And I don't like that. So, Ron has had to fight them off. Literally. He stood up to one of the enormous boys in College and told him to leave me alone. My hero!

Love and hugs, Jess xxxx

# Oct-Dec 2014

I am getting quite tall for a small person. I have been doing so much growing, I am almost the height I should be. Well, give or take several inches. But I'm getting there at last.

October half term had two rather memorable events, although the second one was so exciting it kind of overshadowed the first, which was, I went to Mummy's work. It is quite a trek from home. I know as she moans about it sometimes. And because of that, I haven't been many times. The last of which was absolutely years ago, when I really was small. We sang and we chatted all the way there. Really, I am not sure what all the fuss was about, the journey flew by. The first thing I noticed was the size of the building Mummy works in. It is so enormous it made me cry a little bit. Mummy says it has the same effect on her too sometimes. Anyway, there were some disabled spaces right outside the main doors, so we got to park right out the front, which was cool. Inside the building, actually in the reception area, there were cars. Real ones. It was weird. There the security people took my photo and gave me a badge that I had to wear. And then I went to choir with Mummy and her work friends. I loved it. I really enjoy singing and they do quite a lot of singing at choir, in between all the giggling and chatting that is. I had a great time, and as you'd imagine, they loved me. We then had lunch in the canteen at Mummy's work. It actually looked just like a motorway service station to me. The food was pretty similar too. I had an enormous jacket 'tatoe. Nice. I met some of Mummy's friends in the canteen / restaurant / service station place, and one of them gave me a Harry Potter sticker book. Mummy got one too. We were both well chuffed. We love stickers, and Harry Potter.

The big and truly exciting event of half term though was I took my very first steps. I have to use the word 'steps' loosely as technically it was only 1 and a half steps. But it still involved me standing all by myself and sort of moving my feet. This amazing feat (different sort) was captured on video, and because of which I am now almost famous on you-tube. And when I say almost famous, it had 149 views last count. Which doesn't sound a lot until you consider I probably don't know 149 people! The downside is that the video managed to also capture some slightly embarrassing things, the main one being that I didn't do my impressive walking in my proper Piedro orthotic boots... Nope, I was wearing, of all things, my purple and very fluffy slippers! Oh. My. God.

At Halloween, we took part in a pumpkin challenge arranged by Uncle Billy Bobs and Del. Mine was kind of a cat. Well, that is how it ended up anyway. Amazingly I won the challenge, helped by me being the youngest (by a long, long way), which seemed to work to my advantage considerably with the 'judges'.

We had auditions at school in readiness for our Christmas play, The Wizard of Oz. I was given the part of the Good Witch of the North. I was glad I was suitably cast as a good witch, rather than a bad witch, but I was still not entirely sure I was happy with my part. That was until I saw what I would have to wear. A big, pink party dress, wings and a wand. Well that is SO me, it would be rude not to be the Good Witch now.

So, once that was all agreed and sorted there was just the small task of me learning all my lines and Mummy finding the perfect dress. Well, we both did a sterling job and the play went really very well. I remembered all my words and I looked fabulous. Even if I did have to wear and upturned painted 'Lush' bag on my head as a make-shift crown.

The run up to Christmas was as manic as it ever is. I did loads with school as always. We went out for the day Christmas shopping, had a Decoration Day, went out to the cinema, and I even went out again for a party with school on the minibus. It was fun. There was dancing, which I love, and as a special treat at the end, they gave everybody the most enormous party bag (again!). It was fantastic.

I went to Lapland UK again this year. You would not believe how good you have to be to go this many times in a row. Unfortunately, this year I had to go with Mummy and

Daddy rather than going with my boyfriend and my friends from school. I guess you can't have it your own way all the time. Although I do try! This year, as we knew Lapland was very chilly, I did a better job of wrapping up warm. I wore a top. With a top under my top, and a top on top of my top. And 3 pairs of socks. Ear muffs, Daddy's' hat and... a feather boa!

Lapland was great. We went on a 'Superstars' day, as I am a superstar. This meant we didn't have to rush. There was loads of time to do everything. I made a beautiful reindeer that looked just like Sven from Frozen. So, that is what I named him. I think Arendelle is not far from Lapland anyway, as that too is Frozen, so that kind of makes sense.

At the end of term at school we had a Christmas party and as is the tradition, I got to see Father Christmas. Except this Father Christmas didn't look or sound like the one I had just met the other week in Lapland. The school Santa sounded exactly like my head teacher. Weird.

At our end of term assembly, I was suitably in the festive spirit to spend the whole assembly, in front of all the parents, with a candy cane hanging from my glasses. I did look the part / a wally / festive (delete as appropriate).

Christmas was great. As I am now a big girl I wrapped up presents all by myself this year. I struggle with selotape and often find it doesn't do an overly good job at holding my parcels together. They have this horrible habit of unravelling, all by themselves.

We had Christmas Day at Granny and Pop Pop's this year and Boxing Day at home. This was quite a challenge, as we had rather foolishly decided to redecorate the study and rip up the floor of the utility room just weeks before. But we got there just in time, for about 14 of us to celebrate Christmas together. That is a lot to fit in our kitchen. But we did it. Just. Breathe in. And once you're in your seat, you are not going anywhere. Sit tight.

Love, Jess xxxx

# Jan-Mar 2015

Right at the beginning of the year Daddy got all ill, and we had to have an am-blue-ance car come out. He was wheezing and puffing and sounded just like daft Vader. Nanny and Grandad came around to keep me busy and I read almost a whole Daisy book. And that is a huge amount of pages. But I was still all worried, as there was talk that Daddy might have to go into hospital if he didn't get better at breathing. But in the end, the am-blue-ance man, who was hilarious, and another doctor who came specially out to our house, gave Daddy some medicine so he was able to stay at home. He frightened me out of my life!

Just a week later it was my 12th Birthday and I had a huge and fabulous swimming party. I invited lots of people and we had loads of food and cupcakes. I was too scared to do the flumes, even though I had the offer of someone coming down the flume with me. My teacher and TA (Teaching Assistant) popped in to say hi as well. But neither of them remembered to bring their swimsuits with them. What a pair of cotton-headed-ninny-muggings they are! Watch out, mind that bucket! Splosh!

Just 3-days after my party it all went horribly, horribly wrong. I was at school in my coat ready to come home, waiting for the minibus. And my lovely boyfriend Ron, noticed something was not right. And he told a teacher. Thankfully, after my last fizzy-lip incident (where I had a small stroke), school had set up a plan of action just in case it happened again. Lucky, they did. As that was exactly what was happening. My TA who I love to bits, gave me a hug and realised what was happening, so she phoned my home and spoke to Daddy (he was off work and at home, as he was still recovering from his earlier huffing and puffing threat-of-a-hospital-admission incident the previous week). She explained what was happening and Daddy said he was on his way. Luckily Mummy had just got home from work too, so they both jumped into the car on a Jessie rescue mission.

Meanwhile, I'm still getting cuddles but am feeling more and more fizzy, and weirder and weirder, and more confused and floppy by the minute. My teacher then, rightly so, decided to call for an ambulance to come straight to school. There wasn't time now to wait for Mummy and Daddy. My weirdness, floppiness and wonky face was starting to give everyone the heebie-jeebies, including my friends. So, they moved me to the first aid room, along with a few teachers. I remember the head teacher sitting on the scales in there, which I thought at the time was odd. Mummy and Daddy arrived soon after that and just behind them was the ambulance car. The nice lady doctor person from the ambulance car took one look at me and got on her phone straight away to see how far behind the real ambulance was, and asked them to get a serious move on. Good news, they weren't far behind at all. Before we knew it, we had a room full of people, including three para-magnets (paramedics). I was put in the ambulance with Mummy and two of the para-magnets. They did some tests, there and then, before we went anywhere. And then we couldn't go anyway... the ambulance driver couldn't find the keys to the ambulance! In the confusion and panic of it all, it was actually a strangely funny moment. The para-magnet that was with me in the back, spotted the keys with us, and then we were off. As it was school kick-out time, the roads were really busy, so they said they would put on the lights and siren so we wouldn't have to queue in the traffic. So, that is what we did. Making quite the exit, we were off to 'hostable'. The only slight problem en-route, was when Mummy threatened to throw up as we were travelling very fast and she was sitting sideways. What a light-weight. I'm the poorly person here. The para-magnet phoned the hospital while we were zooming along the dual carriageway, saying that we had a ''FAST (Face; Arms; Smile; Time) positive' child on board and to be ready. That was their code to say I was having a stroke. So, when we did get to hospital there must have been about 20 doctors / nurses /consultants ready and waiting for me. As is always the way with these things though, the closer I got to the hospital, the better I got! I was already recovering by the time I arrived. This meant the huge team that was there initially, was soon dispersed. The paramedics explained to the doctors what they had seen when they had got to school and how bad I had been, and although it was good news that I was already improving, the doctors were not at all happy that this had happened again. So, off I went with Mummy to have lots of tests. Not the sort you get at school thankfully, as I was not ready for spellings at this point. This was more 'touch your nose, touch my finger' and 'squeeze my finger' kind of tests. I did have an MRI that afternoon, which was really good going as they fitted me in 5 minutes after the MRI had shut for the day! But all the doctors in the hospital were very keen to get me looked at, and very closely too.

I had to stay the night there. Daddy came and found us with an overnight bag for me and Mummy. It was decided it was best if Daddy didn't stay, just in case they decided to admit him too! So, we had a bit of tea and then the play assistant asked what I'd like to do. Well, what I really wanted was some quiet time and a chance to watch the TV, as I knew that a whole night of observations (this time it was 'just' every 2 hours) was coming up. And amazingly they found this TV on wheels with loads of films already programmed on it. So, me and Mummy got sorted for the night.

The next day I did a bit of school-type work in hospital, had more tests, had lunch and I was eventually discharged about tea time, on the promise that if anything like this ever happened again, we were to call an ambulance straight away. So, off we went. This whole being up through the night for tests and stuff always whacks me out. So, we had an early night at home and Mummy arranged to work from home, so she could have a bit of a nap if she needed.

So, Daddy puffed and wheezed, Mummy worked, and Nanny and Grandad popped in to see how I was doing. We hadn't even got to lunchtime the next day and I started going all fizzy again. This time though, I knew what was happening and I was getting more and more upset the more the fizziness moved upwards. This time it was Mummy that called the ambulance. By the time the paramedics arrived, my right-hand side was floppy like last time and my mouth went all droopy and then it gets really tricky to talk. They tickled my feet and asked how it felt. I said it felt purple. So off we went again. Lights and sirens all the way back to the hospital. The triage nurse at the entrance to the hospital greeted me by name when they stretchered me off the ambulance and said "back so soon!" And they had the team ready for me again. But like last time, by the time I arrived, I was already starting to recover. So even more tests this time. Another MRI, but this time I got to listen to music. The MRI had to be paused as I was dancing! Apparently, you're not supposed to dance during an MRI. They did lots of other tests too. They rubbed my belly (well my boobies really) with a lump of jelly. They were worried I had a hole in my heart and that was what was causing all the problems. Well the ultrasound thingy did look odd. So, they called back up. And the back-up agreed, there may be a hole. But it is hard to see. So, I'm being referred to the heart specialist at GOSH. I'm already under Neurology and Genetics at GOSH so this will make it a nice hat-trick of GOSH specialists. Meanwhile, more tests, more school-type work (yes, even in hospital!) which this time included clocks, fractions, sums, writing and then we did even more TV/film watching. This time they scaled back on the observations so they weren't so often. So, although we had to spend another night back in hospital, this time we got a lot more sleep. However, being in a hospital it is always so bright, and at 2am we woke up thinking it was properly morning. So, we popped to the loo, and then went to say 'hi' to the nurses on duty. There we bumped into the consultant we had seen both times I had been admitted this week. He had been called out for an emergency, but had popped in via my ward on the way back home to check I was okay. How nice. Anyway, back to bed, and more sleep. We had to wait for some new medicine before I was allowed to go home later that day. And by the time we were finally discharged, we had managed to watch 3 and a half of the Harry Potter films plus 3 other films. Home again, and I need 'oinkment' and a bandage as the para-magnet put a hole in my finger and gave it a heartbeat.

Because of the hole in the heart shenanigans and 2 'fizzy-lips' in 48 hours, I found myself up at GOSH twice over the next month. Once was to see my Neurology consultant and the other for my new heart (Cardiology) consultant. Thankfully no hole was found, just a floppy wall in my heart. So, it's just floppy like the rest of me. No surprises there I guess.

My appointment with the Neurologist had a bed in the room. My first question to her was, "I'm not staying the night…. Am I?" Thankfully, no I wasn't. What a hideous month or so.

I didn't realise turning 12 years old would be so tricky. But at least that is over with now. I do have to take Aspirin now, which I call my 'fizzy-lip medicine'. It is a tablet that gets dissolved in water and I have to have it every single night after tea. The hope is, that this will stop me being ill like that again. I have been really good at remembering to take it, even though it tastes like yuck.

Once I was home and everything had settled down, we invited the teacher that had looked after me at school when I was poorly, to have afternoon tea with us at the jam factory. As is usually the case, I had the high tea option. This is 3 plates, one on top of another. Sandwiches at the bottom. A cream tea with scones and jam and cream in the middle. And then little cakes on the top. It is yummy-licious.

I have been doing some nice playing recently. I like dressing up, as I have brought myself a beautiful Anna (from Frozen) outfit with my birthday money, with a whole load of other Disney stuff. I love Disney, and all things Frozen.

I also like playing with my tiny Sylvanian family animals. I have loads of them and I have got so many different sorts (sheep, rabbits, meerkats, mice and dogs), that I was able to play weddings with them. And I had enough little critters for a full congregation, complete with bride, groom, vicar and even bridesmaids. I even got the wedding march on my iPad. When you do something like this, it has to be done properly.

Love, Jess xxxx

# Apr-Jun 2015

I've been growing fast, especially at night, and I've been getting all tall (for me) and all booby (compared to Mummy). I officially now have 'all the right junk, in all the right places'. As I have been growing out of my clothes, Mummy brought me some new swimsuits. And she was jealous, so she got a matching swimsuit. We look like synchronised swimmers now. I just need to work on the moves.

I have been in knickers now since last summer, well during the day that is. Hence the new normal swimsuit, rather than what I used to wear, my sticky knickers (incontinence swimwear). An amazing thing is, I am now dry in the night as well as in the day. Oh, my God. I can't believe it. No more pull-ups... after over 12 years of being in pull-ups or similar, it is weird to be in knickers all the time.

Apparently, I am getting very much like a teenager. And over 6 months too early as well. REALLY?! What? No, I'm not. Oh. My. God. Leave me alone.  Go away.

Strangely, what is to be known as 'lady business' then started shortly after getting into pants full time. Typical. I'd only just got into knickers and now this. I have to say I handled the whole thing very well. Daddy on the other hand was quite hilarious. The very first one started when I was asleep. Mummy went off to work ever so early as usual, oblivious to what was about to be discovered. Daddy got that pleasure. Thankfully Mummy had got supplies, in readiness. The problem was, Daddy wasn't entirely sure what to do with them!  In utter desperation, Daddy had to call Mummy at work to say "I get the gist. But what are the wings for?". Even from the toilet I could hear Mummy crying with laughter. Poor Daddy. We got there in the end. I was quite pleased to be a proper big girl now. To the extent that I told most people that I'd met that day.

I discovered that I am going to Disney World at the end of the summer holibobs. It was all very exciting. Mummy recorded the very moment I found out and she played the

Disney music 'Flying' while doing so. I had a picture with Mickey Mouse, Auntie Piglet and Uncle Lamby that said "See you next summer Jessie". I'm actually going back to Disney!!!!!! COOL!

So, Disney list-ing has started in earnest. I have been making lists of rides, and restaurants and shows and stuff that I want to do while I am in Disney. So, can someone please go and get the 'lemon maker' so I can make the list extra special. The "what?!" said Mummy. The 'Lemon maker'. You know. It gets all hot and makes things go plastic. Oh. The Laminator.

I went on a Sports Experience day with school and got a free t-shirt, a medal, and got to eat my lunch outside. They were the highlights really. So, that's yet another medal for my ever-growing collection. Fantastic.

As part of me growing up I have just recently discovered Austin Powers. Groovy baby. I love the films. Wish I had a mini-me. Mummy thinks I'm her 'mini-me'. I think she means I'm a 'mini-her'. Anyway, the films have got great dancing, fabulous trousers and seriously groovy-baby music. I just love it.

I had heard of the Jack Petchey awards, as they give them out once a term at school to 1 very lucky person. What I didn't know though, is you could get them from other places. So, I was a mixture of amazed and proud and flabbergasted to be presented with a Jack Petchey award for horse riding. Very well done me.

Something quite funny happened one weekend when Daddy went off sailing. Me and Mummy went to change a jumper at Next, but Mummy parked in the wrong place, so we ended up walking/wheeling past 'Pets at Home' to get to Next. On the way back to the car, we thought we'd pop inside and just have a quick look at the animals. Half an hour, and a lot of giggling later, me and Mummy emerged with a cage, hay, food, and an actual real live hamster!! Oh, my God, I cannot believe we did it. As it was just the two of us, I had to hold the box with my new hamster in, all the way home while Mummy drove. It was called 'Nibbles' for the first half a mile or so, but then I came up with a better name. "Elsa". Perfect. Can't wait to show Daddy my new hamster. She is so small and so cute.

I was briefly famous during half term. I sang in a big choir on stage at the local spring fayre. I didn't know all the words, and hadn't been to all the practices. But I did wear a tiara and a 'One Direction' t-shirt, and I find that sometimes that is just enough to be able to wing it. I am so famous.

Love, Jess xxxx

# Jul-Sep 2015

Well, this growing-up malarkey can be really annoying. I have now, first hand (or first head), and just recently too, discovered acne! Who's she? Never mind - you'll spot her a mile off.

At the school sports day towards the end of term, I got to do a walking race in my Kyle walker. It was my first public performance in my new walker. Usually I have a walking frame that holds me up and keeps me steady. This one doesn't do that. I have to do all the hard work and it can be wobbly and very tricky to manoeuvre. So, it didn't matter that I came last in that race, the cool thing for me was that I did it. And I did it without falling over.

I was in a manual wheelchair race too. I went really fast, and very excitingly, I won it!! And there was some tough competition in that one. As they left that race till last, and as it just had the quickest learners in the school in that race, it means I'm the fastest manual wheeler in the school. Which is cool when your only 12!

I still love horse riding. And on one of my last lessons this term, my Godmother came to watch me, which was amazing, as I have never had an audience before. And that day I completed a 1km ride outdoors and got a certificate to prove it!

After much nagging, I finally had my boyfriend Ron over for a whole day. We played toys at home, while Mummy and Daddy got the car loaded up and ready, and then all of us went out to a park for a picnic. It was fine for a while, but after we had our lunch, which involved Ron managing to get tomato ketchup on his sock, he started to get really bored. And we had got water pistols and make-do stuff and everything specially. Boys!! So, in the end we came back home and played Wii.

At the end of term assembly, I dressed up as a character from Greece. The musical, not the country. I did some singing and had to sing 2 lines all by myself. My favourite one was. "I met a boy, cute as can be". In that assembly, I was officially given my 1km horse riding certificate too.

We also had a summer fete at school to mark the end of term as well. That was really cool as they had: a BBQ (and I had a hot dog); they had a mobile zoo where you could pet all of the animals; and they had loads of stands and stalls and things. I had a go on pretty much everything, which was great fun.

My lady business has gone mad. I didn't like it anyway, but now it's gone crazy. Really horribly bad and lasting for ages and then I'm only fine for a week, and then we are off again. I'll be getting really poorly if this carries on. So, I have had to see a doctor, and they have given me some special pills, mini ones, that I have to take every single day to see if that will help. I hope so, because it is a real nuisance. I'll rattle if I take any more medicine.

After a normal visit to my nice dentist, I was referred to an awful-dentist (orthodontist), who despite the name, turned out to be nice! I've already had my initial assessment, and now I've got to go back and have my impressions done. This is where I have to bite into this big sweetie thing and from that they get a mold of my teeth. Weird. And a bit gross.

As a bit of a last-minute decision, we went to Alton Towers. It is absolutely miles away. While we were there we went to CBeebies land, which I really loved. I met 'Emet' who is from the Lego movie, and I met 'Upsie daisy' and 'Iggle Piggle' from 'The Night garden'. I also did the Postman Pat ride several times, as there was no queue at all, and I delivered all my post just right. Just like Uncle Lamby does. But my favourite was the 'Octonauts' ride. I went on that one three times. It was like a mini rollercoaster. I'm getting in training on all the exciting rides, ready for my return visit to Disney World.

Me and Mummy had to go out shopping and get me some new boobie holders for my new and quickly expanding boobies.

As we are off to America shortly, I have been making passports for my 2 favourite dollies, so they can come too.

Elsa and Anna from 'Frozen'. I'd hate for them not to be able to get through security. So, as part of the passport making process, both of them had to have their photo taken properly. And I'm pleased to say, they sat very still while we took their pictures and their passports are very convincing.

I had a pants party at Granny and Pop Pops house, and Auntie Pigerlert, and Uncle Lamby came down to help me celebrate a whole year of me being dry in the day and more recently, several months at being dry at night. We did: pass the parcel (as it is my favourite); we had a BBQ where I 'ordered' steak; we had party bags; and we even had bunting in the shape of pants, and well, we had everything. Boy, when we decide to do something, we definitely like to do it properly!

My school holiday homework (how dare they give me homework to do in the holidays!!) was to put a scrapbook together of all the things we did. So, I did a page for every week of the holidays, and to do that, it meant we collected bits and bobs all summer. From car park tickets, to cinema stubs, photos to lolly wrappers. And then at the end of the holidays, I did lots of sticking. It looked pretty good by the time I'd finished, and I ended up winning a prize for it at school as it was one of the best scrapbooks ever. Not surprised.

We celebrated Nanny and Grandads Golden anniversary, in a posh way, by all going out in a minibus to dinner at a lovely restaurant and there were even proper speeches. Daddy did one, as it was his Mummy and Daddy. I wrote one too, but in a fit of last minute nerves I decided to leave it at home. Despite that, Mummy persuaded me at the end of the meal to stand up (with help obviously) and do my speech from memory. And I did. And it was in front of loads of people. I did so well, I impress myself sometimes.

Just before I went back to school, to start my third year (third, I know!!!!!!!!) at my now not-so-new school, we went off to Disney World. The real one. In America. We got our passports ready, for both me and the dollies. And we got to stay in my most favourite Disney hotel in the world again. The

Disney Yacht Club. It is rather posh there, so I fit in nicely... I think anyway. We'd been there once before too, and weirdly our room this time was just a couple of doors away from where we stayed last time. It was also only a few doors away from where they keep the elephants. Or so I thought. This came as quite a shock to everyone else, so I took Mummy and Daddy up the corridor to show them the elephant room. Except, apparently, it didn't say that. 'Electrical room'. Oh bum.

Well, Disney was as fabulous as ever. The best bits this time included the new Frozen parade, and there was a really funny cast member who pretended he (yes, HE) was Queen Elsa from Frozen. He was hilarious. I did real proper big girl rides including Everest (it is a rollercoaster in a mountain and has a Yeti), and the Seven dwarves mine train. I went to the sing-along frozen show too, which was just amazing. We had absolutely loads of rain though, as some hurricane was headed our way, but that just meant the parks on some days were unusually empty.

On 'Mary Poppins day' I was given a special Mary Poppins shoe by a cast member, which was really cool. Both me and Mummy had a girly spa morning and we both had a manicure and a pedicure. I was so good they made me princess of the spa and they gave me a tiara. It is weird, but I'm often chosen for stuff like that. I think it is because I am special. That, or I must really be famous!

I went to Fantasmic for the first time ever. As it is on quite late in the evening, and as it is noisy and scary (for me), I hadn't been up to it until now. It was great fun. I like being a big girl. Well, sometimes anyway. It can also be a giant pain in the bottom too. Literally.

On that note, lady business went completely mental on holiday. It was causing me no end of grief for almost all of my holiday, which completely scuppered our plans to do a lot of swimming. Really 'nnoying.

I got to see both Doc Mc.Stuffins and Sofia the First for the first time. They are both TV characters from my favourite Disney Junior shows. I danced and cuddled with them both.

They must have known I was their biggest fan.

We went to the 'Beauty and the Beast' restaurant for Mummy and Daddy's wedding anniversary. In the "Be Our Guest" song it says "try the grey stuff it's delicious". Well I did try the grey stuff. And I can assure you, it is definitely NOT delicious. Disgusting, yes. Delicious, definitely not.

Probably the 2 best moments of that holiday were when we saw Russell and Dug from the film "Up" and Russell wanted to take me home with him. And then there was the time I saw Mickey, and once I'd given him a huge hug, he went off and got Goofy and Minnie. Then he brought them back to me so we could have a photo together and a group hug. It was fabulous, despite Mummy bursting into tears! I just love Disney. When can I go back???

Love, Jess xxxx

# Oct-Dec 2015

Well, the most exciting thing that has happened in ages, and that includes when I went to Disney World with Mummy and Daddy a couple of weeks ago, was a school trip to... Portugal!! Oh. My. God. School have never done anything quite this adventurous before, so they chose 6 well behaved and fabulous learners (or so I assume), and 6 fabulous (but not necessarily well behaved) teachers, to spend 5 days in Portugal as part of a 'learning to be big and independent and very grown-up'. So I could start as I meant to go on, I dragged my own purple suitcase all the way down the hall for it to go in the car. Mummy and Daddy drove me to Stansted airport, where I met up with all the teachers who were to come with us. It was then they handed out special t-shirts, so we would all be matching. They had the name of the school and "Portugal" written on the front. In case we forgot where we were going! It was amazing and I put mine on, there and then, in the middle of the airport! While we were checking in our suitcases and saying our 'goodbyes' to all the parents, the head-teacher from my school joked with me and said that this isn't a holiday at all, and we've got to do lots of school work while we are away. Humph. I hope he really WAS joking!

On the plane, I sat next to my most favourite teacher who was also going to act as my buddy on holiday. I had to hold her hand tight on landing, as I really don't like the feeling when the plane comes in to land at all.

We arrived at the hotel/villa type place in Portugal so late at night, it was already tomorrow. So, we went to bed straight away and left one of my teachers to do all my un-packing for me. My room was cool, as I shared it with a good friend of mine who used to go to my old mainstream school, plus two teachers.

We did absolutely loads of really fabulous stuff while we were in Portugal, including: staying up late; playing games; buying girly stuff, like a hairband and a handbag with my foreign money; going to a fish market (which was quite weird and very smelly and I had to hold my nose); and wheeling my chair though a water fountain, even though the teacher had just categorically said not to do it (I couldn't help it... it was sooooo hot there!). But mostly we: had fun; sat on a sunbed; went in the pool (which was a bit freezing); and relaxed in the hot tub. Some of the learners actually Skyped the head teacher (who was back at school) from the hot tub. It was hilarious. After five fabulous days, we had to come home. At the Portugal airport, I was passport-girl and was in charge of everybody's passport. Heaven help us! This time on the plane I got to sit next to my boyfriend, which was nice. And when we got back to Stansted airport, all the mums and dads, and even the head teacher, were all there waiting for us with a big banner that said 'Welcome Home'. It was there the head asked me where all the school work that I had done was. Well, quick as anything, I said "left it in Portugal!"

Well, home again, and the lady business is still going completely bonkers, which is annoying and a real pain in the bum. Literally. Thankfully the lady business consultant person gave me some new lady business medicine, and it didn't just improve the situation, but it stopped it completely. I'm not sure that was the plan, but I am not complaining one bit, and I am not missing it either.

I have started going to the awful dentist (orthodontist) properly now. To start with you have to go every week! It all began with an x-ray, which was odd because to have it, I was supposed to stand up. But I couldn't. So, Daddy had to help me, but he had to do it without getting x-rayed himself. I then had to have my impressions done, which is where they put this huge sweetie-type thing in your mouth. But it tastes absolutely disgusting, and it even made me gag. But I did it.

Then after that, they fit these weird rings on my back teeth and brace brackets on the fronts of every tooth. Then another visit puts in the wire and joins it all together. Every time I went, for the first day or so afterwards, my mouth hurt quite a bit and I had to have Calpol. Then just as I would start to feel better, it was time to go back and have the next thing done. But before I knew it, all my braces were in place, with purple bands on my brackets, and it wasn't hurting anymore. So... how much longer do I have to have these braces on for??

I still go to Guides every Wednesday evening, and as I've done some growing, I have got some new Guide uniform. But now I am the oldest one in my patrol, the 'Butterflies'. So, it was only fitting that this term I was voted in as the patrol leader.

I had an unusual half term, as for the first time ever, Mummy took part in a "bring your child to work day". Apart from being scared witless when they showed me what happened when an airbag goes off, I had a really good day. The best bit was probably going in a real race car around a real race track. It was a bit like the 'Test track' ride at Disney, but this was real. It was just as fast and exciting. And I got to have 2 goes. I also spray painted a plastic car purple, and helped sculpt a real car out of clay... although I did get a tad messy doing that, and we were finding bits of clay in parts of my wheelchair for weeks later. If this is what Mummy does all day, spray painting, playing and driving fast, then I think I would like to work there too when I'm older.

Just before Christmas, and a month or two after becoming a patrol leader at guides, I found out that they were going to give me a Guide Jack Petchey award! This is the 2nd one in about 6 months. I was so proud of myself. I can't wait for the real and actual award ceremonies when you go up on stage. This one is going to be next October. But I have the Jack Petchey award ceremony for horse riding to do first... that one apparently is next May. Don't know why you have to wait so long. However, I am going to be so famous, again!

On the run-up to Christmas, everything seemed to be going against me, with 3 separate and unrelated problems in less than 2 days. It started with a trip to the nurse for my Flu jab. Now I don't do needles, and when I have to, there is usually a LOT of tears and wailing. This was no exception. However, before I vaguely had time to compose myself, they gave me a pneumonia injection too. How very dare they.

The next thing was, that I went with the Guides to 'Go bananas' as part of the celebration for my Jack Petchey award. It involved loads of climbing up and down and through this massive soft play area. It was great but exhausting fun, for me and both for Mummy and Daddy, who had to carry, manoeuvre and lift me around the obstacles. That was until I had a wobbly moment (it still happens!) and I lost my balance going down a slide, scraping my elbow as I went. I had to have wet towels on my elbow until the stinging stopped. And now my elbow looks like it has 2 slices of pepperoni stuck to it. Not good when less than a day earlier I had had two injections. So now I couldn't use either arm!

Then to finish me off entirely, I had the wire on my brace fitted. Because of all the new metal in my mouth I could hardly talk.  And to add insult to injury, they did it the day before the school play. This would ordinarily be a problem when you are in a play. Even worse when you are the narrator! I'd spent weeks learning those lines and it was a real struggle to talk. However, loaded with Calpol, and battling on like a trooper, I did my best and I did really well, considering.

The Christmas school play this year was Oliver, by Charles Dickens, so I had to wear a mop cap and apron. I looked like a waitress.

It is beginning to become a bit of a tradition, but me and Mummy went to the local garden centre on Christmas eve for a lovely lunch, followed by a wander around their animal winter wonderland and then last but not least, Father Christmas.

2 days before Christmas two of my brace brackets fell out. Luckily, I was able to get an appointment and I got it sorted just before they shut up for Christmas. Phew.

We had Christmas day at Nanny and Grandad's house this year and because they live just around the corner now, I cycled there on my brand new, bright red, big girl, 3-wheeler bike complete with a massive trailer. This proved to be very handy in transporting presents up and down the road.

We then had Boxing day at Granny and Pop Pops. But they live quite a long way away, so we had to go in the car. Lucky I didn't cycle, as I was ill on Boxing day and spent most of the day asleep or lying on the sofa. I was all floppy (floppier than usual anyway), hot and weird (well, weirder than normal). And I was ill for days afterwards. I'm sure I get more than my fair share of poorliness. It's a hard knock life, sometimes.

The problem is, we had tickets to see 'Disney on Ice' just after Christmas. I spent that day on the sofa at home, and during the afternoon I said I still wanted to go, even though I wasn't really well enough. Thankfully we went there in the car, so I was able to snuggle under a blanket there and back, which was handy. Despite running quite a temperature, and having no voice, I still had a really good time. I wanted to sing along to all the Disney songs, but no noise came out, so I mostly just mimed and croaked.

It was worth it all just to see Mickey and Minnie Mouse, and Anna and Elsa. That was medicine enough for me, and I was soon better.

Love, Jess xxxx

# Jan-Mar 2016

Right at the beginning of the year, even before I could fit a birthday in myself, I went to my boyfriend Ron's birthday party at Build-a-bear. But before we could start choosing bears, Ron got stuck in traffic (he wasn't driving!). Meaning we had ages to hang around in the cold. Well, the inevitable happened. Me and Mummy went shopping! And by the time Ron turned up to his own party, not only had I brought a really jazzy pair of pink flowery boots, but I was wearing them too. They were soon known as my 'birthday boots' even though, technically, it wasn't my birthday! After build-a-bear we went on to Pizza Hut, which is my most favourite place to eat. As Ron would say, "Awesome!"

Despite months of training I have actually and officially become a teenager. I am getting really old. Nearly as old as Daddy. As I had loads of lovely presents for Christmas, I asked to have money for my birthday. And I got loads of it. Plus, quite a few iTunes vouchers as well. These are always handy, especially when you get a nice new iPad from Mummy and Daddy for your birthday. The old iPad I had was so old, every new game I wanted, wouldn't download. It was really 'nnoying. Now I can go crazy and get all those games and all that music that I really want. Fantastic.

We did a bit of a detour on the way home after an (orthodontist) awful dentist appointment, and I somehow ended up in Sainsbury's, with all my birthday money! And well, I kind of accidentally brought Lego. Lots and lots of Lego. I've discovered Disney Lego. I brought 2 boxes of "Frozen" Lego, the castle and Oaken's Trading Post. As well as 2 boxes of "Friends" Lego. The supermarket and coffee shop. On the way to the till, the boxes on my lap were stacked so high, they reached to the top of my head!!! Well, that has blown all of my birthday money.

Talking of birthdays, I had a ten-pin bowling party this year. And I even won one game. Then afterwards we had tea with Granny and Pop Pop, as I share a birthday with Pops and

I guess it's only fair he helps me blow out the candles on the cake.

We have finally got a smart telly. It must be clever as it has YouTube and I love YouTube. I could quite literally watch it all day. I especially like watching anything Disney. And people being surprised about going on holiday to Disney, is one of my favourite things. I just wish someone would surprise me!

We did elections at school for the school Council. We haven't had a school Council before, and I thought it would be a good idea if I was on it. So on the poster I made, I said people should vote for me because I am nice, and kind and happy. Well, it must have worked, because I was elected. I even got a shiny blue metal badge that I wear on my uniform and I have to go to meetings and everything. The first thing I'm going to ask for is a pool... and a hot tub... oh, and a cinema.

I have discovered Disney Tsum Tsums. Both the soft and the squishy variety. They are little collectable Disney characters and they are adorable. And I want them all!

Half term came around before I knew it, and as always, it was a week shared between the grandparents. This half term was especially busy. I went: swimming and did 12 lengths; did baking; and went to the library and read 4 books. Now I've got a lot better at reading I've become a real and proper bookworm. I could read all day and every day. I just love it.

I missed the Guide thinking day this year (where lots of different Guide units in the area get together), because I had a sore voice. It was annoying as they were going to make chocolate truffles, and I wanted to 'help' make them so I could eat some.

I went to the Stoke Mandeville Junior Sports camp. I hadn't been for years, but now I'm a bit older, the new and improved set up for the secondary school-age children suited me a lot better. So this time, I was able to choose in advance what sports I would have a go at. So the plan was, to have a go at archery, golf and shooting. Shooting. Oh. My. God! The noise. I didn't even get to hold the gun. Just the noise frightened me out of my life! Not doing that. Golf was okay but a bit boring. And I was a bit rubbish. Archery on the other hand, I loved. The archery instructor was friendly and nice, and he had all the proper equipment so it didn't hurt my fingers. I just loved it. Later in the day, when I wasn't busy, I went back and did archery again. I think this is going to be my new hobby. The problem is, Stoke Mandeville is too far for me to come every week. I'm going to have to find somewhere that does archery a bit nearer to home, so I can have another go.

On World Book day, I went to school dressed as Jessie the cowgirl (from "Toy Story"), which seemed apt. I looked the part too. Yeee haaaaa.

I did a sponsored walk at school, where I had to walk the length of the car park and back in my new walking frame. I am not quite as wobbly as I used to be in it, but it is still very hard work. I did, as you would expect, a fantastic job, and everyone was rightly proud of me.

Right at the end of March was Easter. I'm sure I've still got Easter eggs left over from last year! I like chocolate, I'm just not exactly fast at eating it... unlike Daddy.

So, to avoid a chocolate mountain this year, Mummy did an unusual Easter 'egg' hunt. It was a 'blind bag' hunt complete with clues. I discovered 'blind bags' on YouTube. They are bags with a small toy in, but you don't know which one you'll get. You can get bags for My Little Pony, or Lego or Disney. Problem is, you can buy 5 'blind bags' and end up with exactly the same toy in each. So, Mummy made her own. She got some bags and brought a load of soft and squishy Tsum Tsums and then hid the bags around the house. I then had a list of clues and had to find them. Great fun, and I got loads of fabulous Tsum Tsums as well.

Being Easter, I decided to be a really lovely granddaughter, and using the spare bags from the Easter 'egg' hunt, I made a chocolate crispy nest for each of the grandparents to have on Easter Sunday. Mummy helped with the melting chocolate bit, but I pretty much did the rest. It was good fun, and we had loads of mini eggs to decorate them with. They looked fab in the end, and then we put each one in a bag and put a ribbon round it. Nice!

'Unfortunately,' we had some melted chocolate left over. So, with the help of a big bowl of strawberries, I finished the chocolate up. Waste not, want not.

Love, Jess xxxx

# Apr-Jun 2016

I went up to GOSH again to see the doctor consultant lady. I don't mind going as long as I don't have a plaster, don't stay the night, don't have any needles or blood tests, but do get the chance to buy something with Mummy and Daddy's money. This trip met all those requirements, and after a good chat with my consultant, I bought home a new teddy bear dressed as a nurse, which I called Wendy. I named her that because we got her in the Peter Pan restaurant at GOSH.

I had my first orthotics (that's feet!) appointment in absolutely ages. We were all convinced I would have to start wearing splints again, as that seems to be the current trend with all my friends at school. However, with Mummy and Grandad on the case, and after a remarkably quick appointment, it was agreed that I can stay in boots. I don't have to have wear stupid splints. Fantastic. As they are a right pain in the foot.

Mummy was lucky enough to take me on a weekend Guide camp. The 'camp' was in a big house and had a boaty-cruise theme. We made: cakes with sails; a mirror that looked like a porthole; a bag with a print of an anchor; some soap and lip-gloss. And to top it all, we had a party. As always, guide camp is very busy and very noisy. I think for me, the best bit of all was the talent show. I had brought along my new walking sticks, and had been secretly practicing after school every day. So, when we got to the talent show, my surprise for everyone was to walk across the living room of the house, with my tripod walking sticks, with everyone watching. You could have heard a pin drop. I have never known that many guides to be that quiet. Ever. When I had finished, I was so very proud of myself, I nearly cried.

At school I was picked to go to the Panathlon semi-final. I did a wheelchair relay and Kurling (which is rolling a disc towards a target). I am amazed to say that my team won the gold medal for Kurling. Even more exciting I think, is that my school got the most number of points over all, and actually won the semi-finals! So in about a months' time we will be competing in the County finals.

I went to a place called Jump Street with the Guides. It is a massive trampolining centre, but all the trampolines are in the floor, not up high. The first thing you have to do is get special socks that stop you from falling over. I need more than a pair of non-slip socks to stop me from falling over, but I guess it's the thought that counts. As Mummy is always my guide helper, she had to have a pair of socks too, as she was going to have to go on the trampolines with me. It was fantastic but exhausting fun. We had to have a few breaks while we were there. Some so I could have a drink, as it is hot work. And some so Mummy could pop to the toilet. Quickly! Such fun!

I am becoming more and more independent every day. When I get in from school now, I like to take off my shoes and socks and hair bands and bobbles. However, allegedly I am not quite as neat about it as I could be. I don't get it. I'm a good deal neater than Daddy. I'm not sure quite how tidy you really have to be. Especially in my own room. It is hard being a grown-up teenager sometimes. Also, it's not fair. And I 'ain't not doing it'.

Do you remember a while back I was given a Jack Petchey award for horse riding? Well, I went to my official and proper award presentation ceremony. I put on a posh dress especially and as we had managed to get 4 tickets at the last moment, we invited Nanny and Grandad to come along too. The ceremony was at the Civic Theatre, and because it was for horse riding I wondered if the horses would be there too. But they weren't invited. I was one of the first people on stage. It was a really fantastic and exciting moment getting my boxed medal in front of all the people watching and clapping. There were photos and posing too, which I am good at. Afterwards, on my way back to my seat, when me and Mummy were still backstage, I completely burst into tears. I was so proud of myself and so excited all at once, my emotions went crazy. I can't wait for my Guide ceremony now!

We have some good highs and some pretty impressive lows sometimes. If Jack Petchey was a good high, less than a week later a stint in hospital was a pretty bad low. We are not sure, and we never will be, but it is believed I tried to do 'walk sleeping' (I think that is what they called it). Problem is, if you walk in your sleep when you can't even walk when you are awake, it means you crash to the floor in a very noisy heap in the middle of the night and bang your head very, very hard on the floor. I apparently knocked myself into next week. I had a really bad case of concussion, we think anyway. But as I don't do anything normally, I wasn't likely to do this normally either. I don't remember anything. In fact, not only do I not remember falling out of bed, but when I'd completely recovered, I didn't remember the last few days either! So, according to both Mummy and Daddy, they were woken up with a huge bang, like someone was kicking a door, and they found me sitting on the floor near my bedroom door. Quite a way from my bed. I was all confused and sleepy and not sure what was going on. Then apparently, I got all fidgety and more confused. And then I went all floppy, and my speech went all slurred. So yet again, Mummy called for an ambulance. Because we ended up with both a fast response ambulance car and an ambulance, we had three para-magnets (paramedics) in the house at once. By this point I couldn't even lift my head, or talk or anything. I'd gone all weird. So, off we went. Me and Mummy in the ambulance, Daddy following in the car. Naughty Daddy actually got there before we did this time! Which is good going. I spent hours in resus, or wherever it is they hold all the really poorly people. I apparently had an MRI at one o'clock in the morning. And I must have been completely out of it, as I didn't even make a fuss. Hours and hours later, I was a bit better and had started to recognize Mummy and Daddy, so they moved me onto a high dependency children's' ward, which was so much more friendly than resus.

It was about then, someone spotted that I had a big graze across my face and they then realized I must have hit my head when I fell out of bed, or sleep walked, or whatever it was I did. Then, just to prove I definitely had got concussion, I was horribly sick everywhere. Several times. I hate being sick. And I hate it when I am in hospital. The good news is, that by the next lunchtime, I was home again. And because I had been poorly, I had some special treats. A prize out of the prize bag, a helium balloon, a visit at home from my most favourite teacher, and they even arranged for me to Face Time my friends at school. And after a few technical hitches (all our end), that was good fun too. It made me feel loads better. The weird bit was me having no memory of the last couple of days at all. I even forgot that I had built a Lego aeroplane the day before. Thankfully the Jack Petchey award ceremony had been 4 days earlier and I completely remember that.

We had our summer holiday in the May half-term, and not in the summer at all. Which was a tad strange to say the least. As it was only a week or so after my 'falling out of bed' incident, we nearly didn't go. But we all really needed a holiday, more than ever. So, we went. To Portugal. It was hot and nice. There was a nice Italian man in charge of Entertainment who gave me a kiss on the cheek, twice!! And there was a really friendly waiter-man who always looked after me at dinner time. We went for a swim in the pool every day. But it was freezing. We did a couple of day trips. One to a shopping place where we brought fudge. And it was weird, because it was the same place as the fish market I went to when I went to Portugal with the school. I even showed Mummy and Daddy the fish. They were still really smelly!!

We did a trip to a water park as well. It was there I found out that dolphins have babies. Well, baby dolphins anyway. I did loads of fab rides and watched some cool shows. It was a great day out.

We even managed to get down to the beach in the Algarve, and I saw a rock pool for the first time in my life. The water was pretty chilly though. It was tiring fun playing in the sand and around the rock pools, so much so that I needed a lift back to my wheelchair. Luckily daddy is still strong enough to carry me. Just.

Less than a week after getting back from Portugal, was the school Panathlon final. I did both the wheelchair relay and Kurling again. And, yet again I won the gold for Kurling. Oh. My. God. A gold in the finals. That means I have now got 6 Panathlon medals, as I've been to the competition for the last 3 years. So, I have had them put in a really special frame. I also have about 6 other medals, but they are less exciting and not so pretty, so they're just on my pin board at the moment. But I am quite proud of my rather impressive medal collection. What have you done today to make you feel proud?

After going to the Junior Sports camp at Stoke Mandeville a few months ago, I finally managed to get some real archery lessons near home. In fact, they are in the same town that I go to school. Daddy was supposed to take me to my first lesson, but was too poorly. Lightweight. So, Mummy took me instead. No-one but me turned up to the lesson. So, to keep me company, Mummy had a go too. By the time our 1st two-hour lesson was over, I'd found my new hobby. And weirdly, so had Mummy! I had a great teacher, and I was lucky enough to have the same teacher for all four of my lessons. Daddy (and Mummy) came along for the next three lessons with me. The teacher even built me a wooden stand that holds my bow, as I struggle to hold it steady for long. That way I can concentrate on just shooting the arrows. Sometimes I hit the target. But mostly I just shoot grass. By the time we'd finished all of our lessons, we decided we would need to join the club, and hence would have to get our own kit, as we'd all inadvertently become a bit hooked on archery. That meant me, Mummy and Daddy spent hours, and hours and hours in an archery supplies shop… and apparently, we spent an absolute fortune there too. By the time we left, I had a pink bag (to match most of my clothes), purple quiver (to match my wheelchair) and a red bow stand (to match my glasses). All the other kit I got though was pretty boring colours. My bow is real wood but feels nice, my glove is a boring brown (but is funny because it only has 3 fingers) and my arrows are black and white. But all in all, I am really quite excited by all my new stuff. I at least look the part now.

In some respects, despite the middle-of-the-night emergency trip to hospital in an ambulance, my holiday to Portugal, winning the gold medal in the final of the Panathlon competition, the Jack Petchey award ceremony and discovering that archery is my new and most favourite hobby, THE most amazing thing that happened was, GOSH, finally, after 13 years of tests and looking… have got me a diagnosis! Oh. My. God. A proper answer for everything. Not just for the wobbliness, or the floppiness, or the struggling at school, or even just for the 'fizzy lip' episodes I have. They found one answer that explains it all. It doesn't have a catchy title or anything. It is so unusual that the diagnosis is about 10 words long! To put it simply. When I was first made, right at the very, very beginning, there was a spelling mistake in my genes. Not my jeans, like I first thought. But my genes. It explains absolutely everything. And I'm the only one in the whole world with this exact mutation. I always thought I was 1 in a million. Well now it is official. I am 1 in 7 billion (1:7,000,000,000!!) You couldn't get more special or unique than that if you tried!

Love, Jess xxx

THE END (…for now!)

# Epilogue

A year on and all is fine. No further 'fizzy-lip' episodes. No regression.

The diagnosis showed that the 'fizzy-lip' episodes, were not actually strokes after all, even though they looked exactly like a stroke, because they didn't cause any damage to the brain. So, that is good news.

The prognosis is still uncertain. But, I guess that is true for everyone. No-one knows what their future holds. But we'll ensure that her full potential, whatever that is, is reached. That every possible opportunity is seized. And that it is done with the love and support of all our family and friends. So in that respect, she is a very lucky girl.

As has been the case so far, we will deal with whatever is thrown at us in the future, and we'll do the best we can when that happens. You can't ask more than that.

# ABOUT THE AUTHOR

Rebecca Green is honestly one of the most unlikely people to ever write a book. English was always her worst subject... assuming you discount French, which you need to, as that was just appalling. This book kind of happened by accident! It was never meant to be a book.

What started as a regular update to family and friends, grew, and grew. It just kept going, because the news and updates were never ending. It also became a therapy to get the problems and issues out there, and onto paper.

I hope you enjoyed our journey. And forgave any dodgy spellings or punctuation. I'm sure my old English teacher has her red pen out as we speak.

Hey, ho. We can't all be perfect!

17373684R00203

Printed in Poland
by Amazon Fulfillment
Poland Sp. z o.o., Wrocław